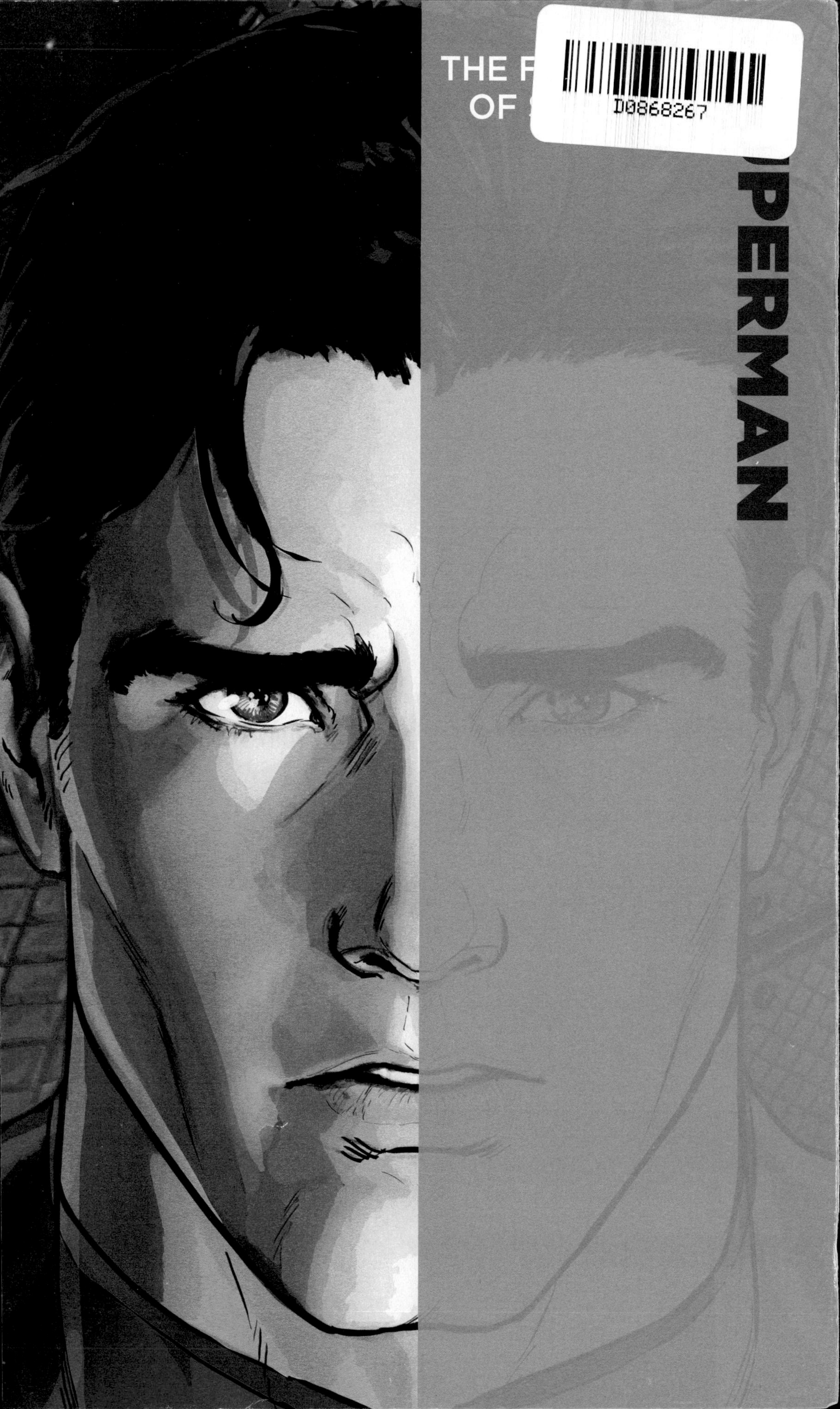
THE F
OF S
PERMAN

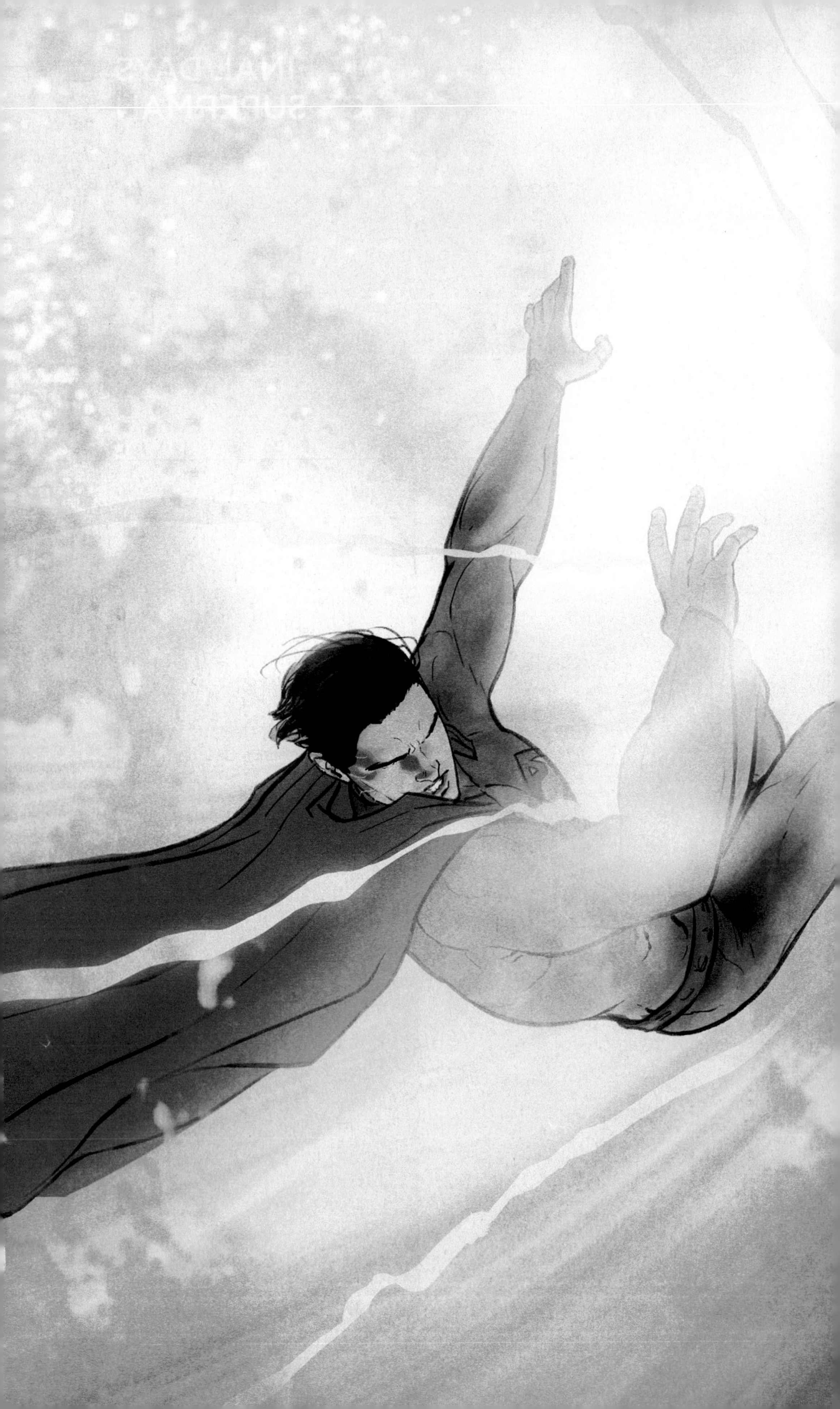

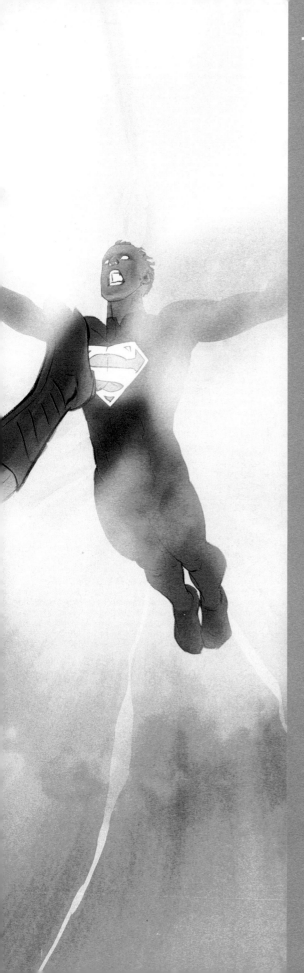

SUPERMAN

THE FINAL DAYS OF SUPERMAN

WRITTEN BY
PETER J. TOMASI

PENCILS BY
ED BENES
DALE EAGLESHAM
SCOT EATON
MIKEL JANÍN
JORGE JIMÉNEZ
DOUG MAHNKE
PAUL PELLETIER

COLOR BY
JEROMY COX
MIKEL JANÍN
TOMEU MOREY
WIL QUINTANA
ALEJANDRO SÁNCHEZ
ALEX SINCLAIR

INKS BY
CHRISTIAN ALAMY
SANDRA HOPE ARCHER
ED BENES
DALE EAGLESHAM
WAYNE FAUCHER
MIKEL JANÍN
JORGE JIMÉNEZ
JOHN LIVESAY
JAIME MENDOZA
TOM NGUYEN

LETTERS BY
ROB LEIGH

COLLECTION COVER ART BY
MIKEL JANÍN

SUPERMAN CREATED BY
JERRY SIEGEL & JOE SHUSTER
BY SPECIAL ARRANGEMENT
WITH THE JERRY SIEGEL FAMILY

WONDER WOMAN CREATED BY
WILLIAM MOULTON MARSTON

BATMAN CREATED BY
BOB KANE WITH **BILL FINGER**

ANDREW MARINO Assistant Editor – Original Series
EDDIE BERGANZA Group Editor – Original Series
JEB WOODARD Group Editor – Collected Editions
SUZANNAH ROWNTREE Editor – Collected Edition
STEVE COOK Design Director – Books
DAMIAN RYLAND Publication Design

BOB HARRAS Senior VP – Editor-in-Chief, DC Comics

DIANE NELSON President
DAN DiDIO Publisher
JIM LEE Publisher
GEOFF JOHNS President & Chief Creative Officer
AMIT DESAI Executive VP – Business & Marketing Strategy, Direct to Consumer & Global Franchise Management
SAM ADES Senior VP – Direct to Consumer
BOBBIE CHASE VP – Talent Development
MARK CHIARELLO Senior VP – Art, Design & Collected Editions
JOHN CUNNINGHAM Senior VP – Sales & Trade Marketing
ANNE DePIES Senior VP – Business Strategy, Finance & Administration
DON FALLETTI VP – Manufacturing Operations
LAWRENCE GANEM VP – Editorial Administration & Talent Relations
ALISON GILL Senior VP – Manufacturing & Operations
HANK KANALZ Senior VP – Editorial Strategy & Administration
JAY KOGAN VP – Legal Affairs
THOMAS LOFTUS VP – Business Affairs
JACK MAHAN VP – Business Affairs
NICK J. NAPOLITANO VP – Manufacturing Administration
EDDIE SCANNELL VP – Consumer Marketing
COURTNEY SIMMONS Senior VP – Publicity & Communications
JIM (SKI) SOKOLOWSKI VP – Comic Book Specialty Sales & Trade Marketing
NANCY SPEARS VP – Mass, Book, Digital Sales & Trade Marketing

SUPERMAN: THE FINAL DAYS OF SUPERMAN

DC Comics, 2900 West Alameda Ave., Burbank, CA 91505
Printed by LSC Communications, Salem, VA, USA. 4/21/17. First Printing.
ISBN: 978-1-4012-6914-2

Library of Congress Cataloging-in-Publication Data is available.

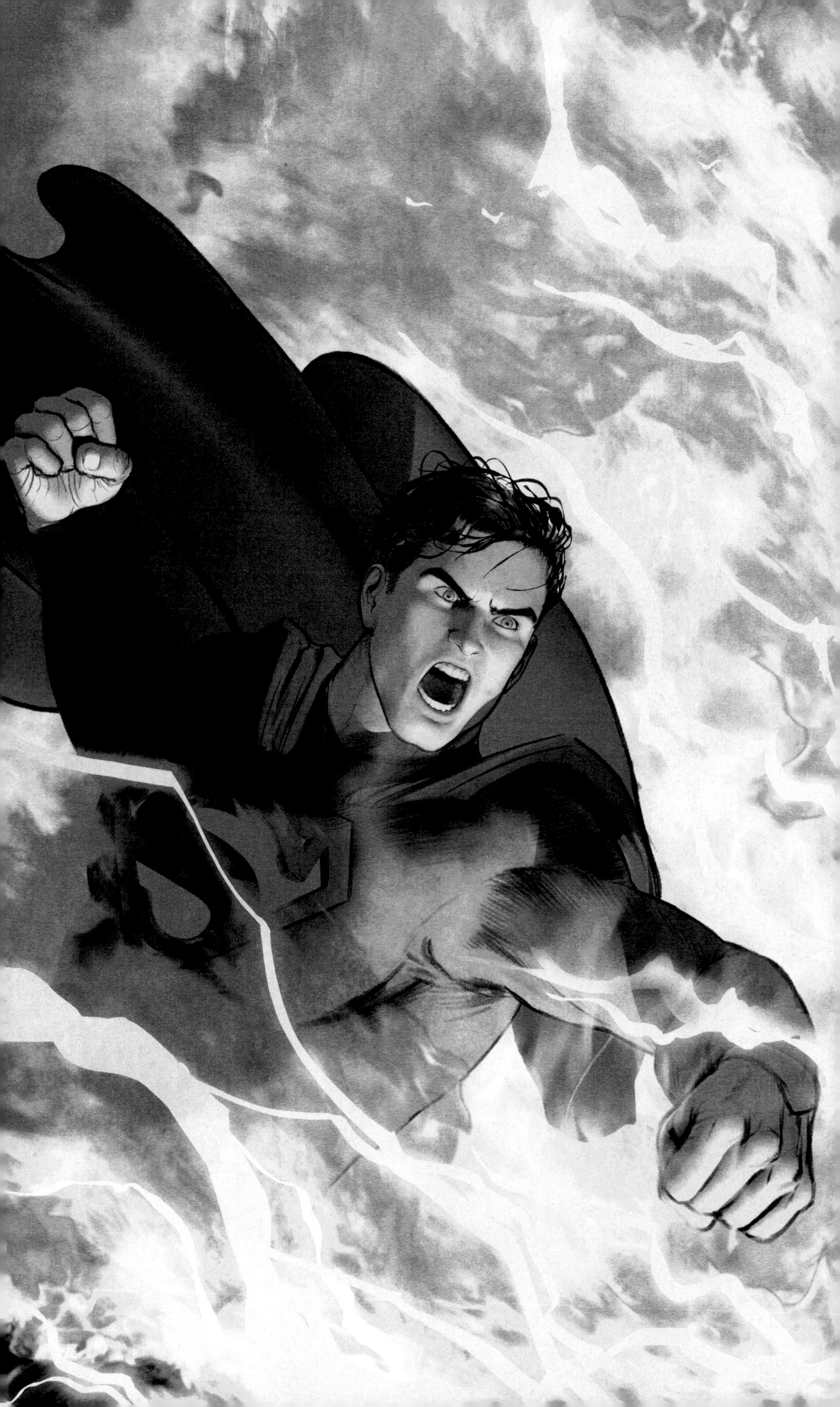

THE FINAL DAYS OF SUPERMAN PART 1: THIS MORTAL COIL

PETER J. TOMASI writer **MIKEL JANÍN** artist **MIKEL JANÍN** colorist **ROB LEIGH** letterer **MIKEL JANÍN** cover

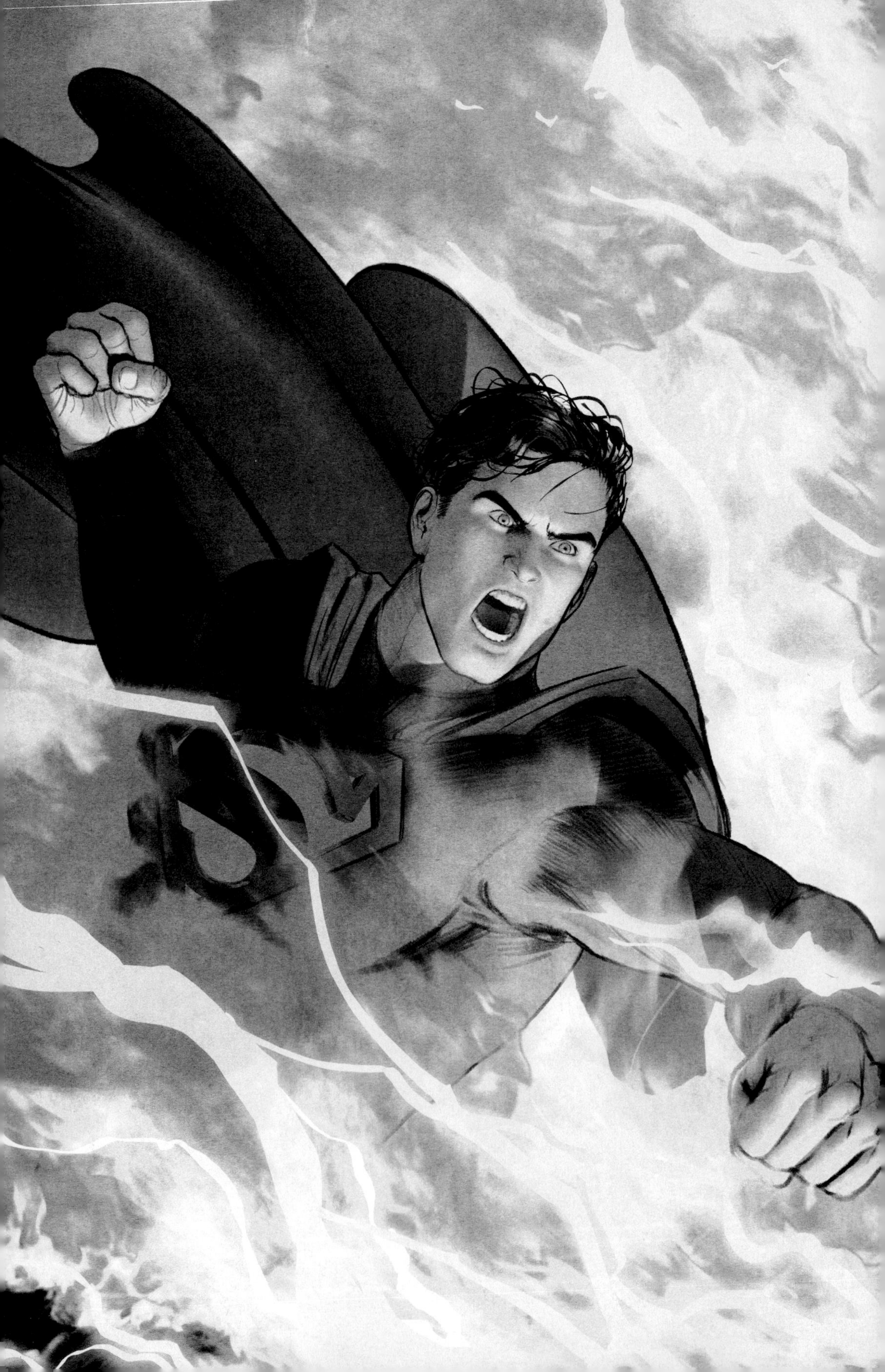

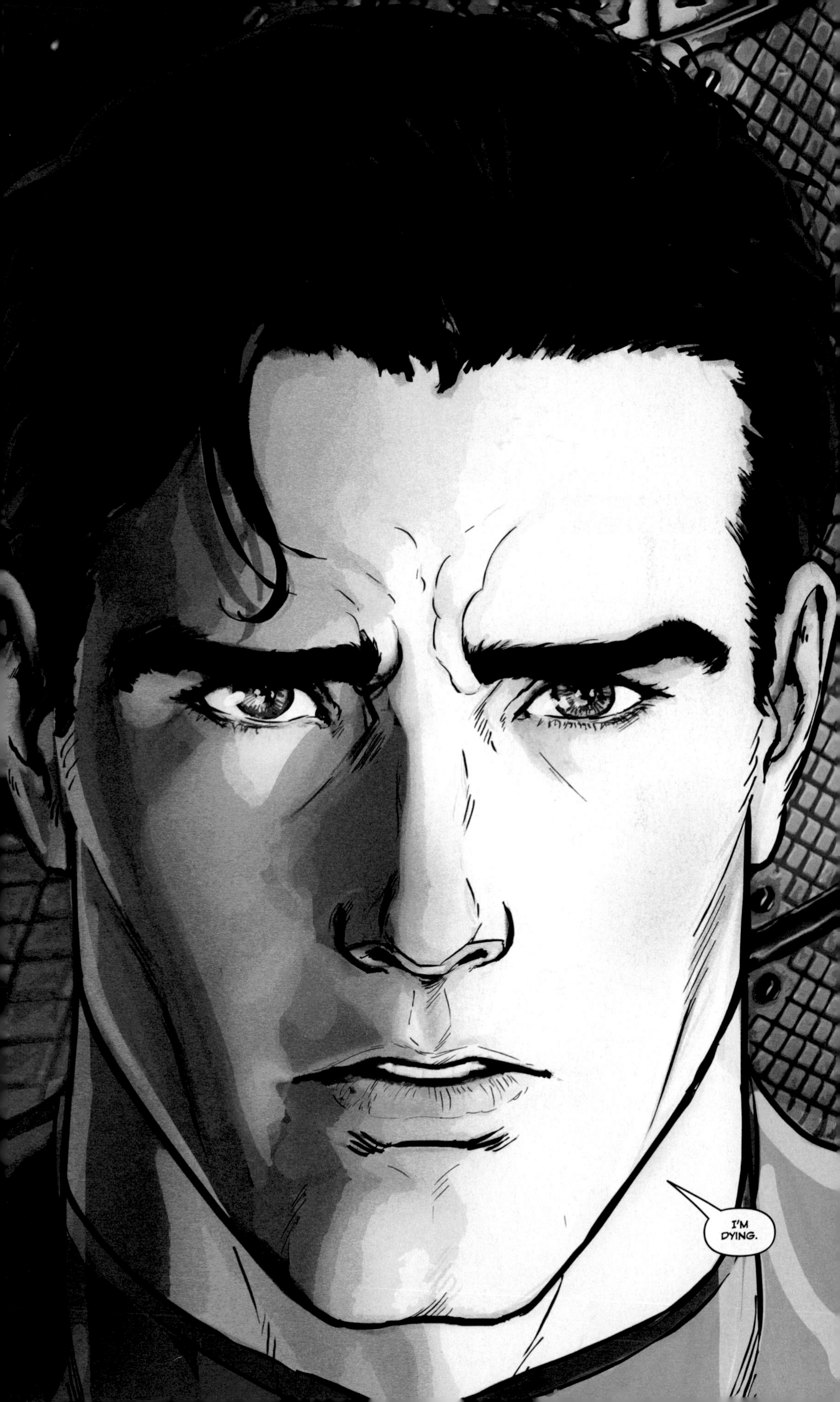
I'M DYING.

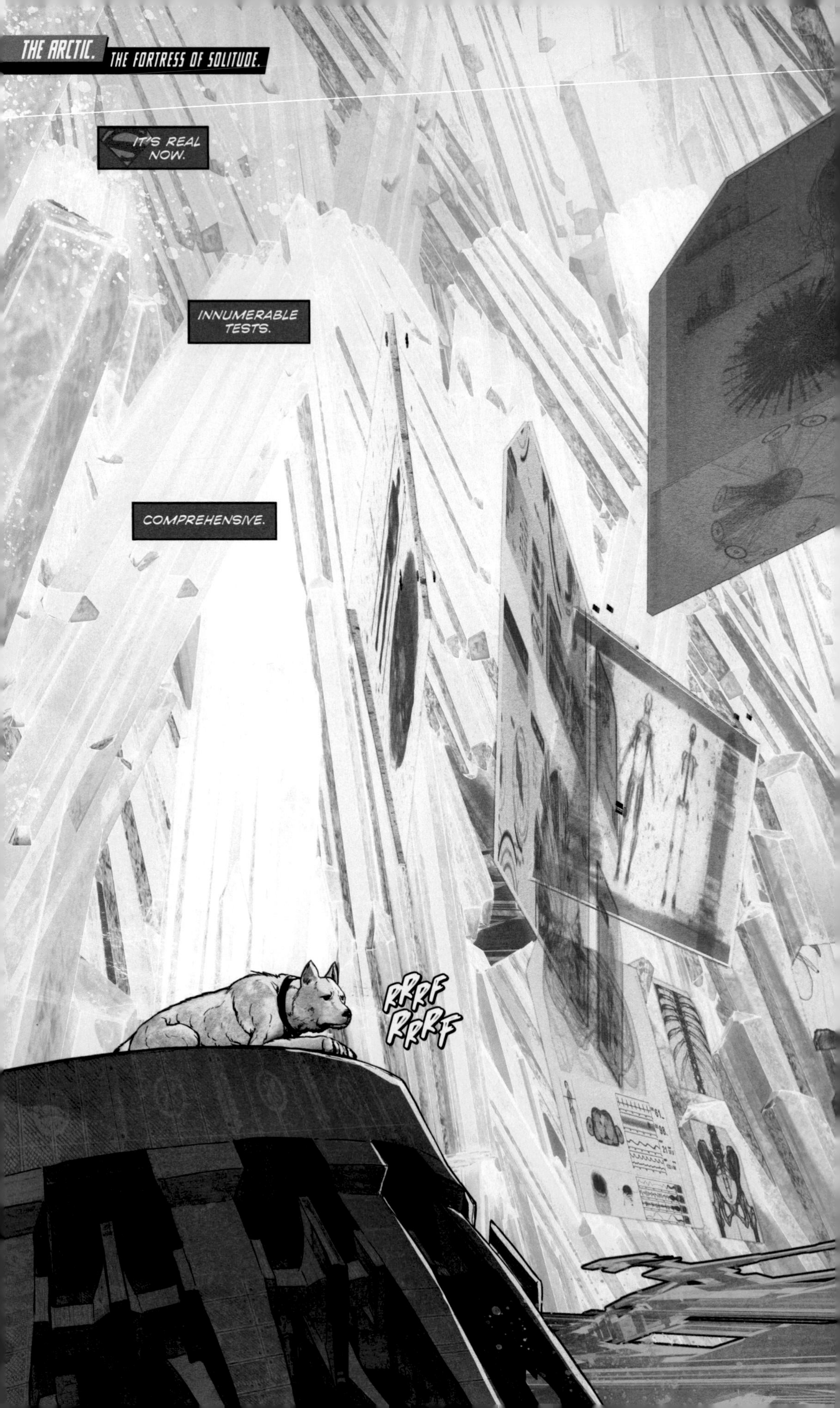
THE ARCTIC.
THE FORTRESS OF SOLITUDE.
IT'S REAL NOW.
INNUMERABLE TESTS.
COMPREHENSIVE.
RRRF RRRF

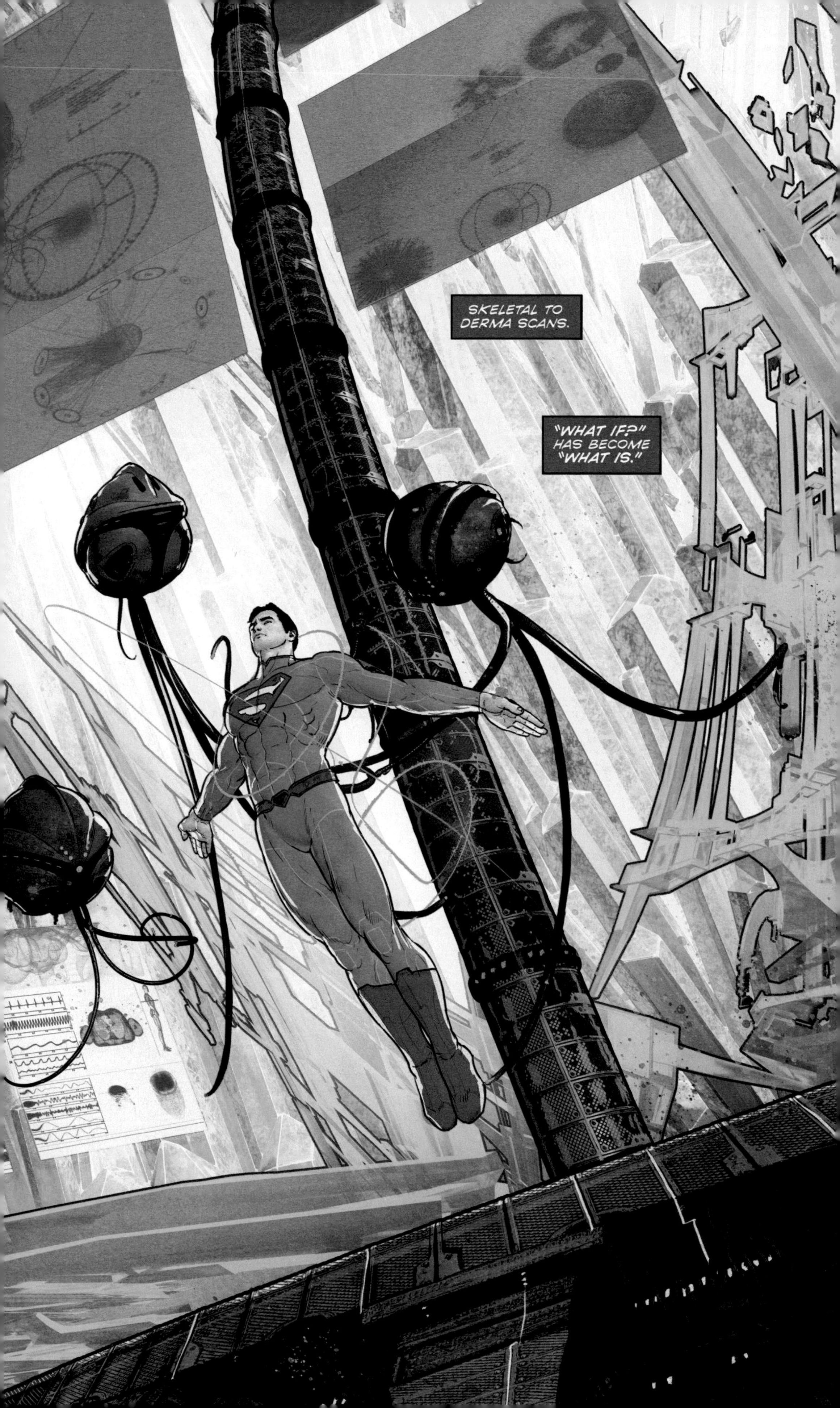
SKELETAL TO DERMA SCANS.
"WHAT IF?" HAS BECOME "WHAT IS."

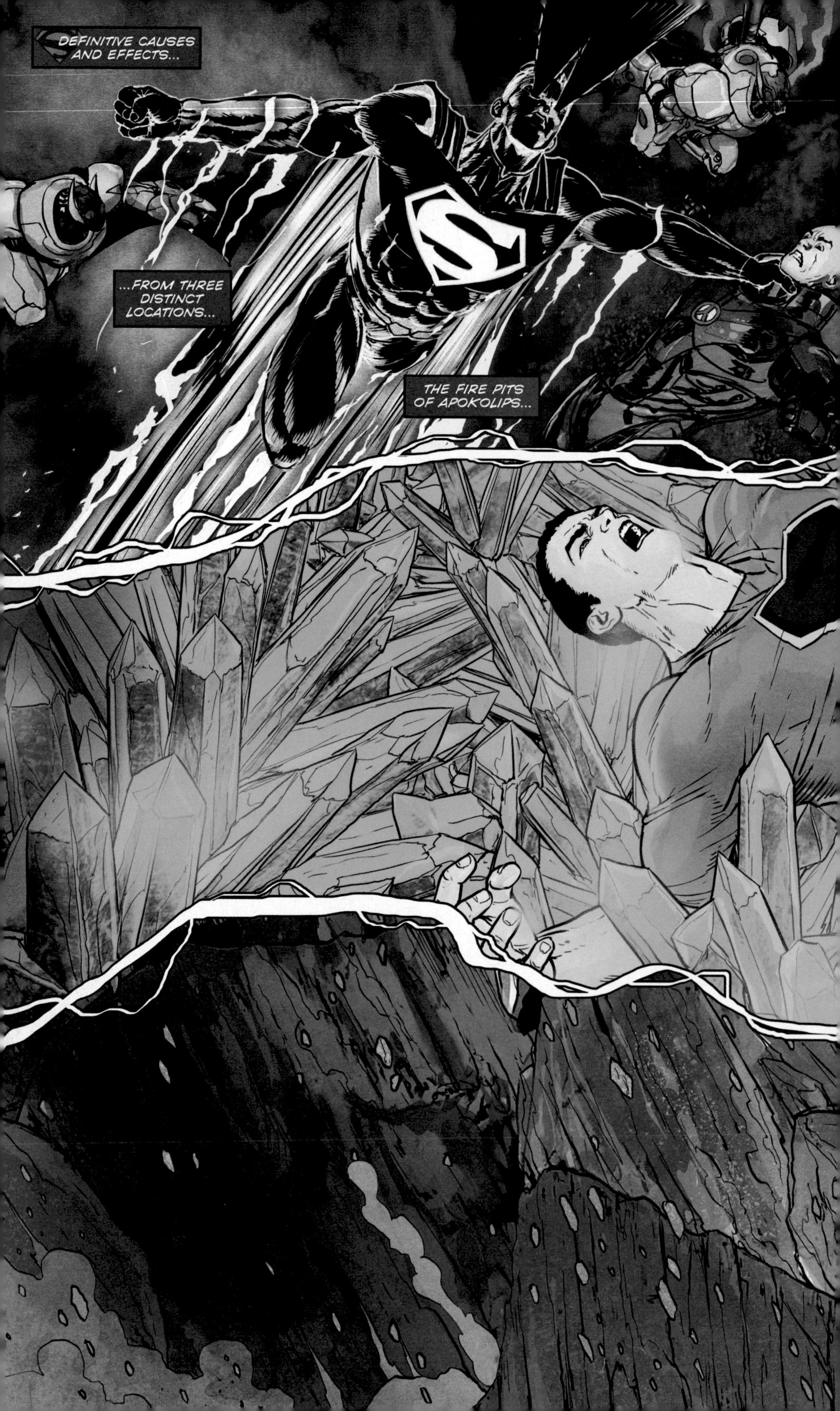
DEFINITIVE CAUSES AND EFFECTS...
...FROM THREE DISTINCT LOCATIONS...
THE FIRE PITS OF APOKOLIPS...

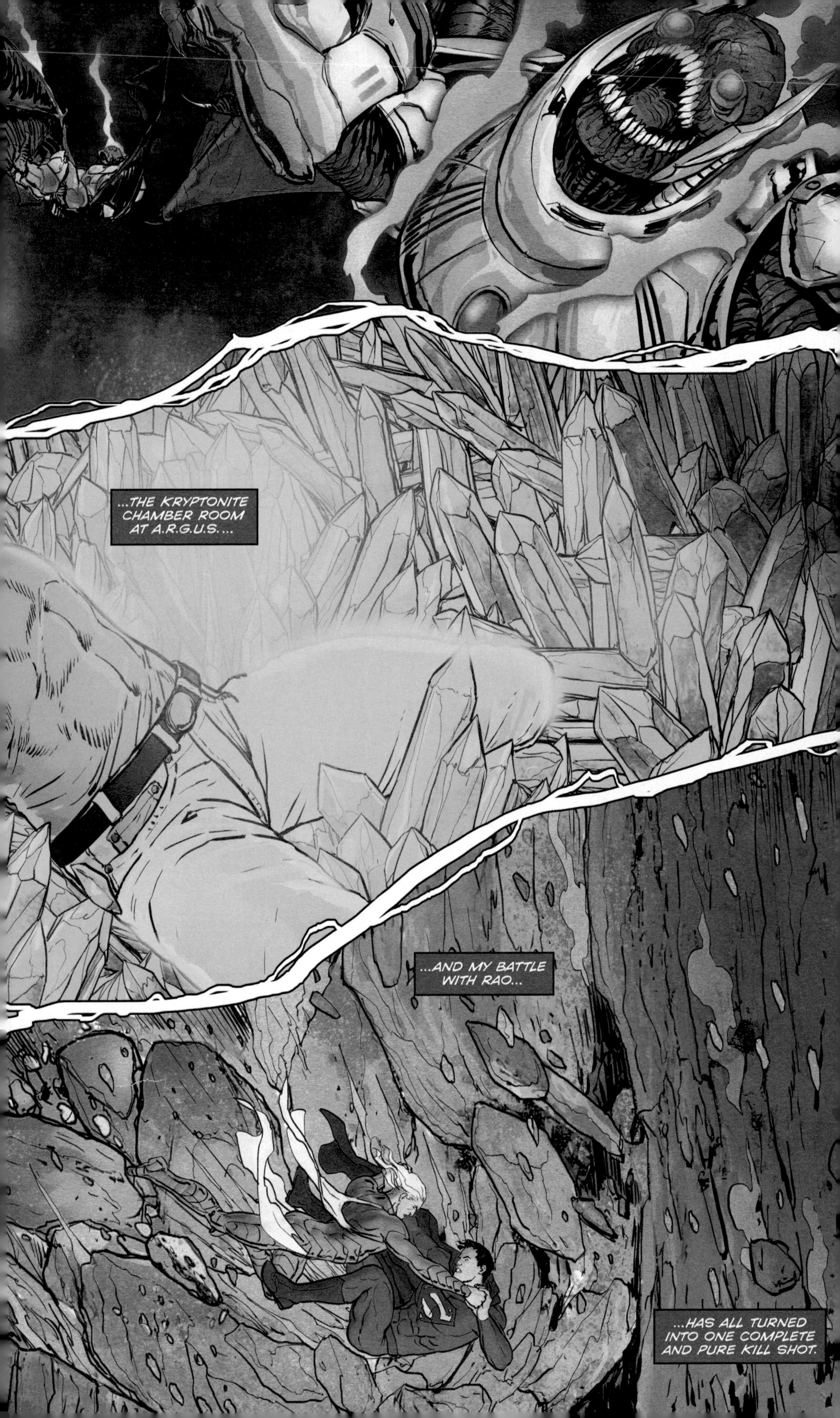
...THE KRYPTONITE CHAMBER ROOM AT A.R.G.U.S....
...AND MY BATTLE WITH RAO...
...HAS ALL TURNED INTO ONE COMPLETE AND PURE KILL SHOT.

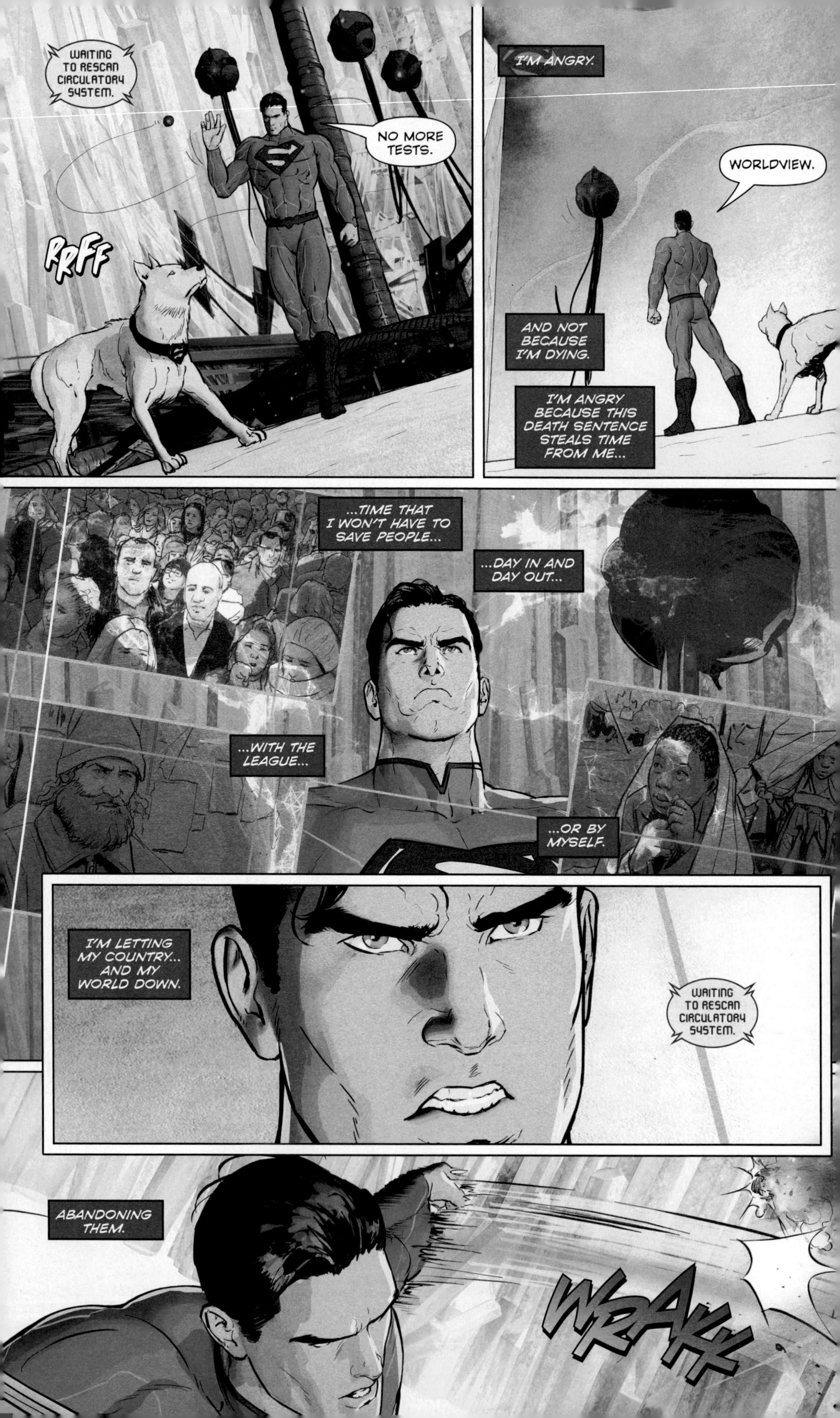
WAITING TO RESCAN CIRCULATORY SYSTEM.
NO MORE TESTS.
RRFF
I'M ANGRY.
WORLDVIEW.
AND NOT BECAUSE I'M DYING.
I'M ANGRY BECAUSE THIS DEATH SENTENCE STEALS TIME FROM ME...
...TIME THAT I WON'T HAVE TO SAVE PEOPLE...
...DAY IN AND DAY OUT...
...WITH THE LEAGUE...
...OR BY MYSELF.
I'M LETTING MY COUNTRY... AND MY WORLD DOWN.
WAITING TO RESCAN CIRCULATORY SYSTEM.
ABANDONING THEM.
WRAKK

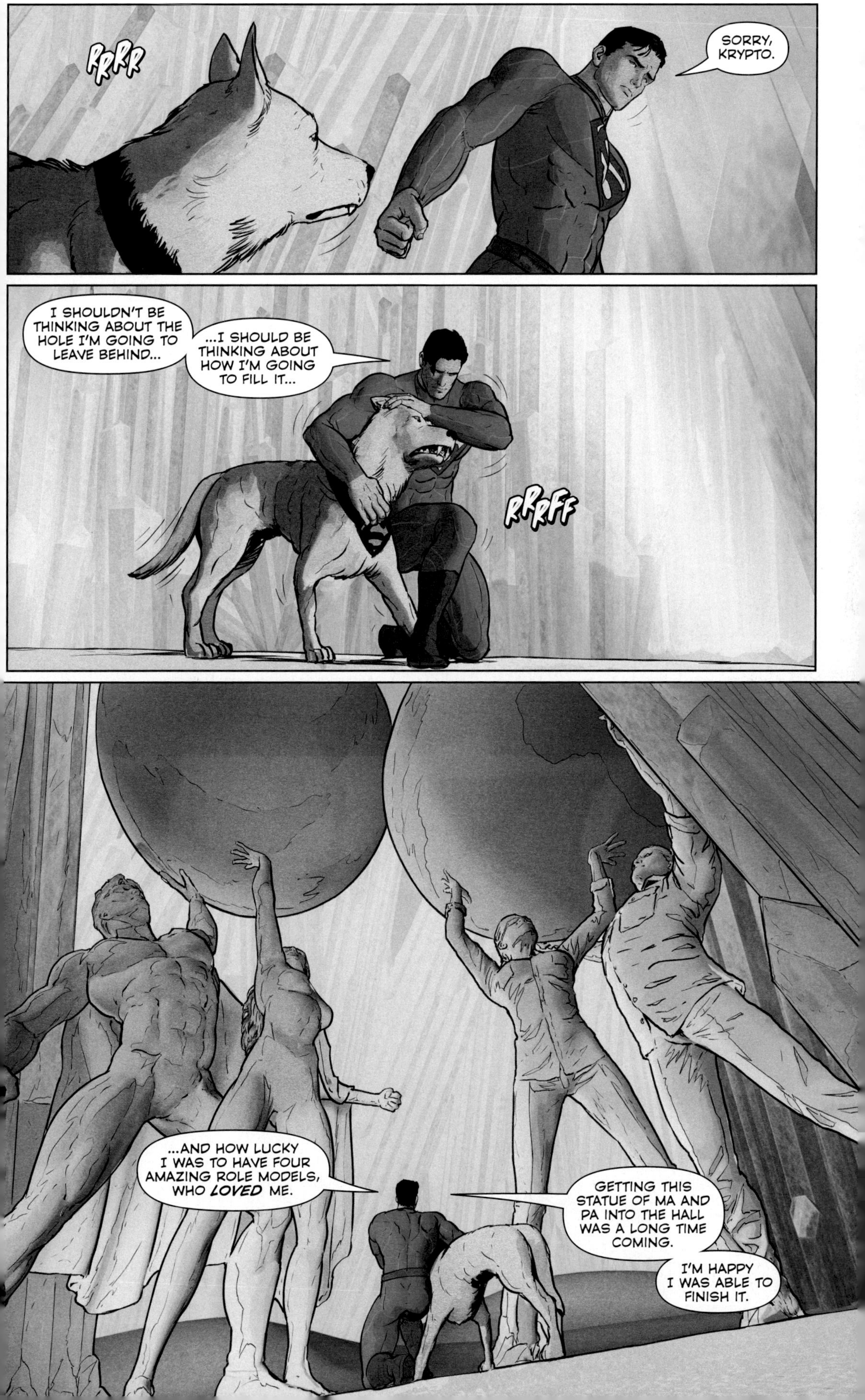
RRRR
SORRY, KRYPTO.
I SHOULDN'T BE THINKING ABOUT THE HOLE I'M GOING TO LEAVE BEHIND...
...I SHOULD BE THINKING ABOUT HOW I'M GOING TO FILL IT...
RRRFF
...AND HOW LUCKY I WAS TO HAVE FOUR AMAZING ROLE MODELS, WHO *LOVED* ME.
GETTING THIS STATUE OF MA AND PA INTO THE HALL WAS A LONG TIME COMING.
I'M HAPPY I WAS ABLE TO FINISH IT.

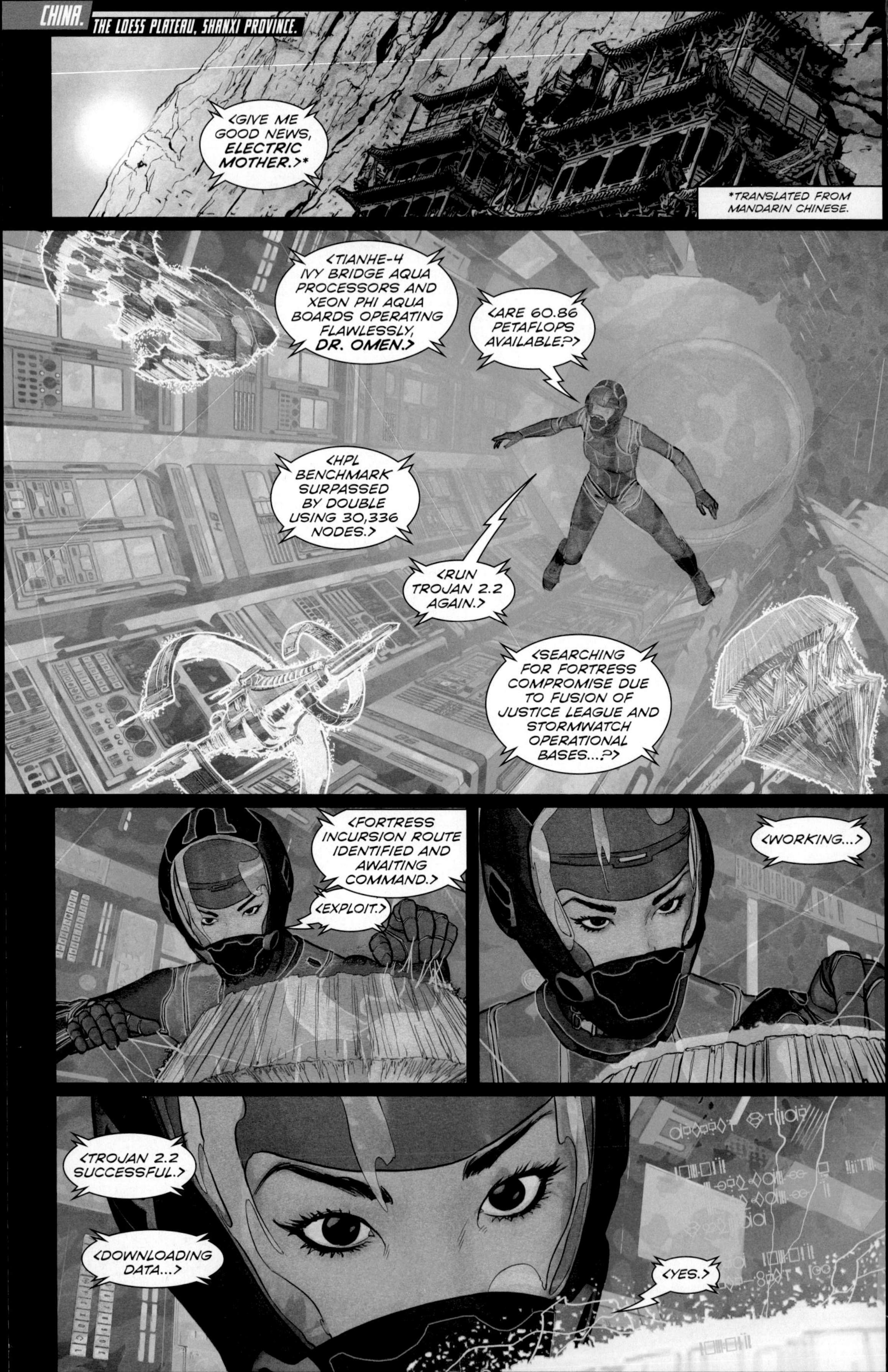
CHINA. THE LOESS PLATEAU, SHANXI PROVINCE.
<GIVE ME GOOD NEWS, **ELECTRIC MOTHER.**>*
*TRANSLATED FROM MANDARIN CHINESE.
<TIANHE-4 IVY BRIDGE AQUA PROCESSORS AND XEON PHI AQUA BOARDS OPERATING FLAWLESSLY, **DR. OMEN.**>
<ARE 60.86 PETAFLOPS AVAILABLE?>
<HPL BENCHMARK SURPASSED BY DOUBLE USING 30,336 NODES.>
<RUN TROJAN 2.2 AGAIN.>
<SEARCHING FOR FORTRESS COMPROMISE DUE TO FUSION OF JUSTICE LEAGUE AND STORMWATCH OPERATIONAL BASES...?>
<FORTRESS INCURSION ROUTE IDENTIFIED AND AWAITING COMMAND.>
<EXPLOIT.>
<WORKING...>
<TROJAN 2.2 SUCCESSFUL.>
<DOWNLOADING DATA...>
<YES.>

BRRRT BRRRT

RRARF RRARPF

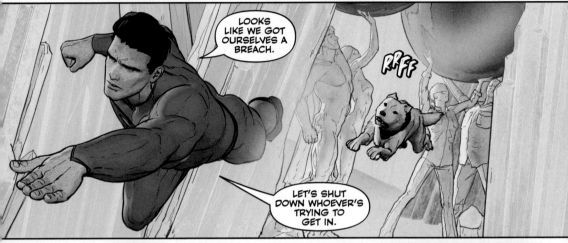

LOOKS LIKE WE GOT OURSELVES A BREACH.

RRFF

LET'S SHUT DOWN WHOEVER'S TRYING TO GET IN.

COMPUTER, STATUS?

ENTITY IDENTIFICATION?

FIREWALL GAP DISCOVERED. OUTSIDE SCANNING INITIATED.

ACCESS HALTED.

UNKNOWN.

POSSIBLE ANOMALY DUE TO RECENT FUSION ATTEMPT BY VANDAL SAVAGE. NO FOCAL POINT DISCOVERED.

INITIATE TRACE SEARCH ANYWAY. FIREWALL REBUILD.

RRFF

READ MY MIND, BOY.

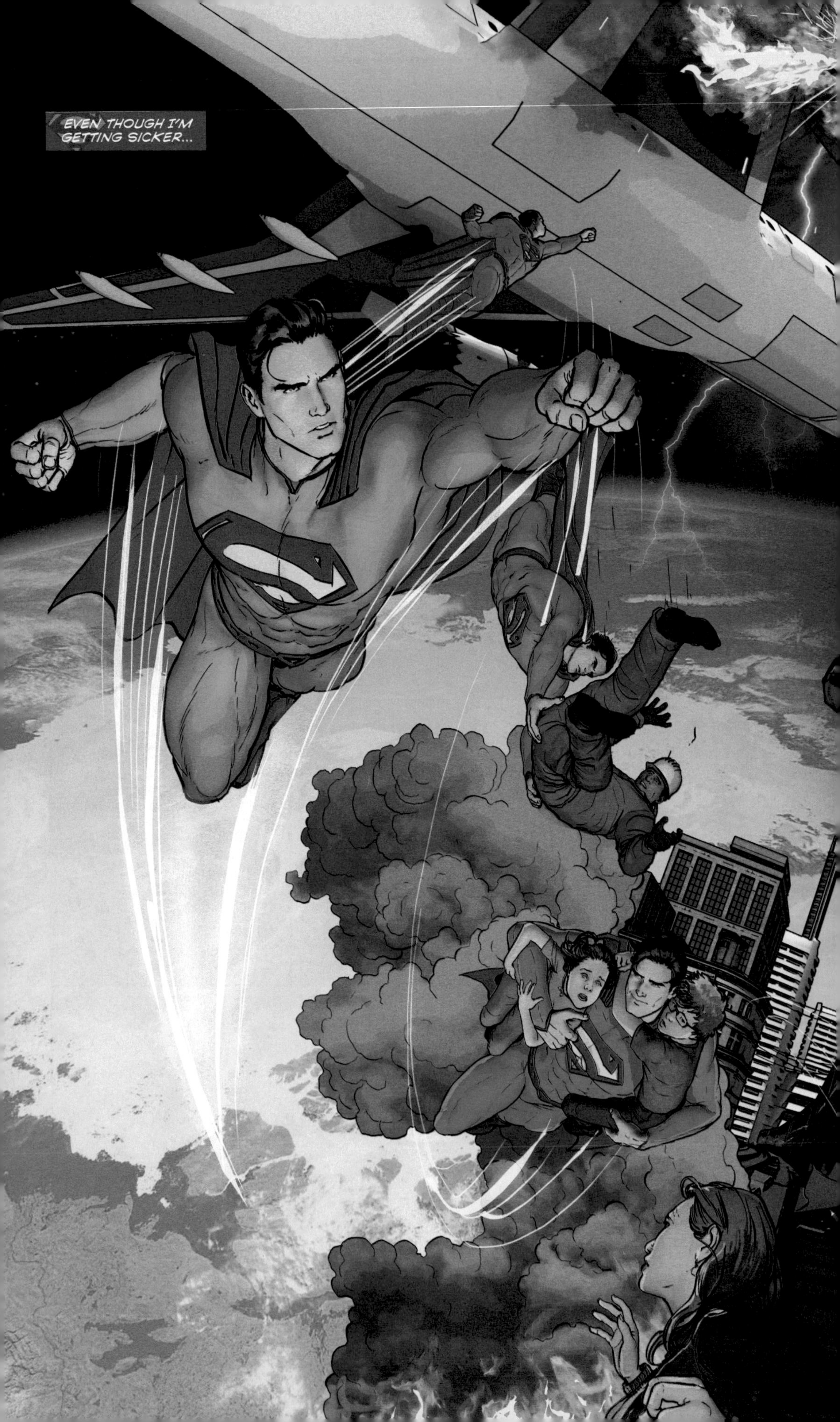
EVEN THOUGH I'M GETTING SICKER...

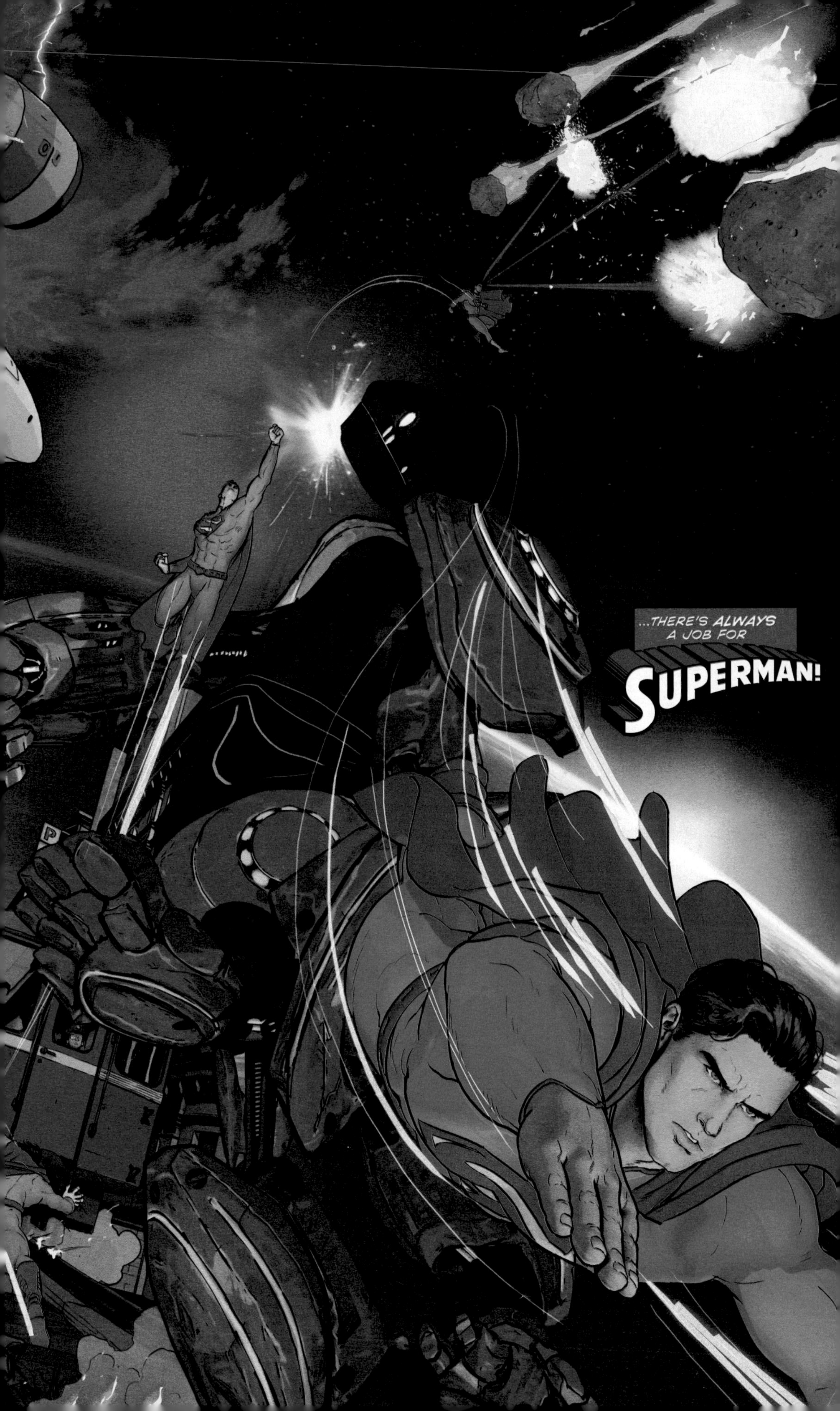
...THERE'S ALWAYS A JOB FOR
SUPERMAN!

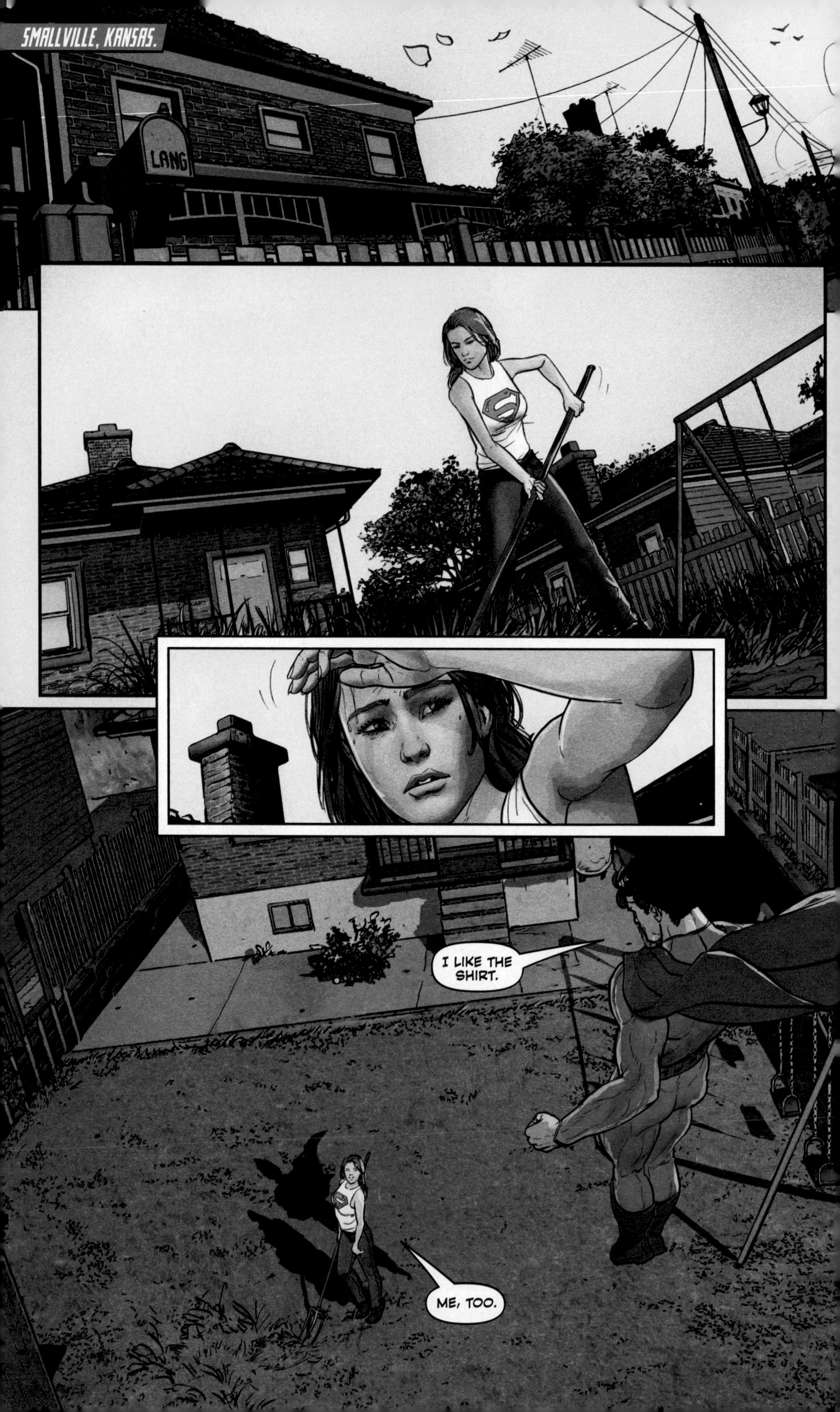
SMALLVILLE, KANSAS.
LANG
I LIKE THE SHIRT.
ME, TOO.

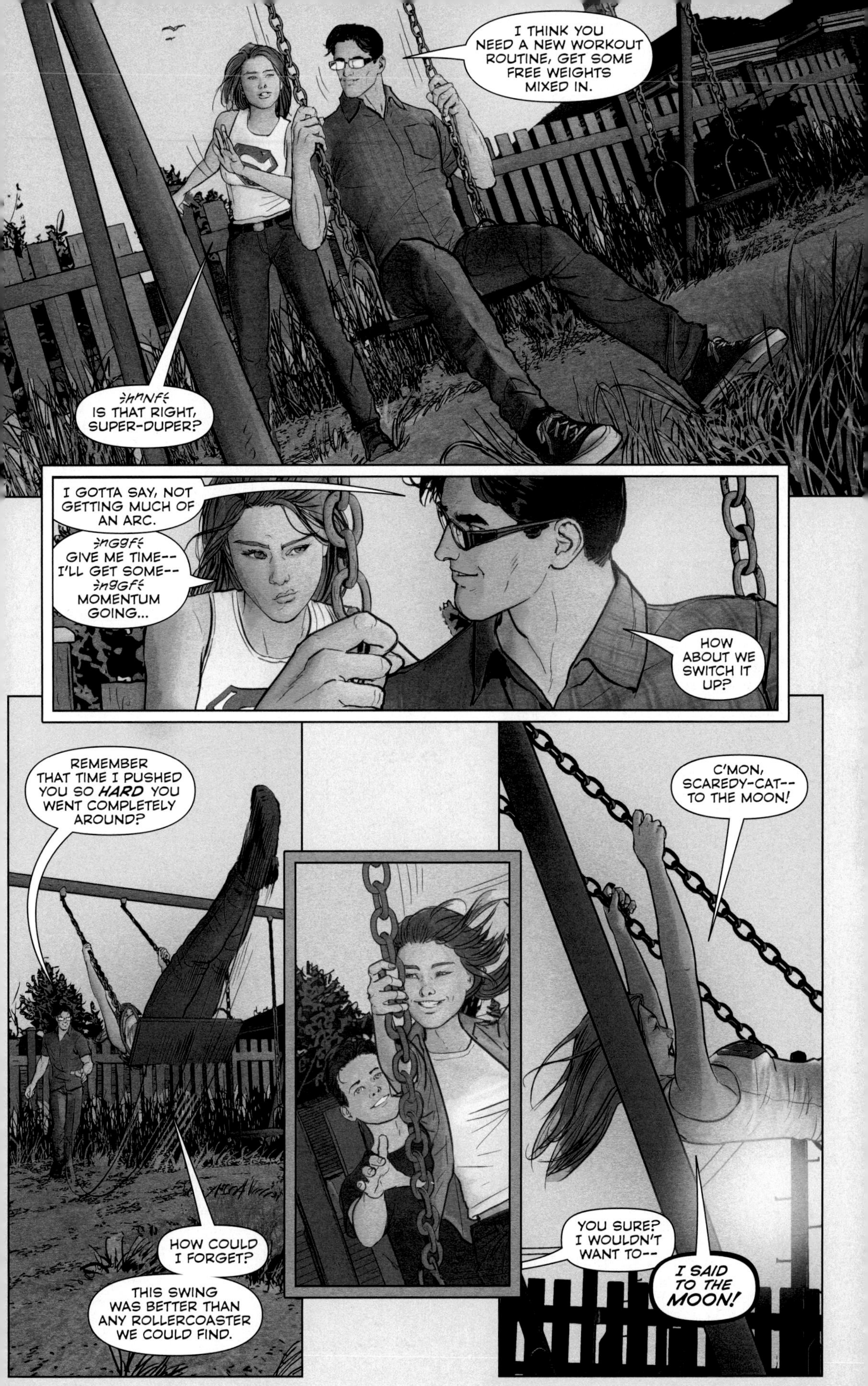

I THINK YOU NEED A NEW WORKOUT ROUTINE, GET SOME FREE WEIGHTS MIXED IN.
hnnf IS THAT RIGHT, SUPER-DUPER?
I GOTTA SAY, NOT GETTING MUCH OF AN ARC.
nggf GIVE ME TIME-- I'LL GET SOME-- nggf MOMENTUM GOING...
HOW ABOUT WE SWITCH IT UP?
REMEMBER THAT TIME I PUSHED YOU SO HARD YOU WENT COMPLETELY AROUND?
HOW COULD I FORGET?
THIS SWING WAS BETTER THAN ANY ROLLERCOASTER WE COULD FIND.
C'MON, SCAREDY-CAT-- TO THE MOON!
YOU SURE? I WOULDN'T WANT TO--
I SAID TO THE MOON!

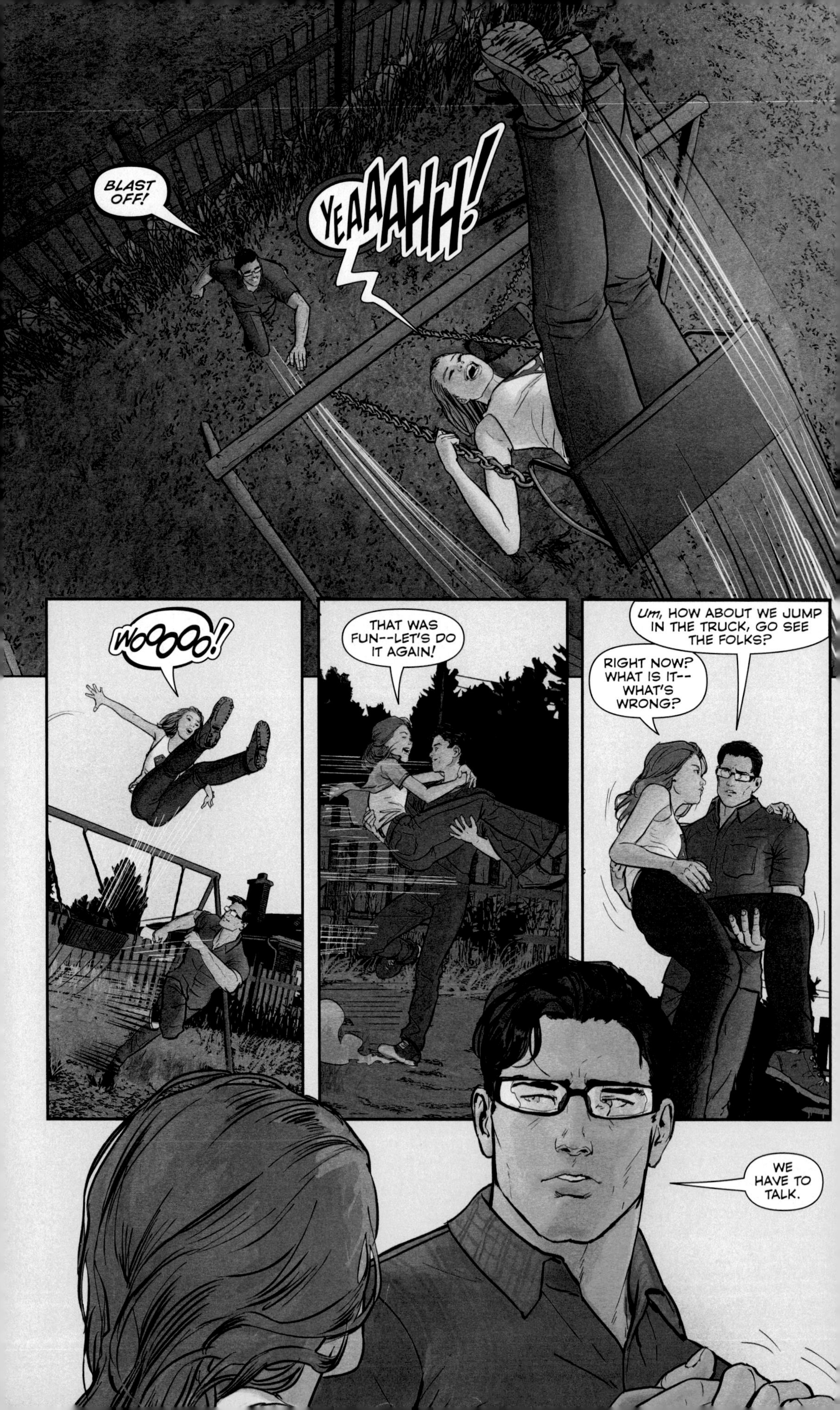
BLAST OFF!
YEAAAHH!
WOOOOO!
THAT WAS FUN--LET'S DO IT AGAIN!
Um, HOW ABOUT WE JUMP IN THE TRUCK, GO SEE THE FOLKS?
RIGHT NOW? WHAT IS IT-- WHAT'S WRONG?
WE HAVE TO TALK.

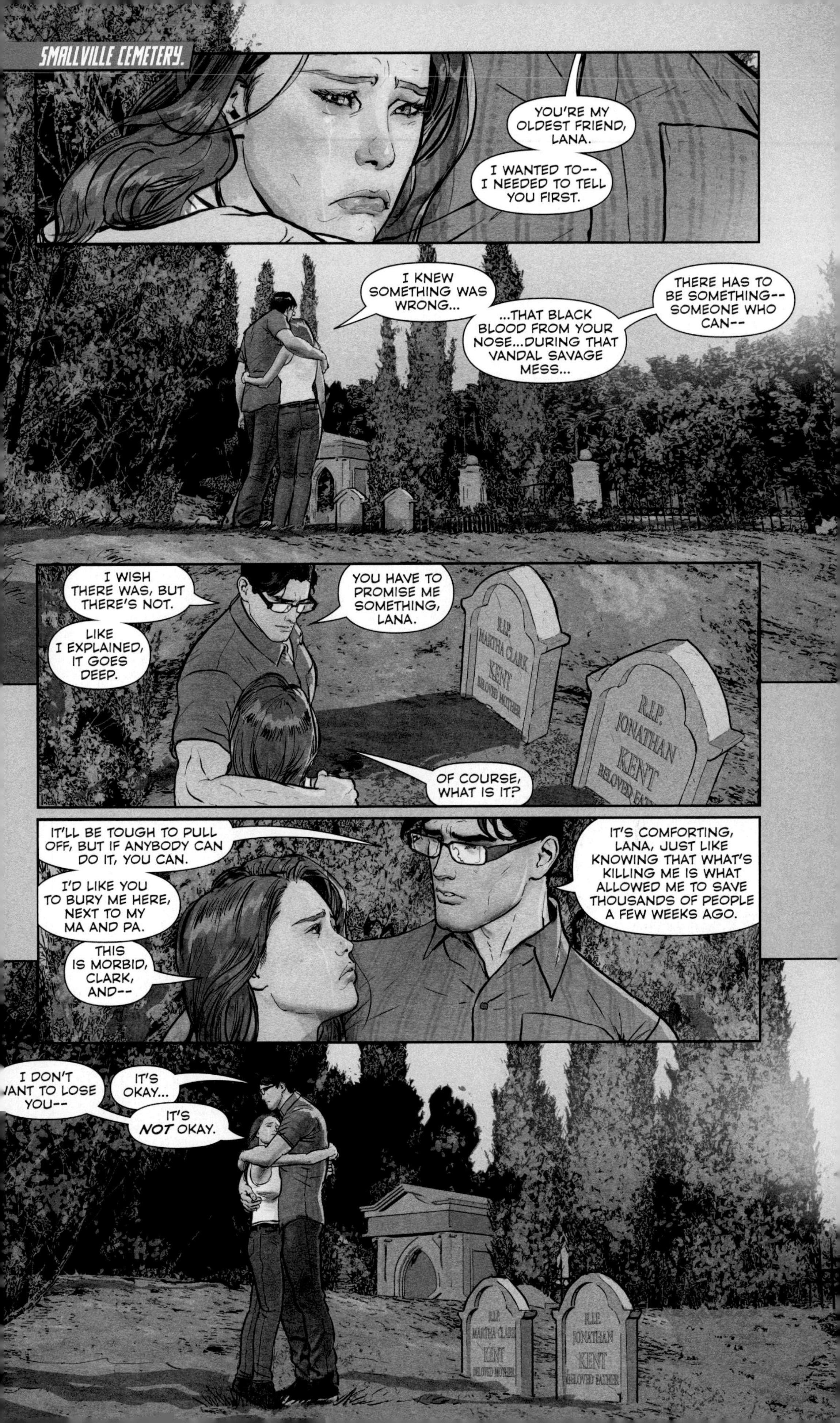
SMALLVILLE CEMETERY.
YOU'RE MY OLDEST FRIEND, LANA.
I WANTED TO-- I NEEDED TO TELL YOU FIRST.
I KNEW SOMETHING WAS WRONG...
...THAT BLACK BLOOD FROM YOUR NOSE...DURING THAT VANDAL SAVAGE MESS...
THERE HAS TO BE SOMETHING-- SOMEONE WHO CAN--
I WISH THERE WAS, BUT THERE'S NOT.
LIKE I EXPLAINED, IT GOES DEEP.
YOU HAVE TO PROMISE ME SOMETHING, LANA.
R.I.P. MARTHA CLARK KENT BELOVED MOTHER
R.I.P. JONATHAN KENT
OF COURSE, WHAT IS IT?
IT'LL BE TOUGH TO PULL OFF, BUT IF ANYBODY CAN DO IT, YOU CAN.
I'D LIKE YOU TO BURY ME HERE, NEXT TO MY MA AND PA.
THIS IS MORBID, CLARK, AND--
IT'S COMFORTING, LANA, JUST LIKE KNOWING THAT WHAT'S KILLING ME IS WHAT ALLOWED ME TO SAVE THOUSANDS OF PEOPLE A FEW WEEKS AGO.
I DON'T WANT TO LOSE YOU--
IT'S OKAY...
IT'S *NOT* OKAY.
R.I.P. MARTHA CLARK KENT BELOVED MOTHER
R.I.P. JONATHAN KENT BELOVED FATHER

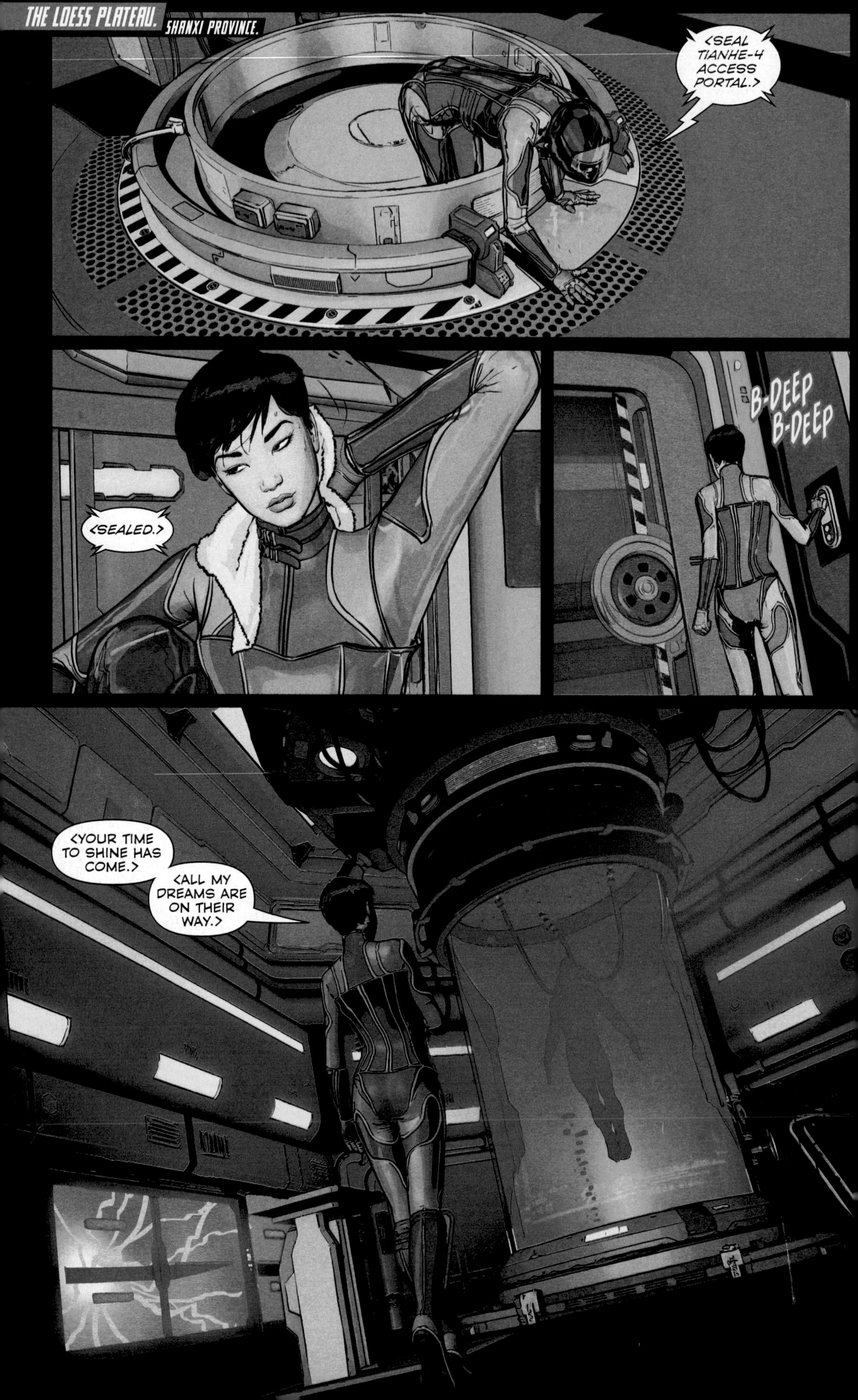
THE LOESS PLATEAU.
SHANXI PROVINCE.
<SEAL TIANHE-4 ACCESS PORTAL.>
<SEALED.>
B-DEEP B-DEEP
<YOUR TIME TO SHINE HAS COME.>
<ALL MY DREAMS ARE ON THEIR WAY.>

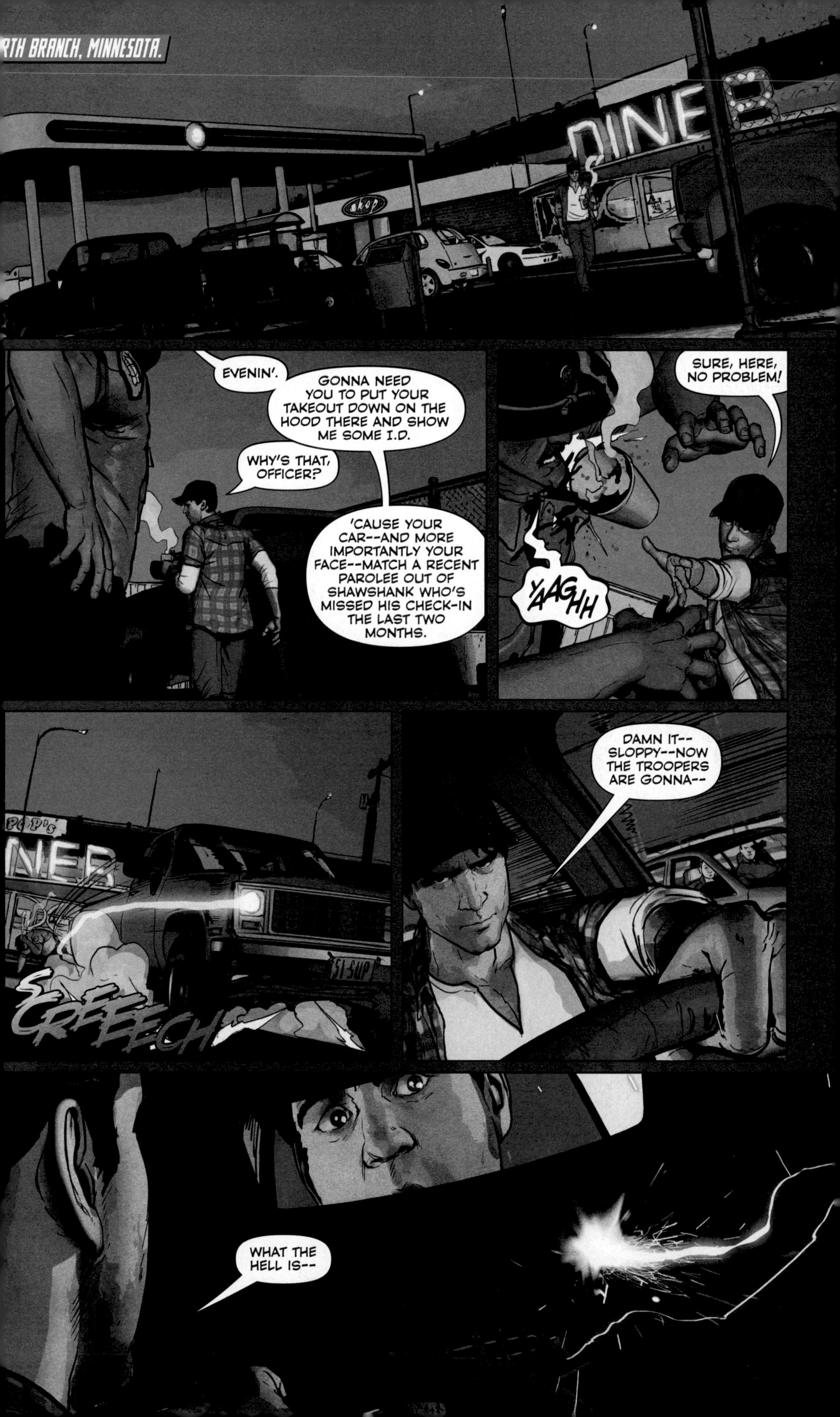
RTH BRANCH, MINNESOTA.
DINE
EVENIN'.
GONNA NEED YOU TO PUT YOUR TAKEOUT DOWN ON THE HOOD THERE AND SHOW ME SOME I.D.
WHY'S THAT, OFFICER?
'CAUSE YOUR CAR--AND MORE IMPORTANTLY YOUR FACE--MATCH A RECENT PAROLEE OUT OF SHAWSHANK WHO'S MISSED HIS CHECK-IN THE LAST TWO MONTHS.
SURE, HERE, NO PROBLEM!
YAAGHH
NER
SCREEECH
DAMN IT-- SLOPPY--NOW THE TROOPERS ARE GONNA--
WHAT THE HELL IS--

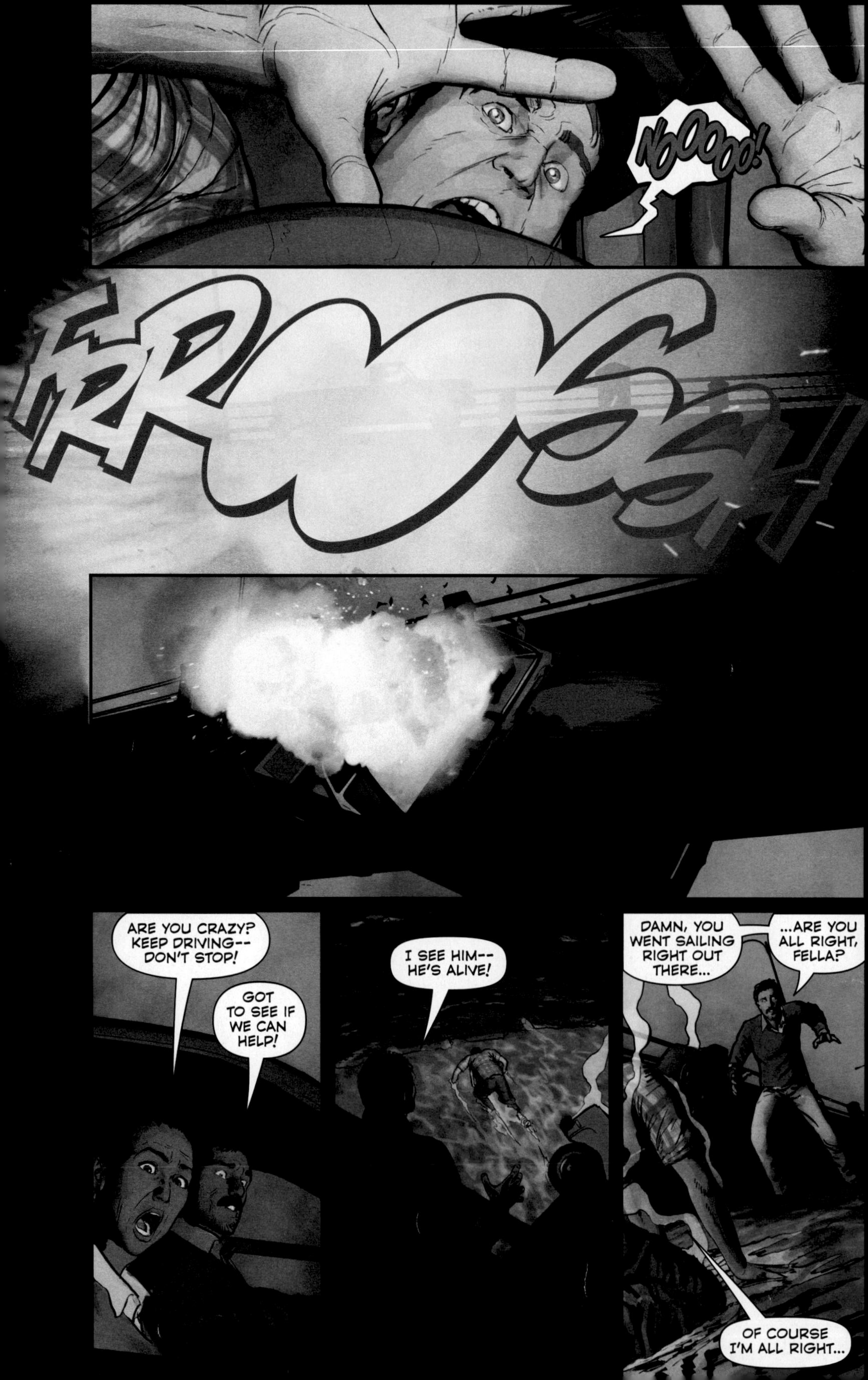
NOOOOOO!
FRROOSSH
ARE YOU CRAZY? KEEP DRIVING-- DON'T STOP!
GOT TO SEE IF WE CAN HELP!
I SEE HIM-- HE'S ALIVE!
DAMN, YOU WENT SAILING RIGHT OUT THERE...
...ARE YOU ALL RIGHT, FELLA?
OF COURSE I'M ALL RIGHT...

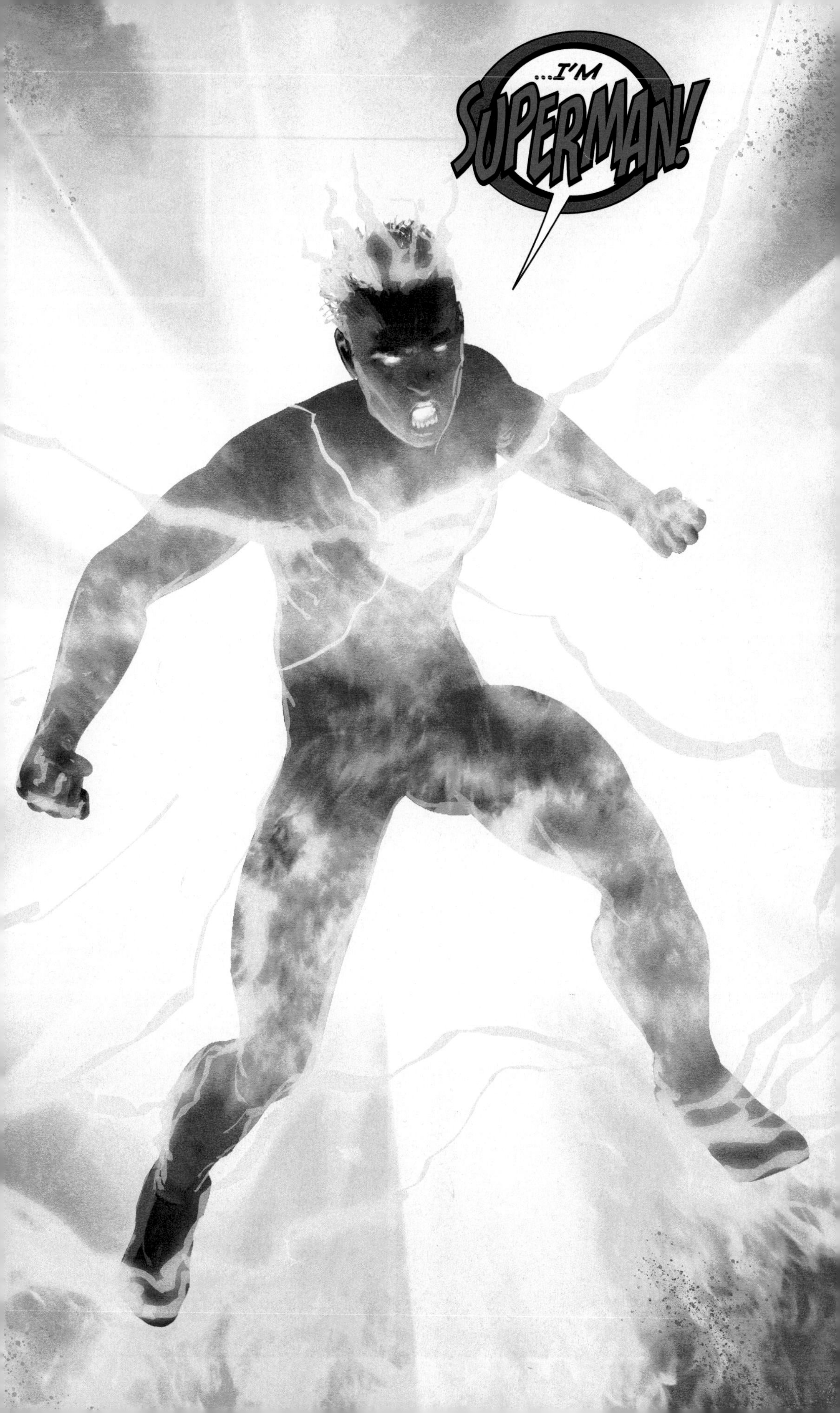
...I'M SUPERMAN!

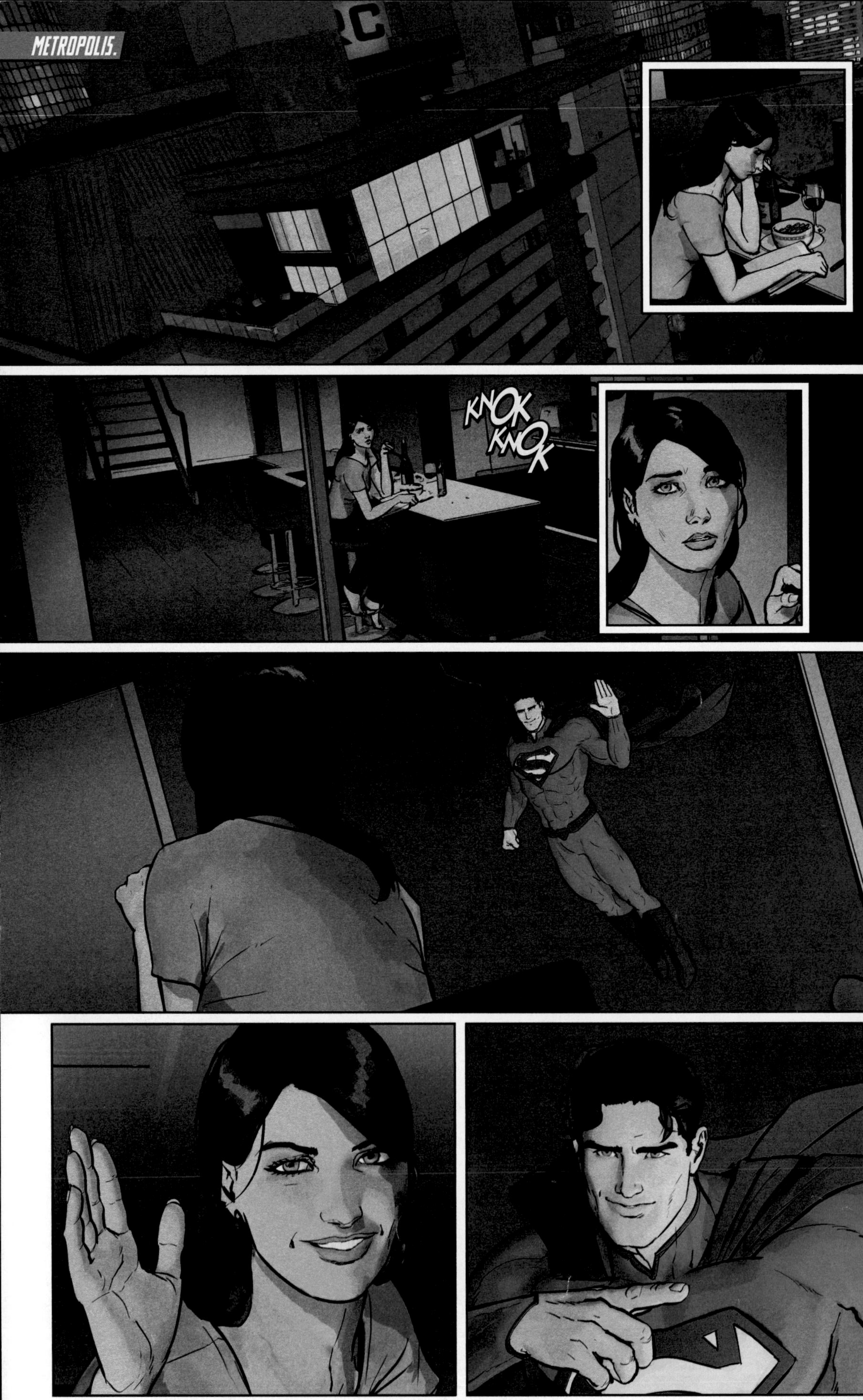
METROPOLIS.
KNOK
KNOK

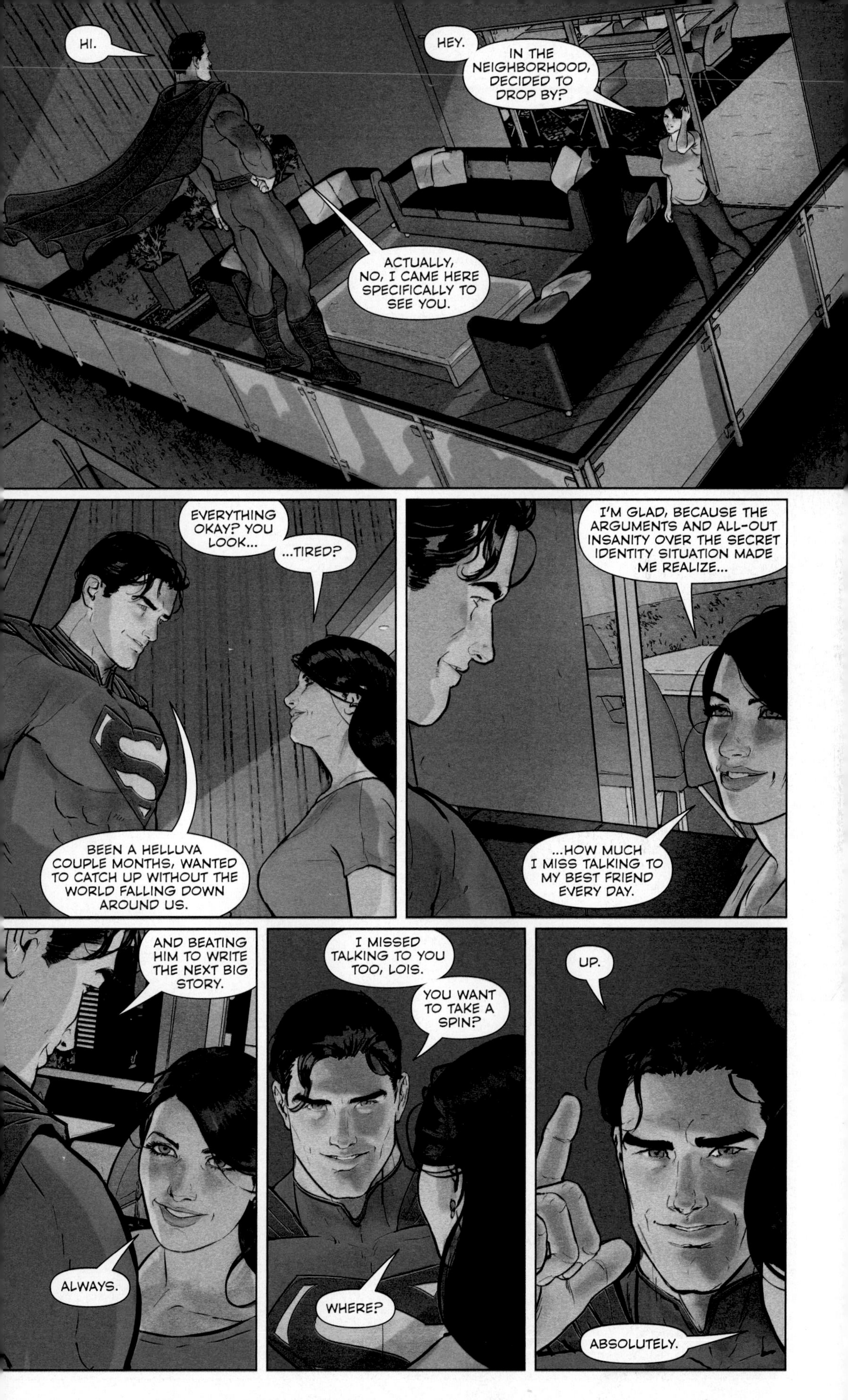
HI.
HEY.
IN THE NEIGHBORHOOD, DECIDED TO DROP BY?
ACTUALLY, NO, I CAME HERE SPECIFICALLY TO SEE YOU.
EVERYTHING OKAY? YOU LOOK...
...TIRED?
BEEN A HELLUVA COUPLE MONTHS, WANTED TO CATCH UP WITHOUT THE WORLD FALLING DOWN AROUND US.
I'M GLAD, BECAUSE THE ARGUMENTS AND ALL-OUT INSANITY OVER THE SECRET IDENTITY SITUATION MADE ME REALIZE...
...HOW MUCH I MISS TALKING TO MY BEST FRIEND EVERY DAY.
AND BEATING HIM TO WRITE THE NEXT BIG STORY.
ALWAYS.
I MISSED TALKING TO YOU TOO, LOIS.
YOU WANT TO TAKE A SPIN?
WHERE?
UP.
ABSOLUTELY.

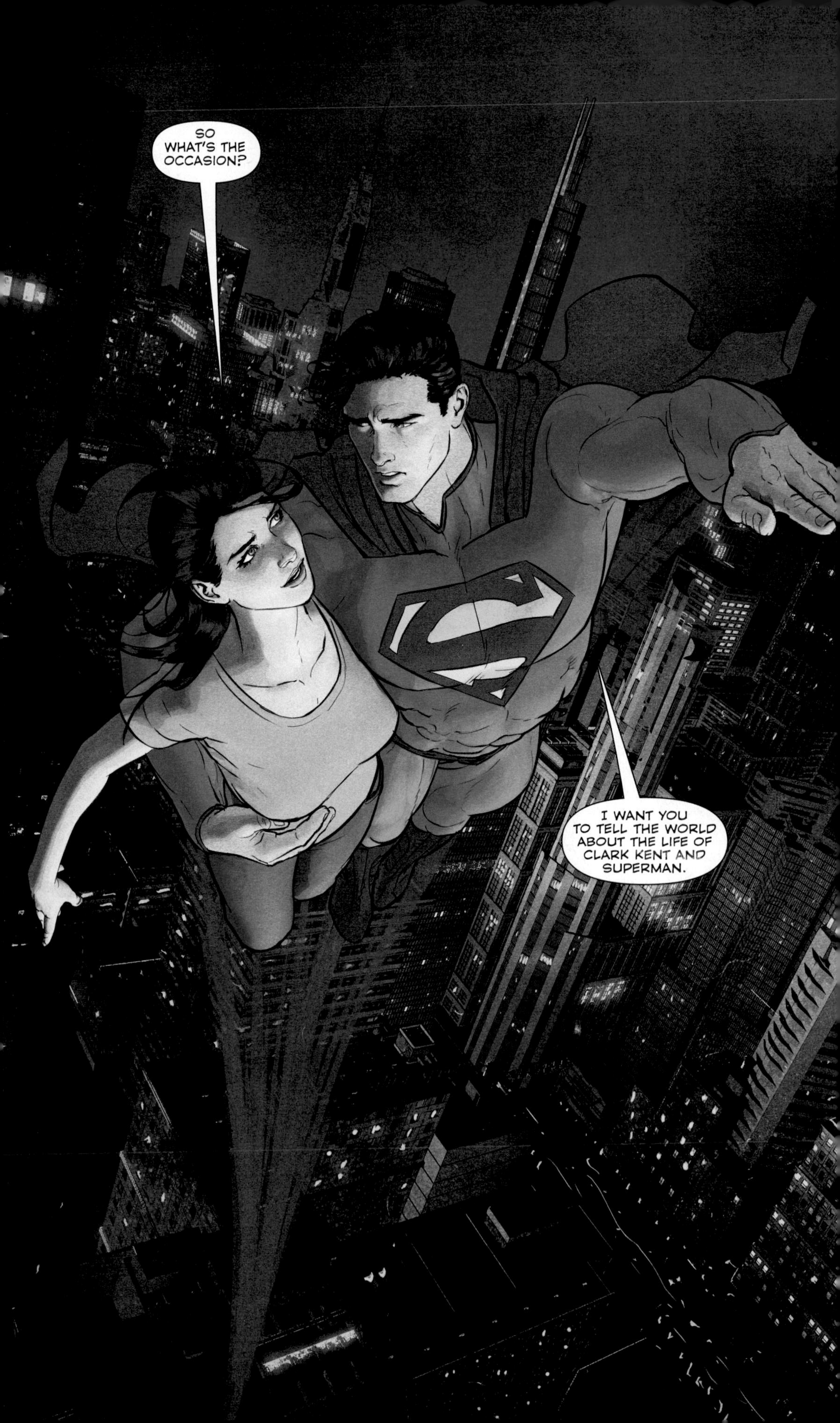
SO WHAT'S THE OCCASION?
I WANT YOU TO TELL THE WORLD ABOUT THE LIFE OF CLARK KENT AND SUPERMAN.

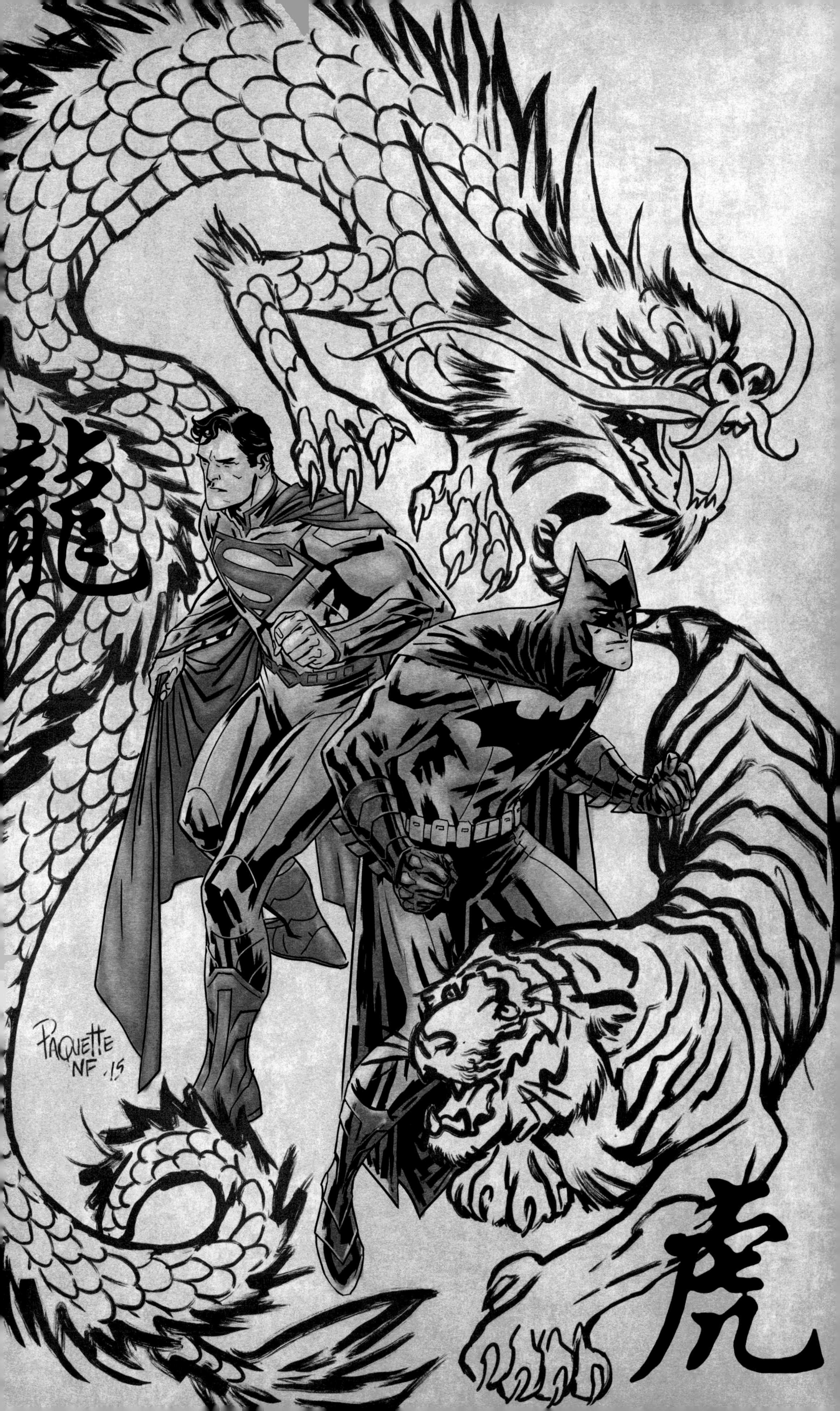
龍
虎
PAQUETTE
NF .15

THE FINAL DAYS OF SUPERMAN PART 2: DARK DISCOVERY

PETER J. TOMASI writer **DOUG MAHNKE** penciller **JAIME MENDOZA** inker **WIL QUINTANA** colorist **ROB LEIGH** letterer **YANICK PAQUETTE NATHAN FAIRBAIRN** cover

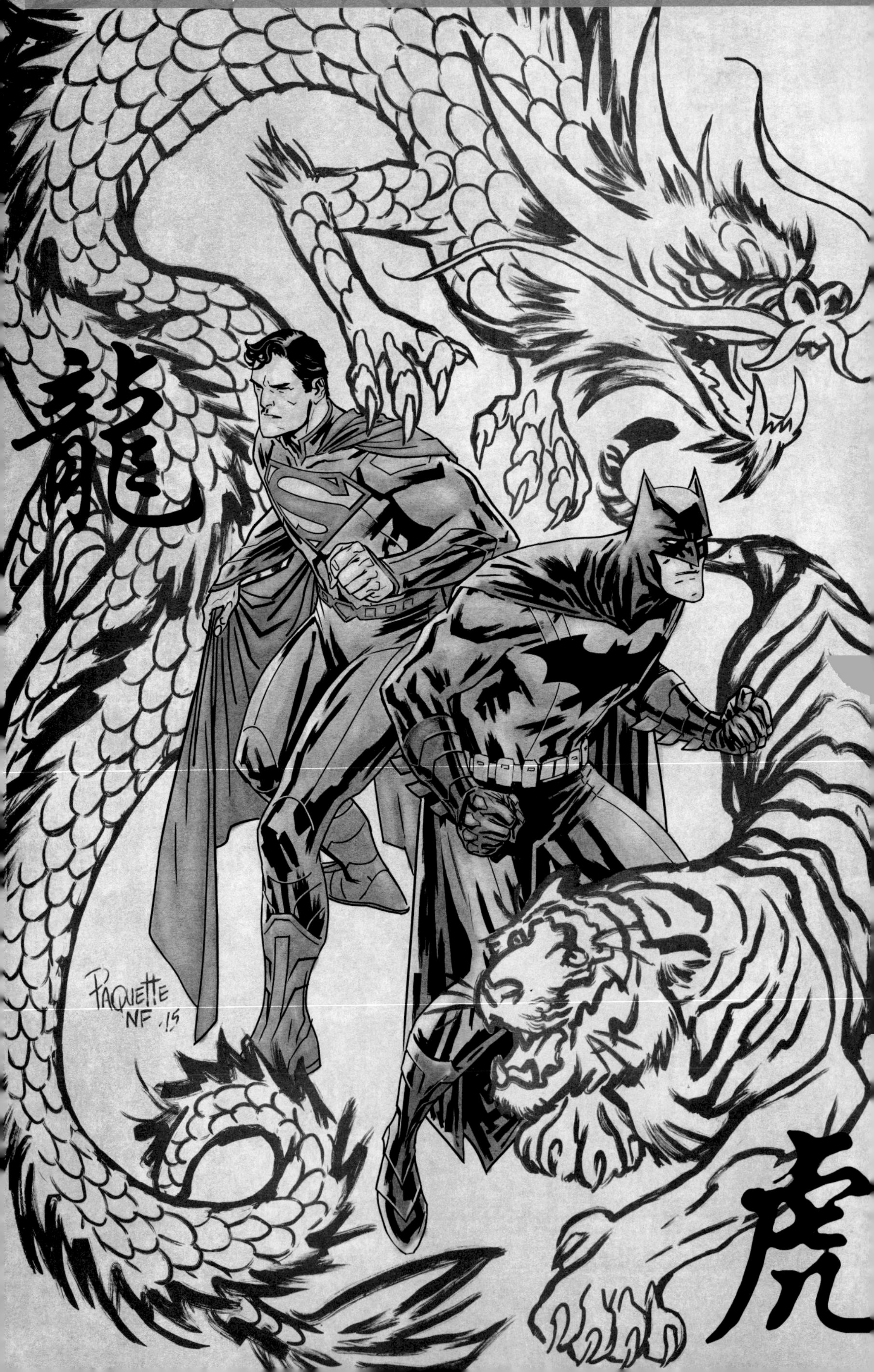

龍
PAQUETTE NF .15
虎

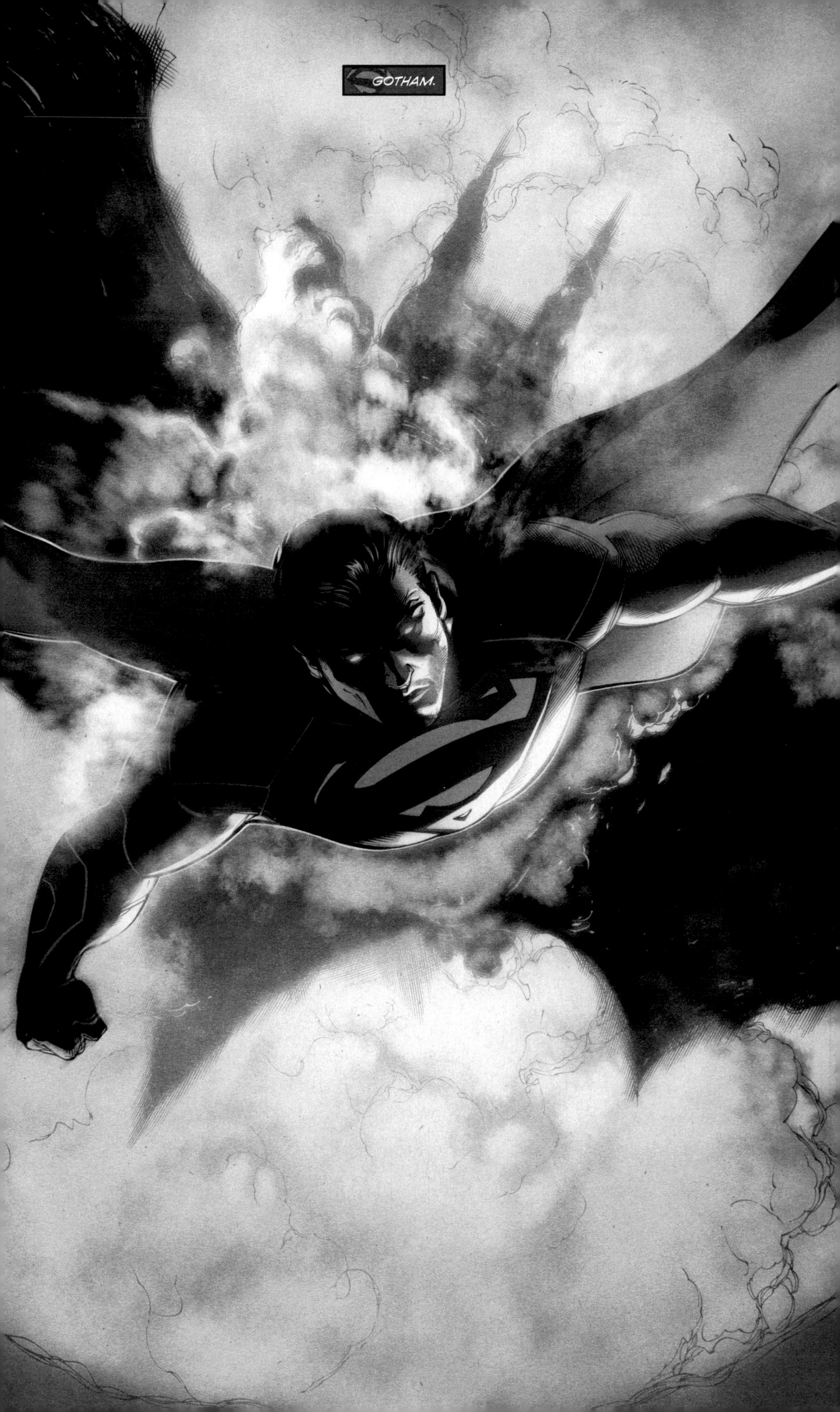
GOTHAM.

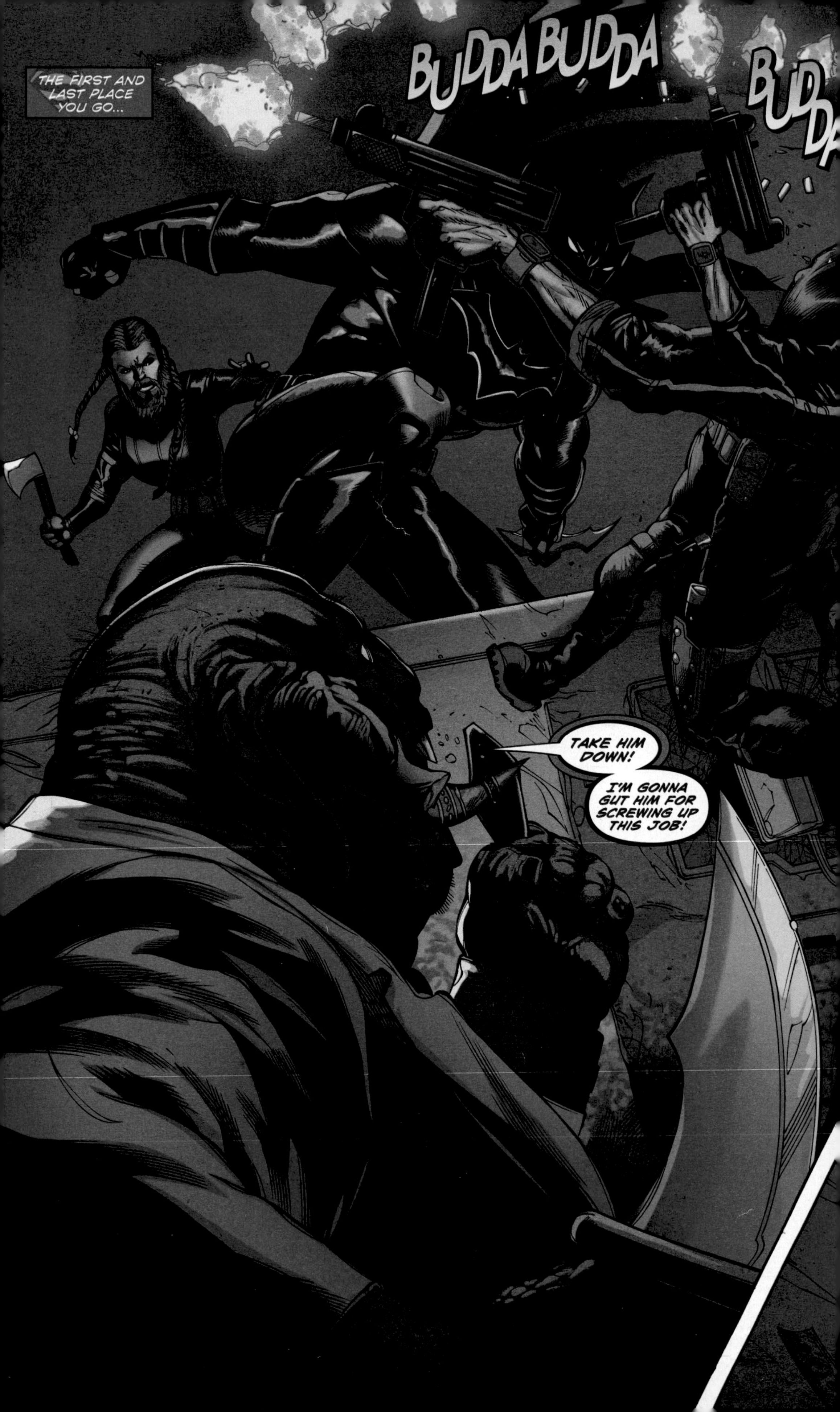
THE FIRST AND LAST PLACE YOU GO...
BUDDA BUDDA
BUDDA
TAKE HIM DOWN!
I'M GONNA GUT HIM FOR SCREWING UP THIS JOB!

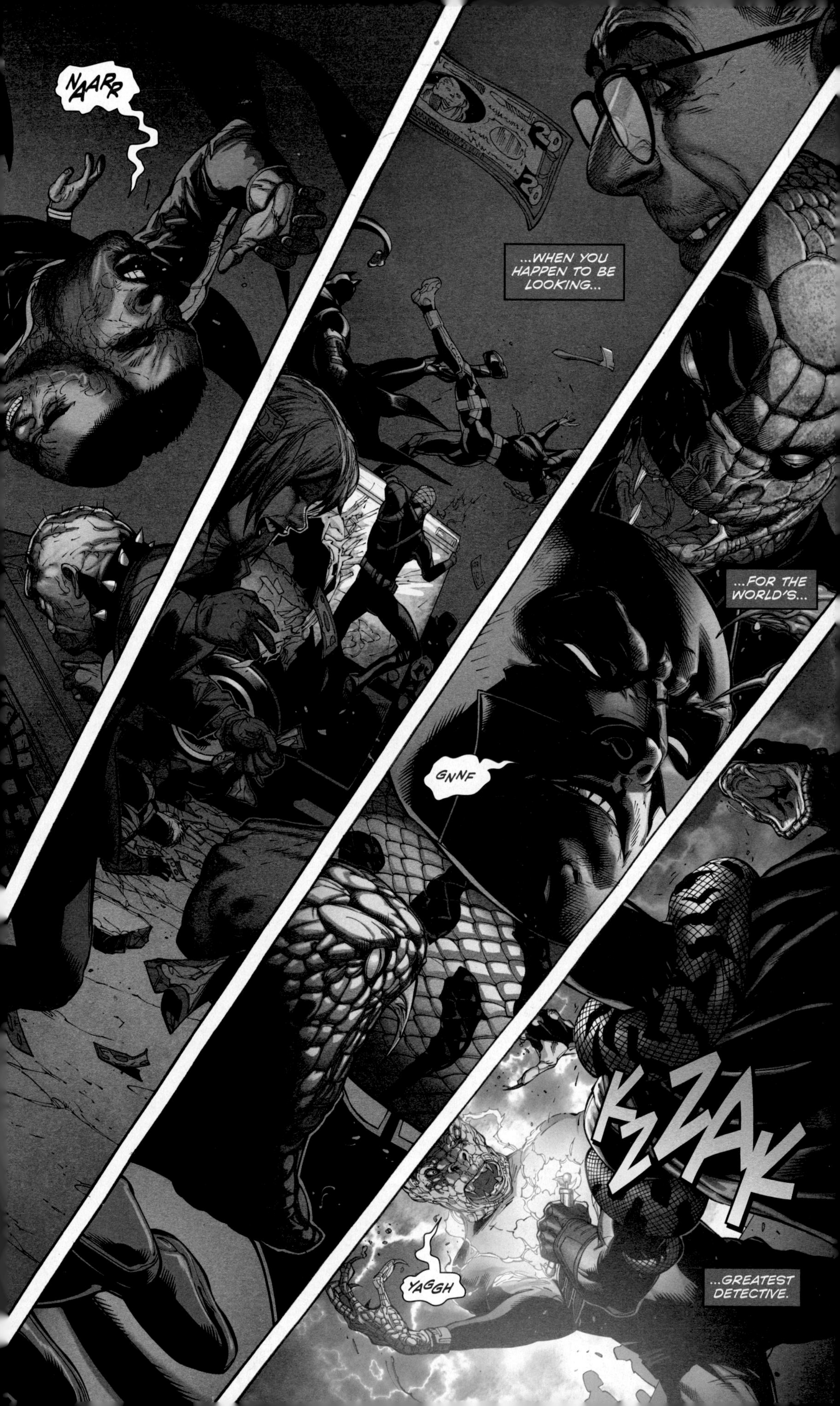
NAARR
...WHEN YOU HAPPEN TO BE LOOKING...
...FOR THE WORLD'S...
GNNF
KZZAK
YAGGH
...GREATEST DETECTIVE.

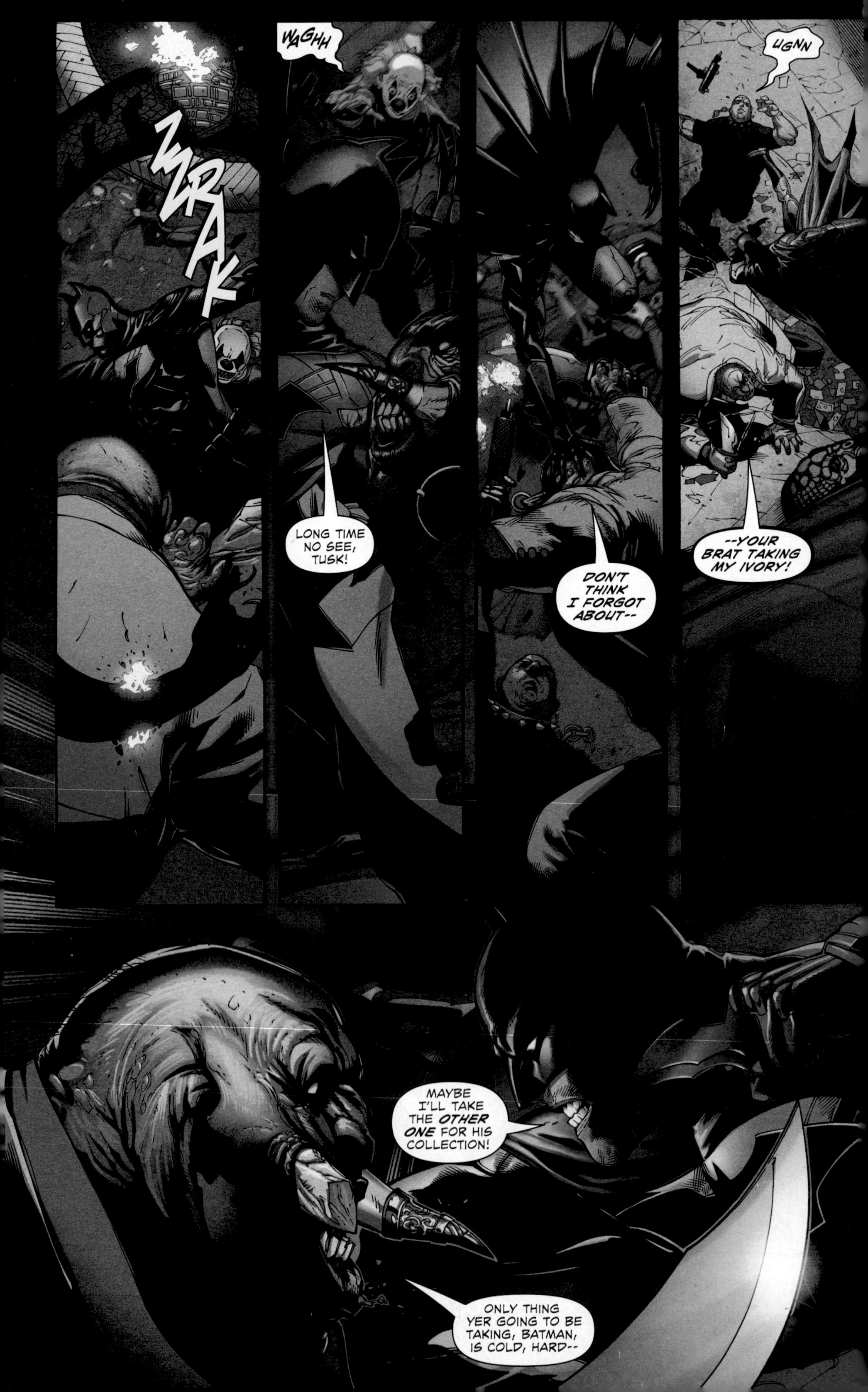

ZZRAK
WAGHH
LONG TIME NO SEE, TUSK!
DON'T THINK I FORGOT ABOUT--
UGNN
--YOUR BRAT TAKING MY IVORY!
MAYBE I'LL TAKE THE OTHER ONE FOR HIS COLLECTION!
ONLY THING YER GOING TO BE TAKING, BATMAN, IS COLD, HARD--

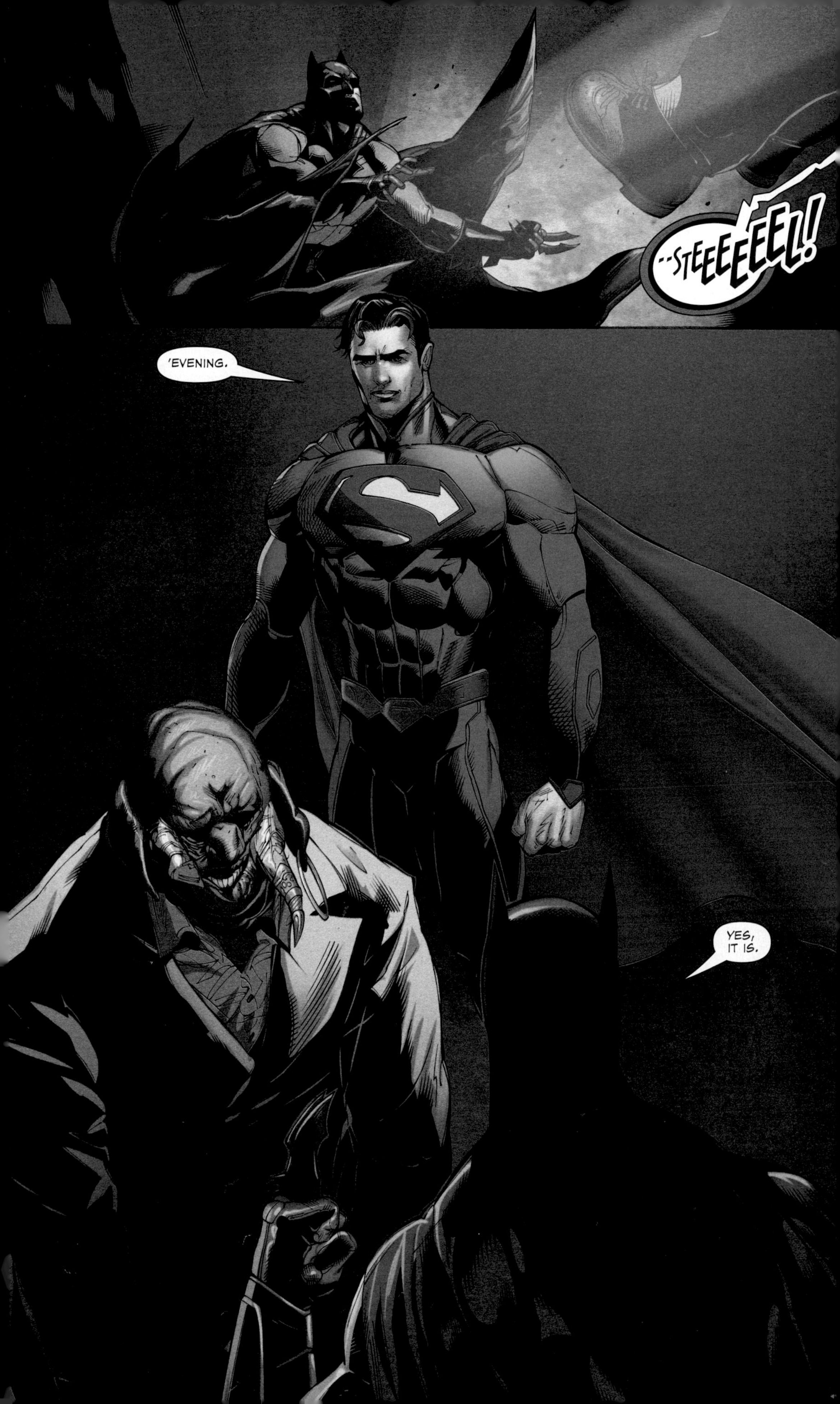
--STEEEEEEL!!
'EVENING.
YES,
IT IS.

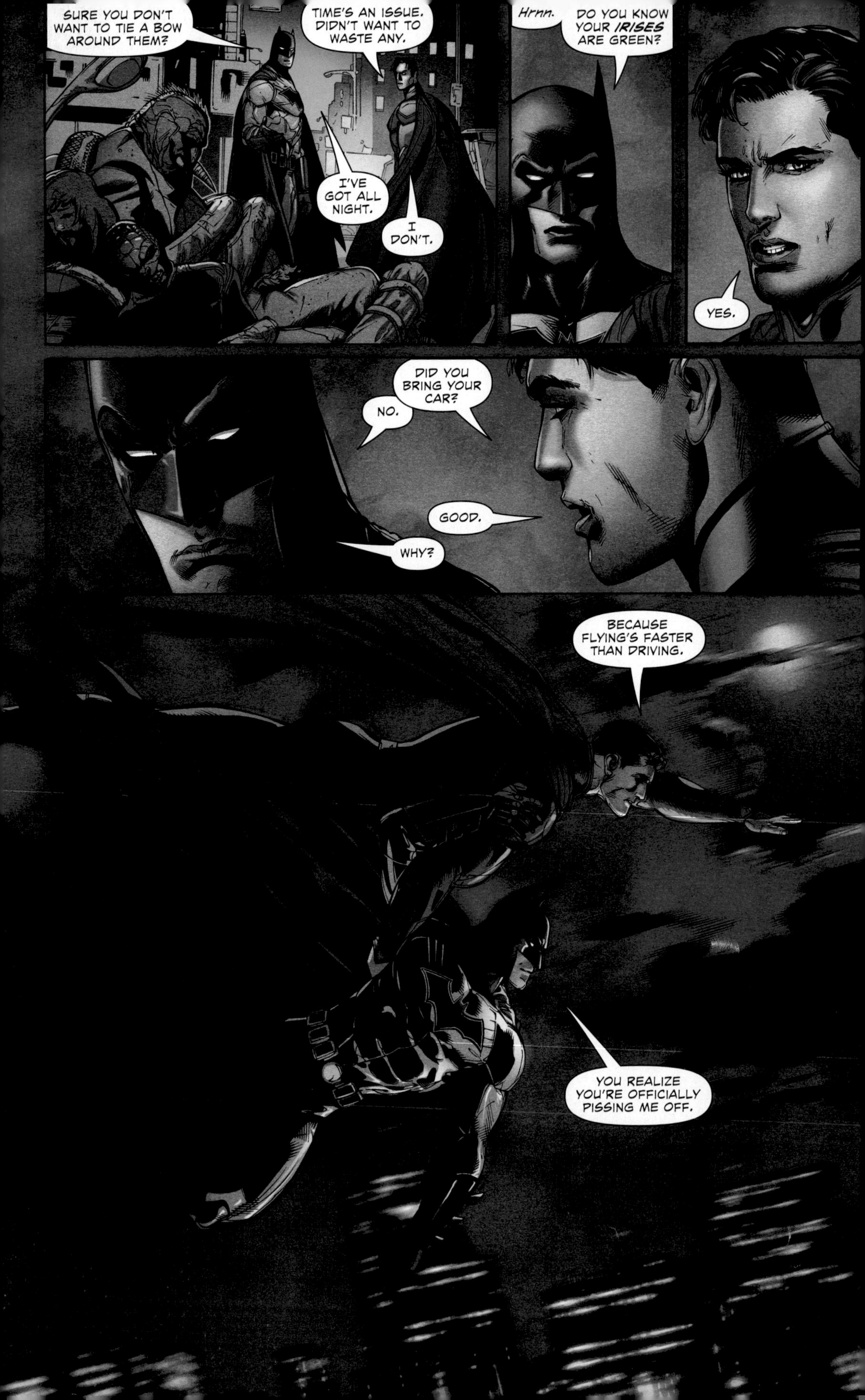
SURE YOU DON'T WANT TO TIE A BOW AROUND THEM?
TIME'S AN ISSUE. DIDN'T WANT TO WASTE ANY.
I'VE GOT ALL NIGHT.
I DON'T.
Hrnn.
DO YOU KNOW YOUR IRISES ARE GREEN?
YES.
DID YOU BRING YOUR CAR?
NO.
GOOD.
WHY?
BECAUSE FLYING'S FASTER THAN DRIVING.
YOU REALIZE YOU'RE OFFICIALLY PISSING ME OFF.

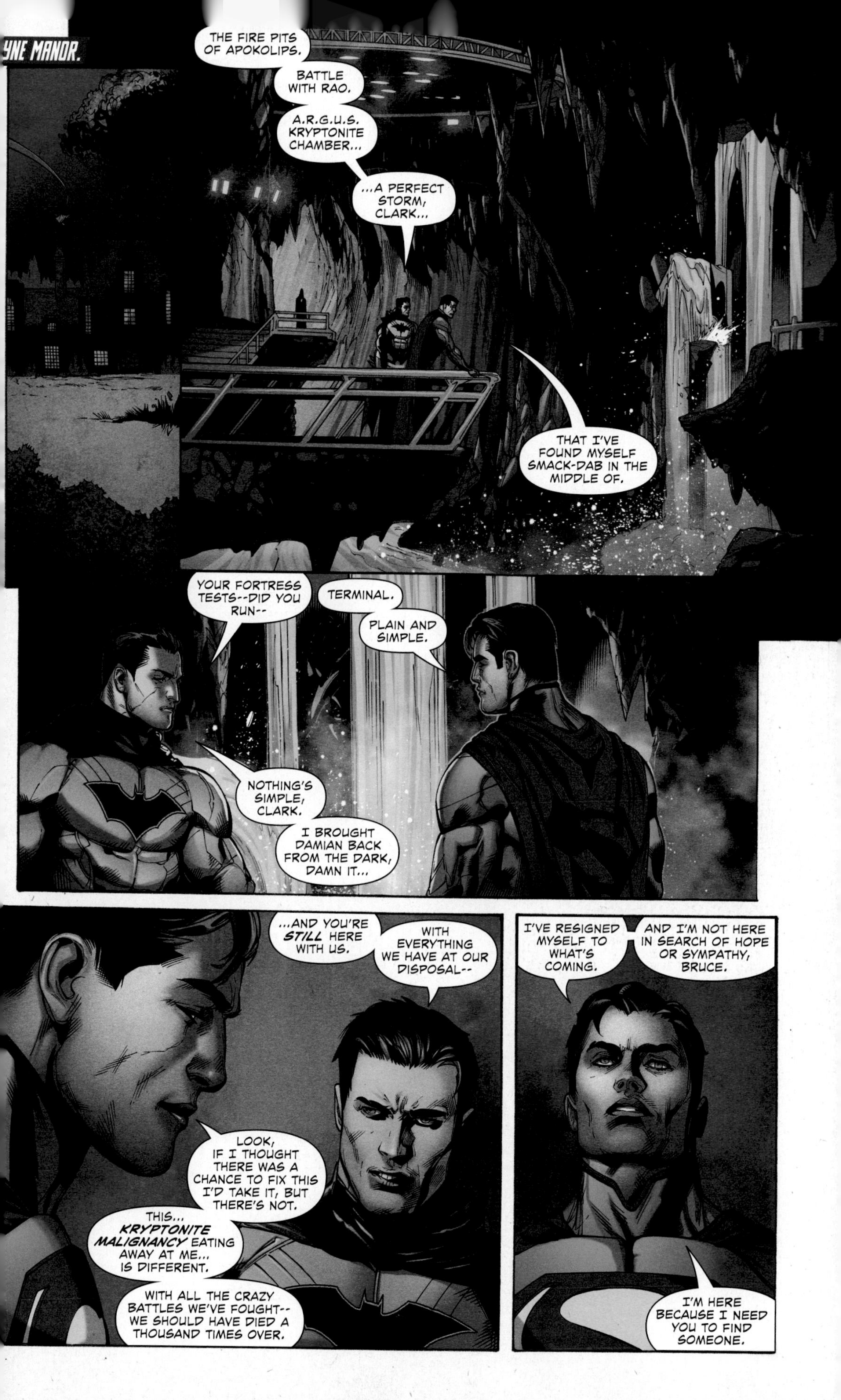
YNE MANOR.
THE FIRE PITS OF APOKOLIPS.
BATTLE WITH RAO.
A.R.G.U.S. KRYPTONITE CHAMBER...
...A PERFECT STORM, CLARK...
THAT I'VE FOUND MYSELF SMACK-DAB IN THE MIDDLE OF.
YOUR FORTRESS TESTS--DID YOU RUN--
TERMINAL.
PLAIN AND SIMPLE.
NOTHING'S SIMPLE, CLARK.
I BROUGHT DAMIAN BACK FROM THE DARK, DAMN IT...
...AND YOU'RE STILL HERE WITH US.
WITH EVERYTHING WE HAVE AT OUR DISPOSAL--
LOOK, IF I THOUGHT THERE WAS A CHANCE TO FIX THIS I'D TAKE IT, BUT THERE'S NOT.
THIS... KRYPTONITE MALIGNANCY EATING AWAY AT ME... IS DIFFERENT.
WITH ALL THE CRAZY BATTLES WE'VE FOUGHT--WE SHOULD HAVE DIED A THOUSAND TIMES OVER.
I'VE RESIGNED MYSELF TO WHAT'S COMING.
AND I'M NOT HERE IN SEARCH OF HOPE OR SYMPATHY, BRUCE.
I'M HERE BECAUSE I NEED YOU TO FIND SOMEONE.

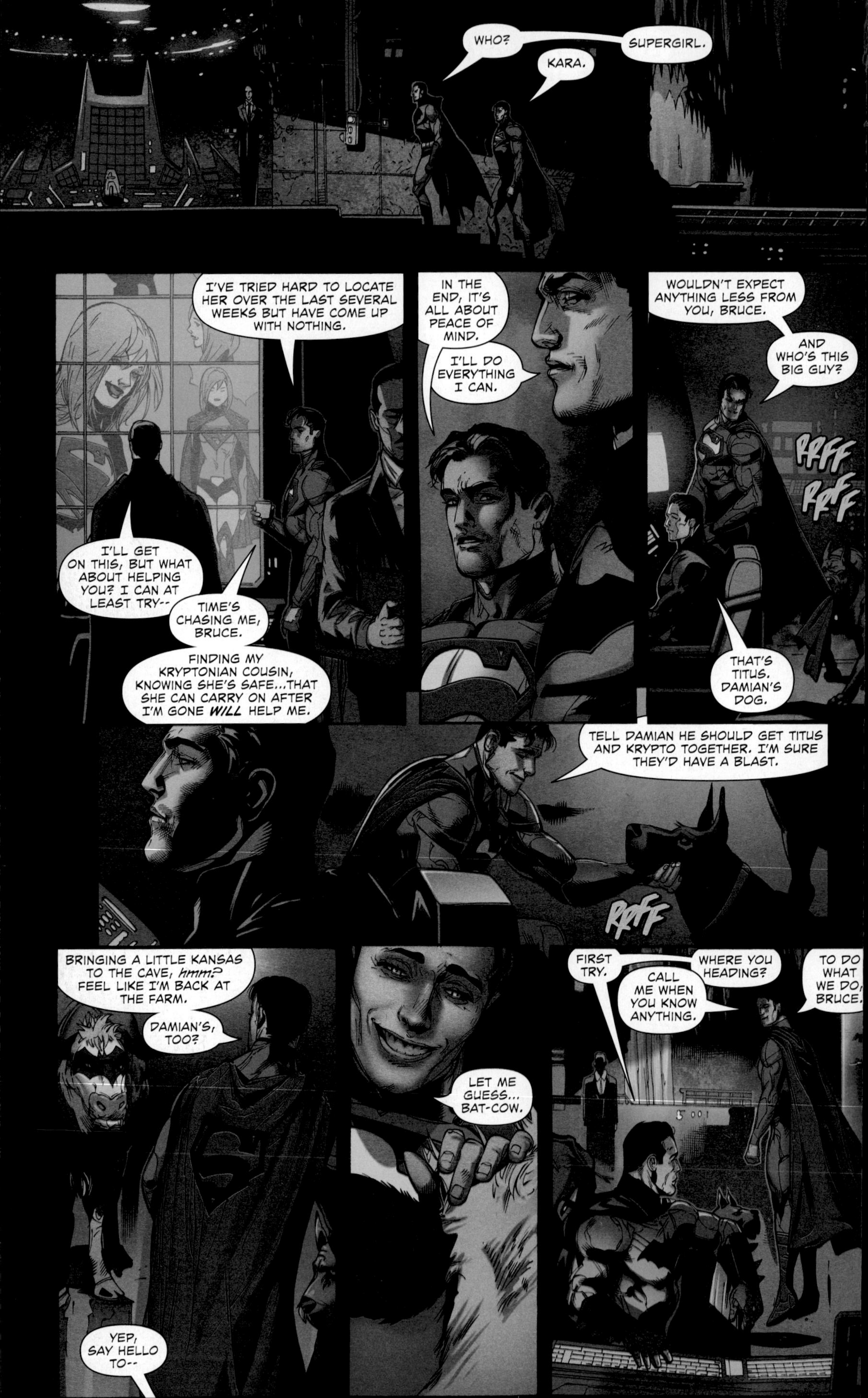
WHO?
SUPERGIRL.
KARA.
I'VE TRIED HARD TO LOCATE HER OVER THE LAST SEVERAL WEEKS BUT HAVE COME UP WITH NOTHING.
I'LL GET ON THIS, BUT WHAT ABOUT HELPING YOU? I CAN AT LEAST TRY--
TIME'S CHASING ME, BRUCE.
FINDING MY KRYPTONIAN COUSIN, KNOWING SHE'S SAFE...THAT SHE CAN CARRY ON AFTER I'M GONE WILL HELP ME.
IN THE END, IT'S ALL ABOUT PEACE OF MIND.
I'LL DO EVERYTHING I CAN.
WOULDN'T EXPECT ANYTHING LESS FROM YOU, BRUCE.
AND WHO'S THIS BIG GUY?
RRFF RRFF
THAT'S TITUS. DAMIAN'S DOG.
TELL DAMIAN HE SHOULD GET TITUS AND KRYPTO TOGETHER. I'M SURE THEY'D HAVE A BLAST.
RRFF
BRINGING A LITTLE KANSAS TO THE CAVE, hmm? FEEL LIKE I'M BACK AT THE FARM.
DAMIAN'S, TOO?
YEP, SAY HELLO TO--
LET ME GUESS... BAT-COW.
FIRST TRY.
CALL ME WHEN YOU KNOW ANYTHING.
WHERE YOU HEADING?
TO DO WHAT WE DO, BRUCE.

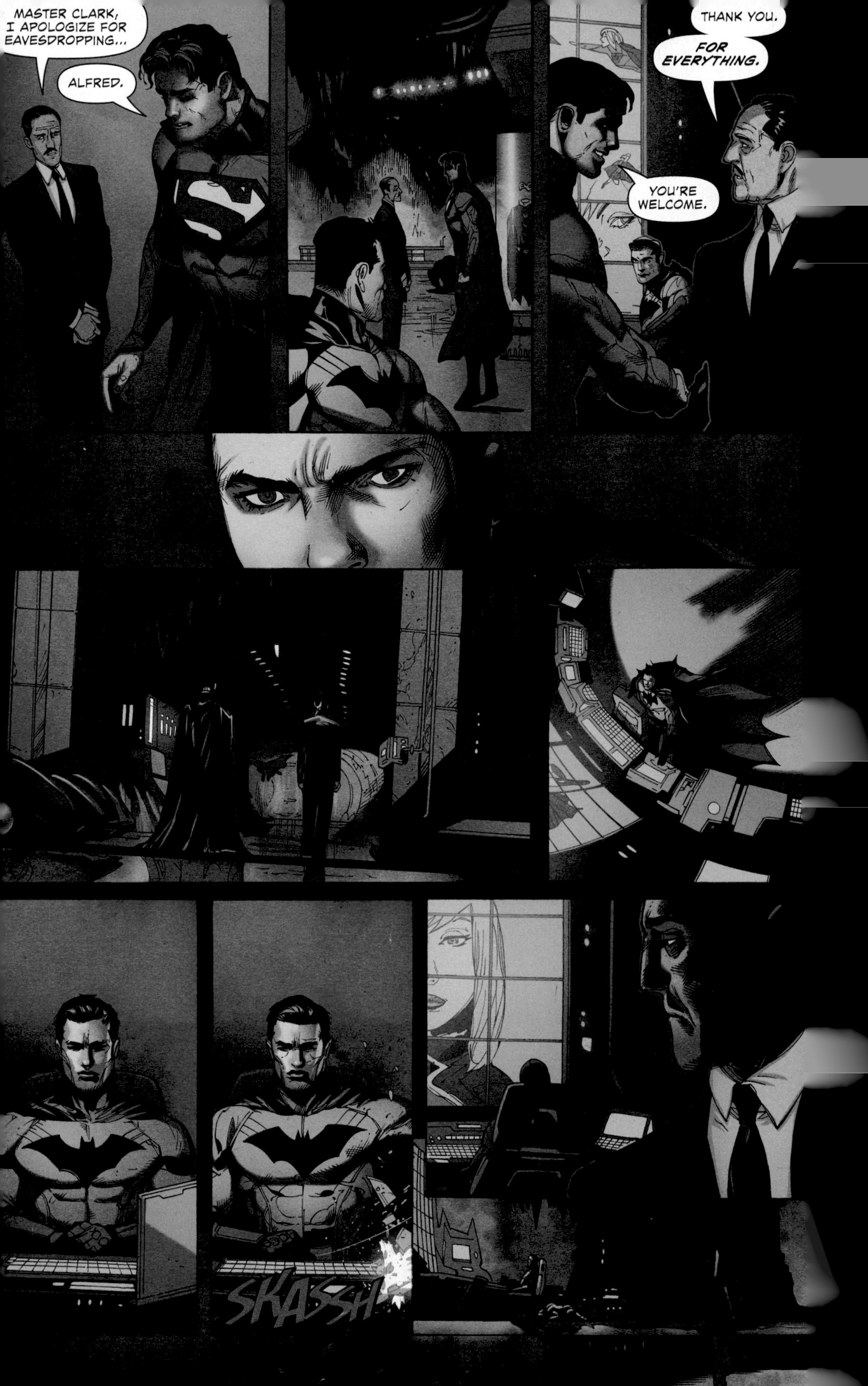
MASTER CLARK, I APOLOGIZE FOR EAVESDROPPING...
ALFRED.
THANK YOU.
FOR EVERYTHING.
YOU'RE WELCOME.
SKASSH

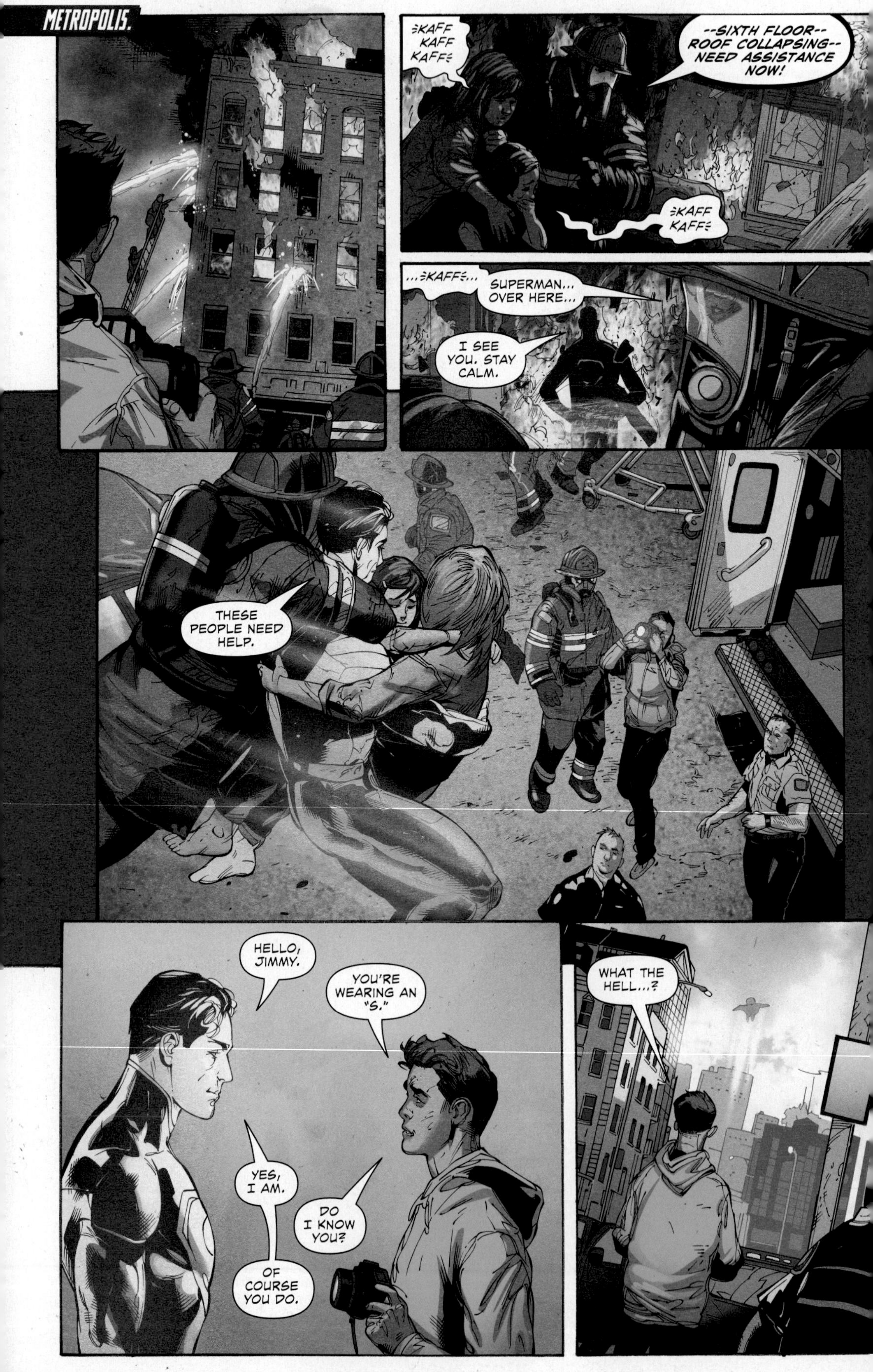
METROPOLIS.
KAFF KAFF KAFF
--SIXTH FLOOR-- ROOF COLLAPSING-- NEED ASSISTANCE NOW!
KAFF KAFF
...KAFF...
SUPERMAN... OVER HERE...
I SEE YOU. STAY CALM.
THESE PEOPLE NEED HELP.
HELLO, JIMMY.
YOU'RE WEARING AN "S."
YES, I AM.
DO I KNOW YOU?
OF COURSE YOU DO.
WHAT THE HELL...?

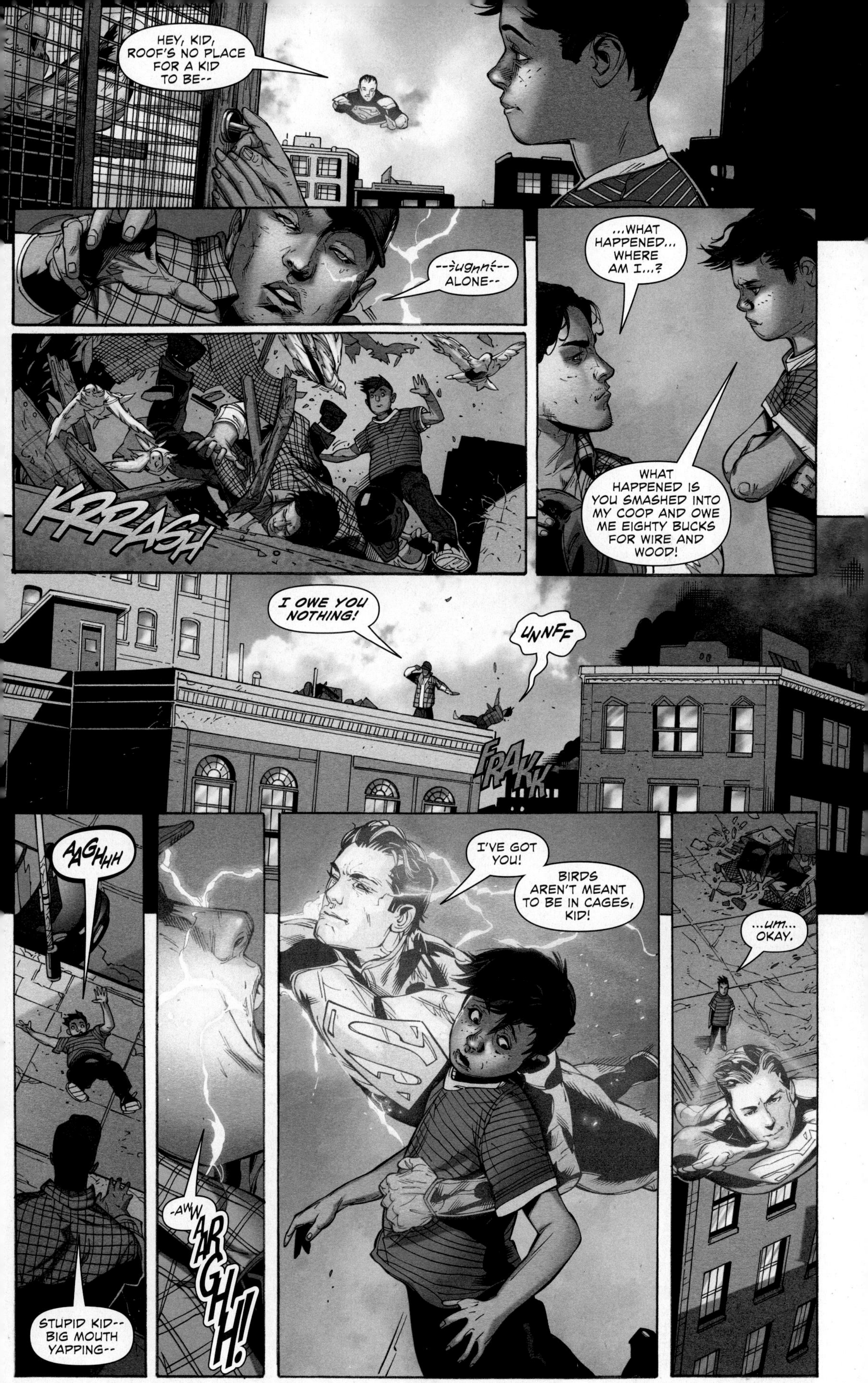
HEY, KID, ROOF'S NO PLACE FOR A KID TO BE--
--ugnn--
ALONE--
KRRASH
...WHAT HAPPENED... WHERE AM I...?
WHAT HAPPENED IS YOU SMASHED INTO MY COOP AND OWE ME EIGHTY BUCKS FOR WIRE AND WOOD!
I OWE YOU NOTHING!
UNNFF
FRAKK
AAGHHH
STUPID KID-- BIG MOUTH YAPPING--
-AWWARGHH!
I'VE GOT YOU!
BIRDS AREN'T MEANT TO BE IN CAGES, KID!
...um... OKAY.

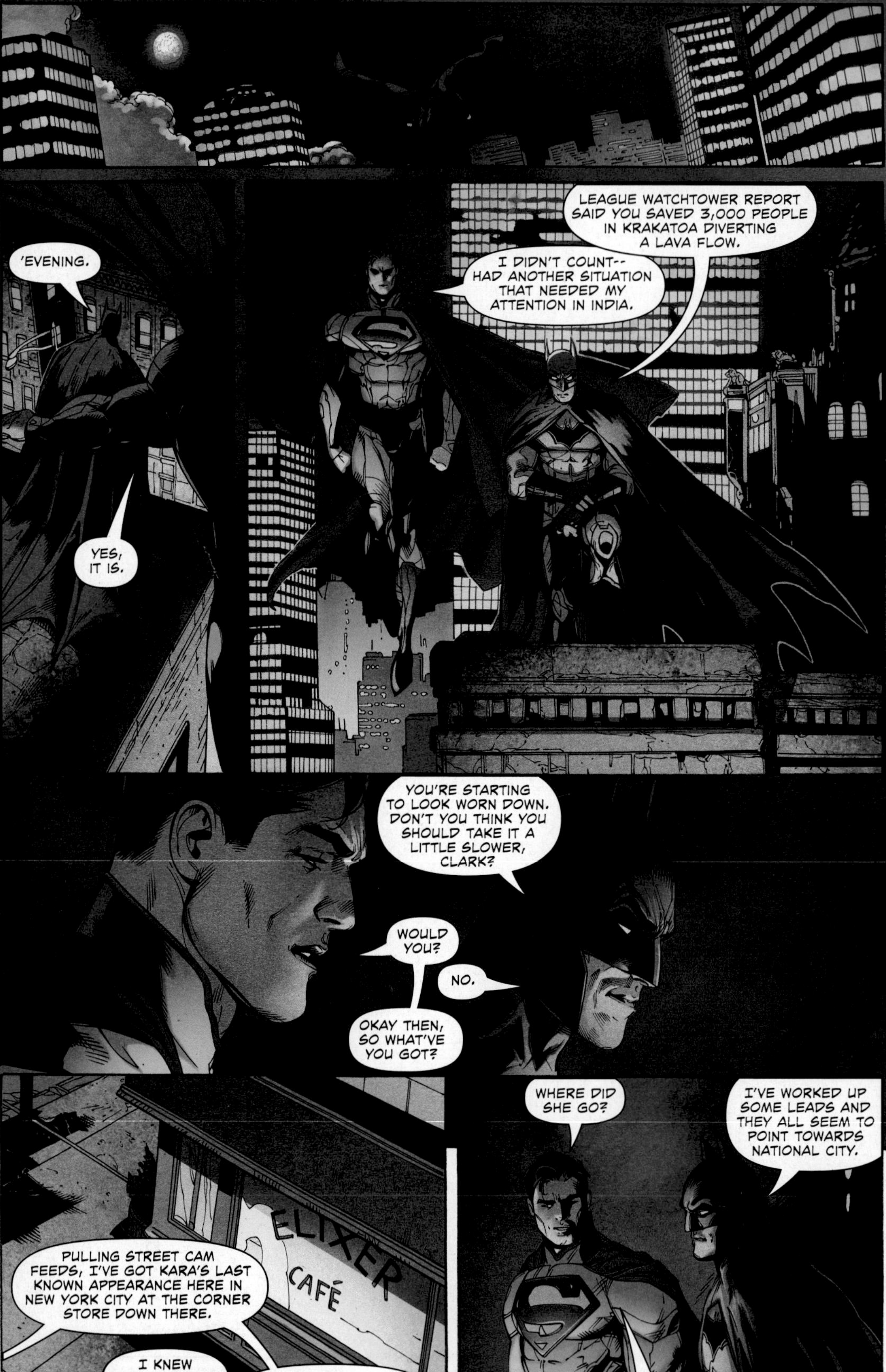
'EVENING.
LEAGUE WATCHTOWER REPORT SAID YOU SAVED 3,000 PEOPLE IN KRAKATOA DIVERTING A LAVA FLOW.
I DIDN'T COUNT-- HAD ANOTHER SITUATION THAT NEEDED MY ATTENTION IN INDIA.
YES, IT IS.
YOU'RE STARTING TO LOOK WORN DOWN. DON'T YOU THINK YOU SHOULD TAKE IT A LITTLE SLOWER, CLARK?
WOULD YOU?
NO.
OKAY THEN, SO WHAT'VE YOU GOT?
ELIXER
CAFÉ
PULLING STREET CAM FEEDS, I'VE GOT KARA'S LAST KNOWN APPEARANCE HERE IN NEW YORK CITY AT THE CORNER STORE DOWN THERE.
I KNEW THAT. WHEN DID SHE LEAVE?
SEVERAL WEEKS AGO. SHE WAS WORKING AS A BARISTA FOR A WHILE AND THEN TOOK OFF.
WHERE DID SHE GO?
I'VE WORKED UP SOME LEADS AND THEY ALL SEEM TO POINT TOWARDS NATIONAL CITY.
THEN THAT'S MY NEXT--

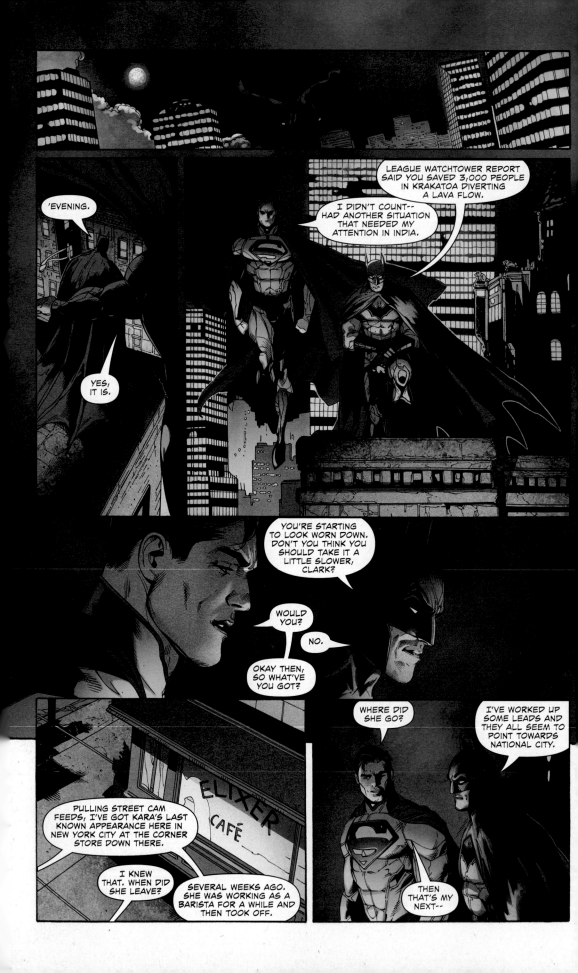

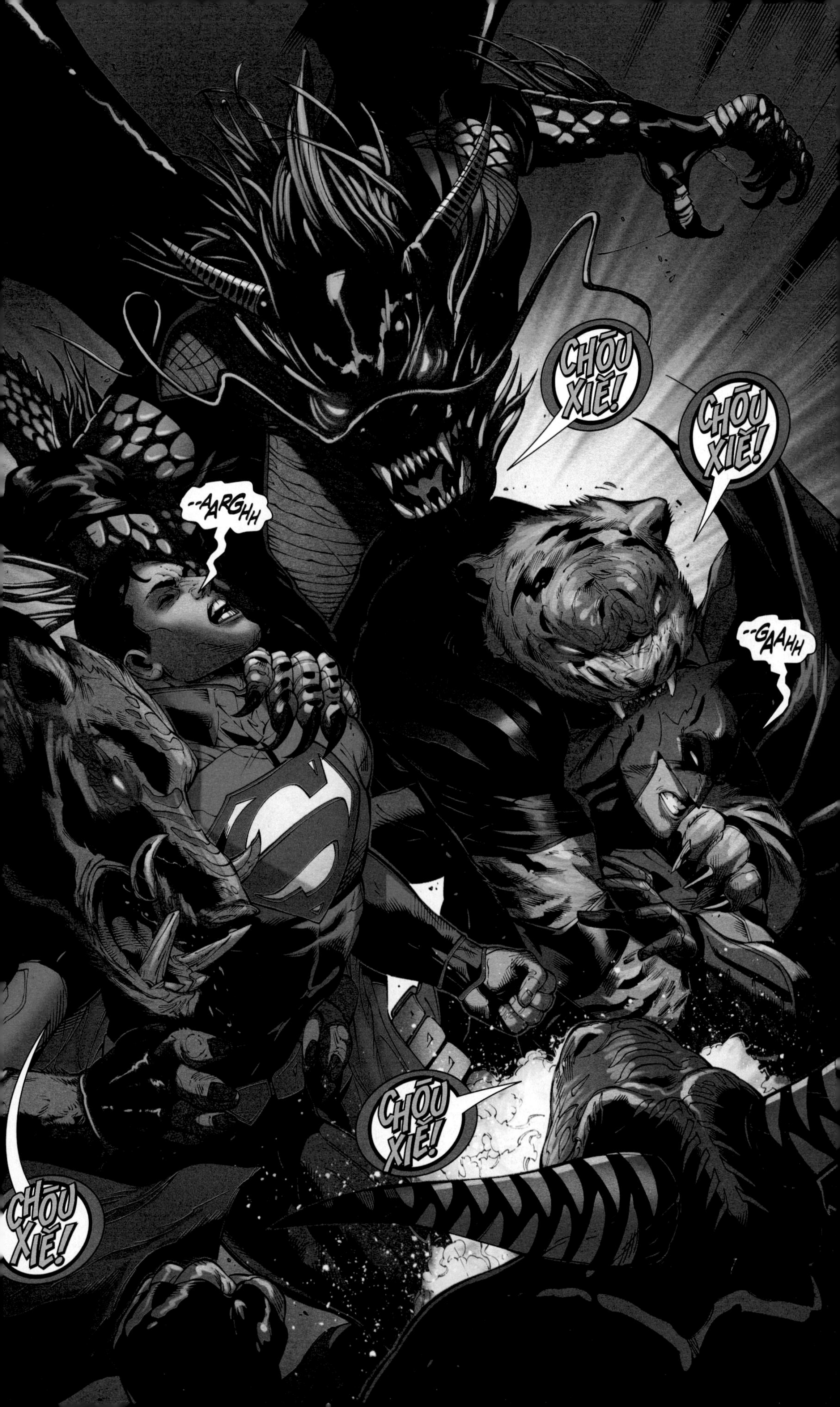
CHŌU XIĚ!
CHŌU XIĚ!
--AARGHH
--GAAHH
CHŌU XIĚ!
CHŌU XIĚ!

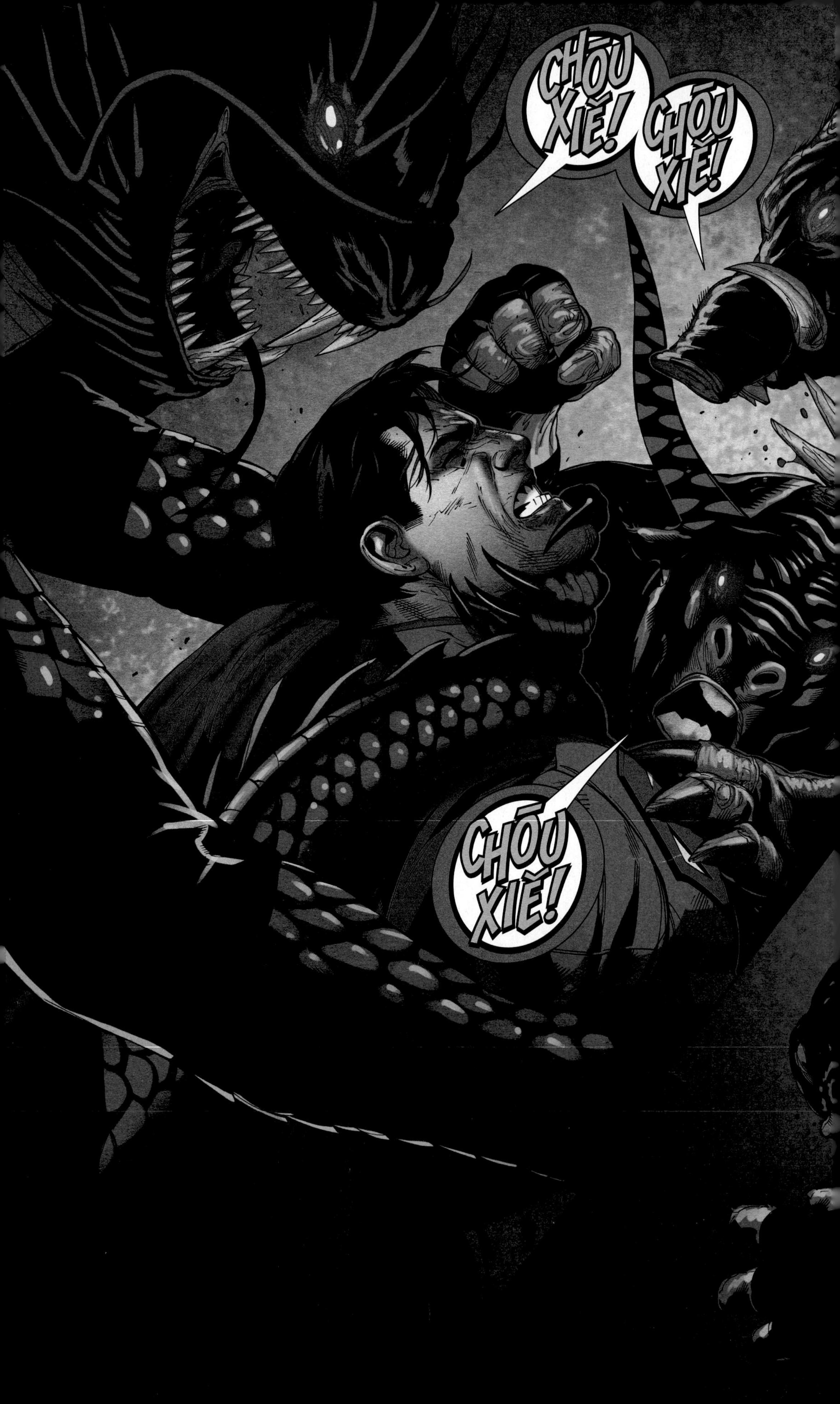
CHŌU XIĚ!
CHŌU XIĚ!
CHŌU XIĚ!

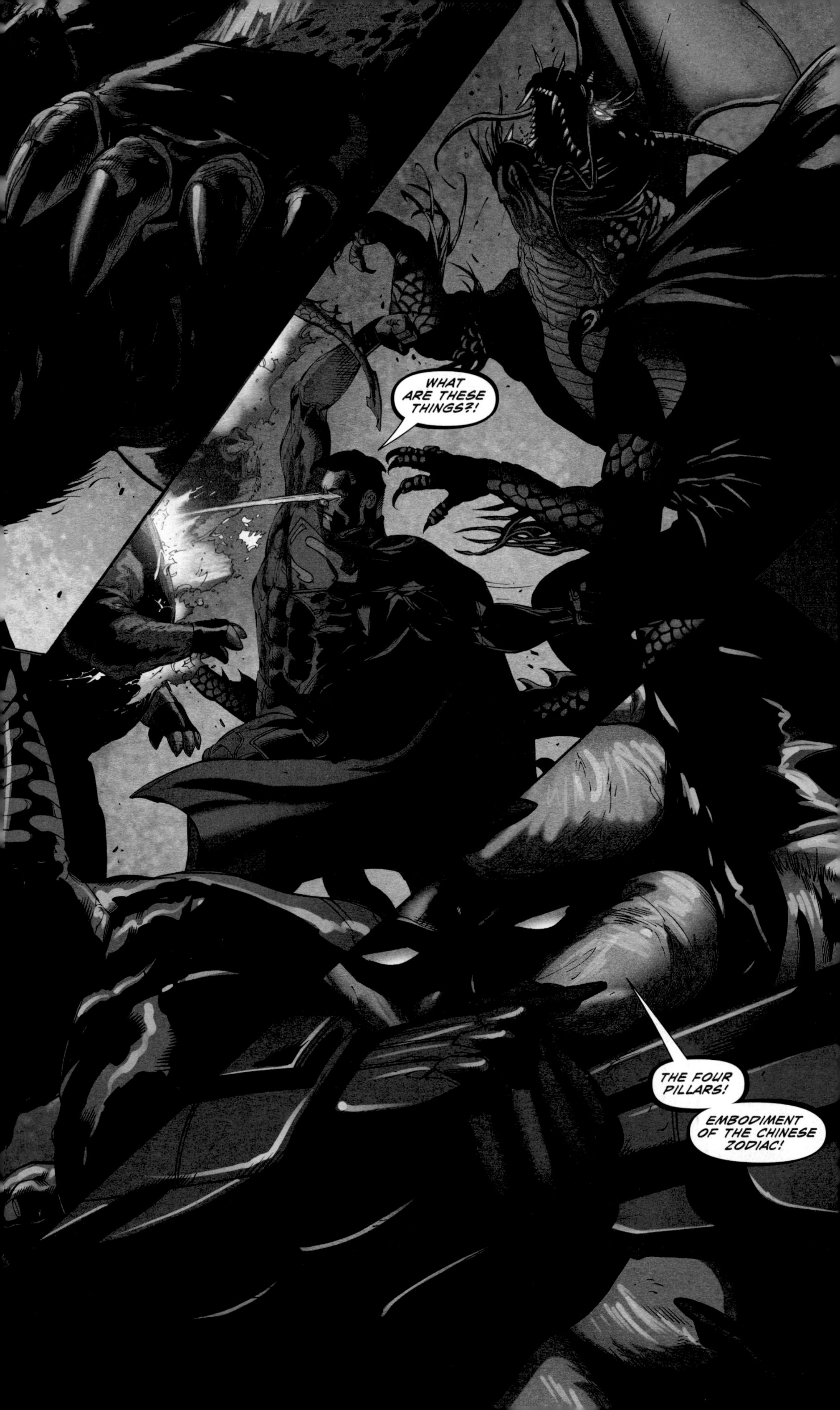
WHAT ARE THESE THINGS?!
THE FOUR PILLARS!
EMBODIMENT OF THE CHINESE ZODIAC!

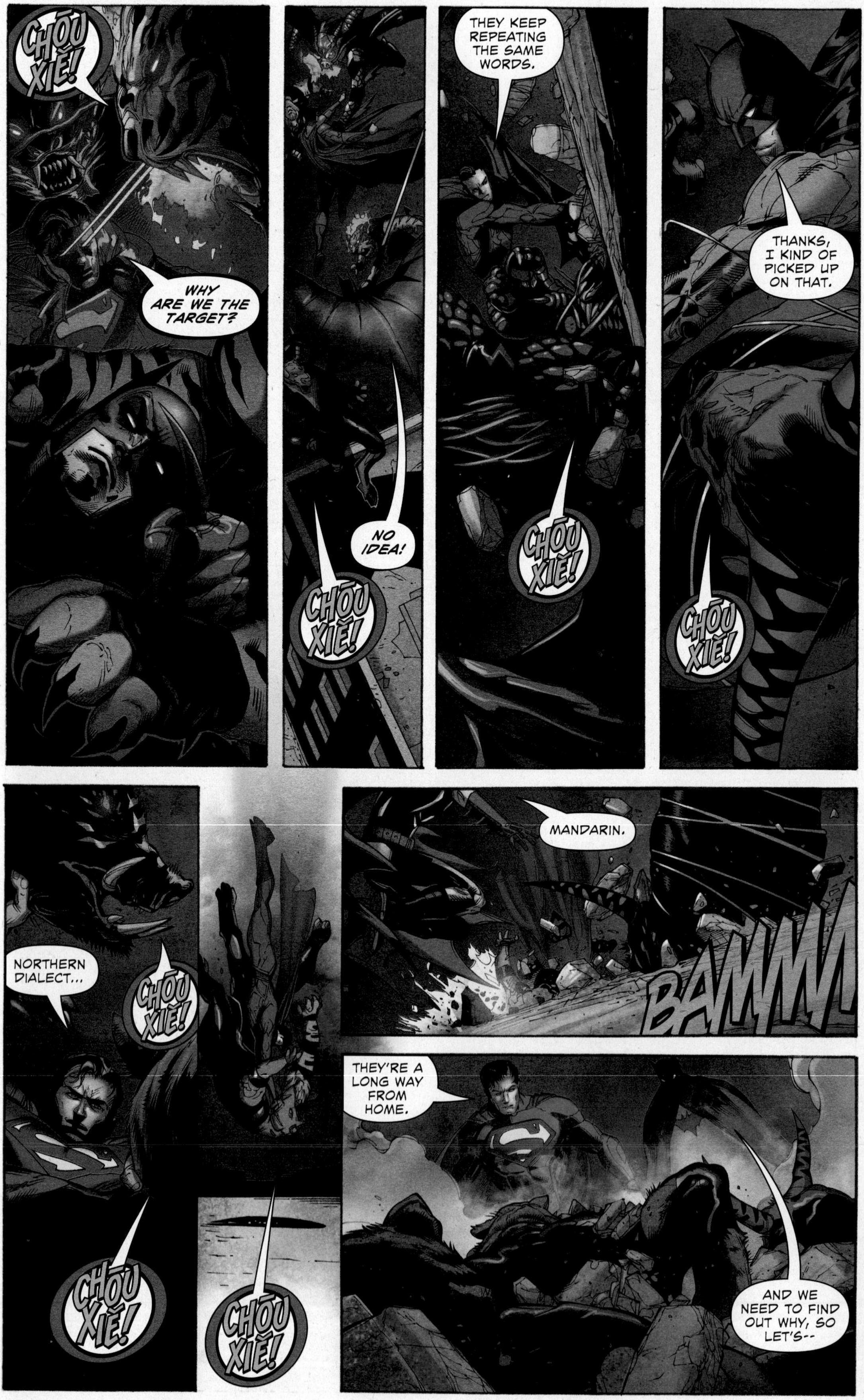
CHŌU XIĚ!
WHY ARE WE THE TARGET?
NO IDEA!
CHŌU XIĚ!
THEY KEEP REPEATING THE SAME WORDS.
CHŌU XIĚ!
THANKS, I KIND OF PICKED UP ON THAT.
CHŌU XIĚ!
NORTHERN DIALECT...
CHŌU XIĚ!
CHŌU XIĚ!
CHŌU XIĚ!
MANDARIN.
BAMMM
THEY'RE A LONG WAY FROM HOME.
AND WE NEED TO FIND OUT WHY, SO LET'S--

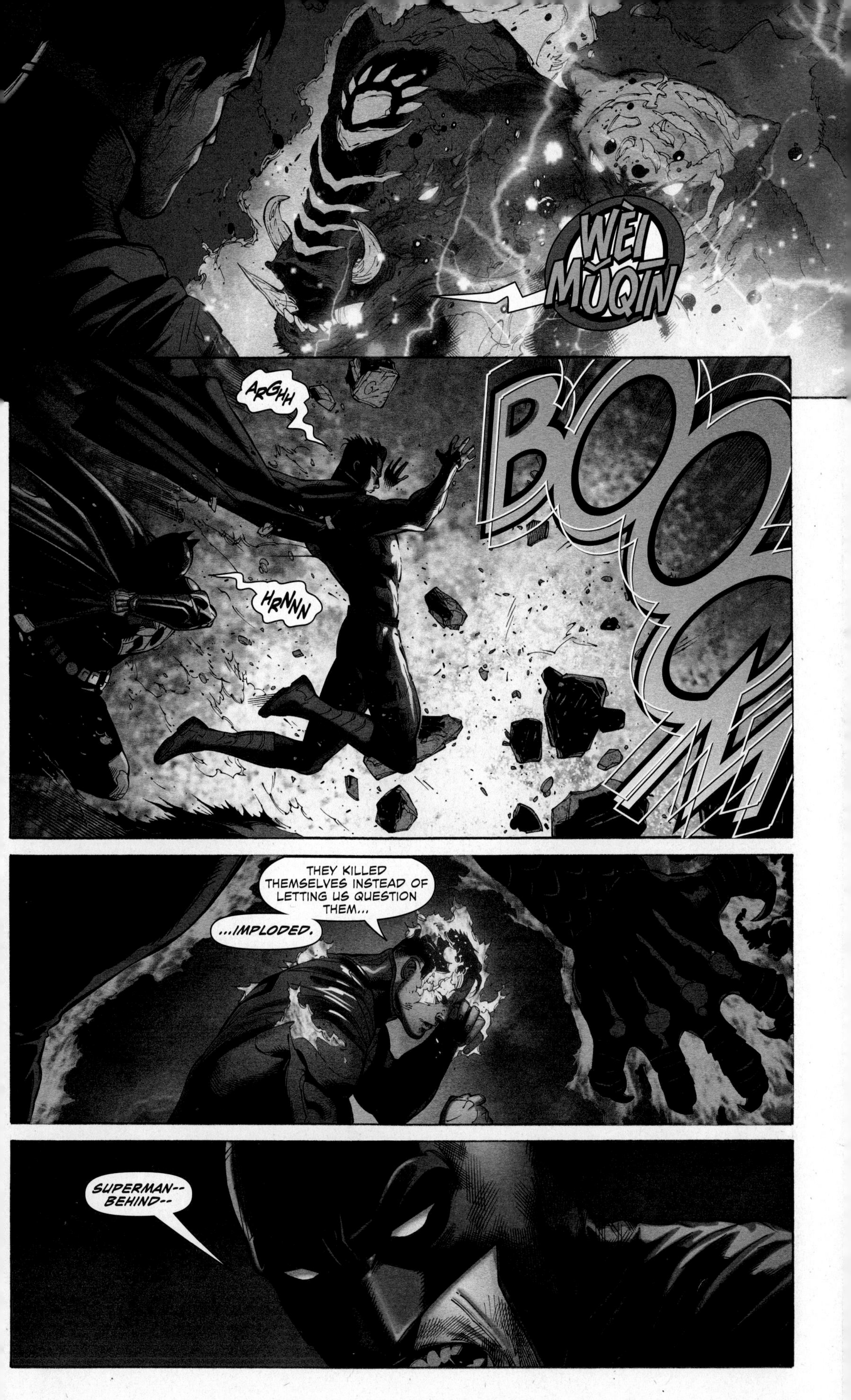
WÈI MǓQIN
ARGHH
HRNNN
BOOM
THEY KILLED THEMSELVES INSTEAD OF LETTING US QUESTION THEM...
...IMPLODED.
SUPERMAN-- BEHIND--

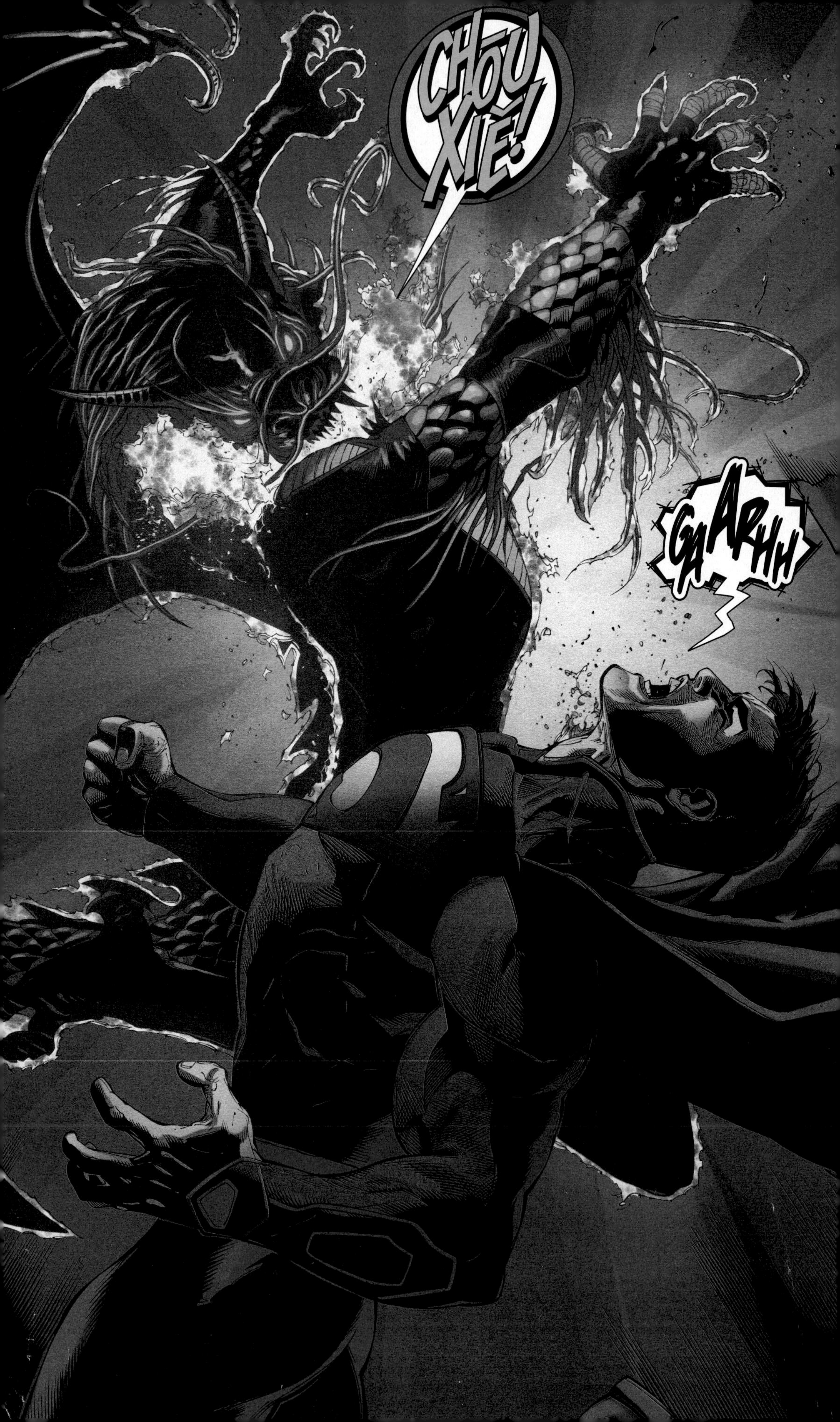
CHŌU XIĚ!
GAARHH

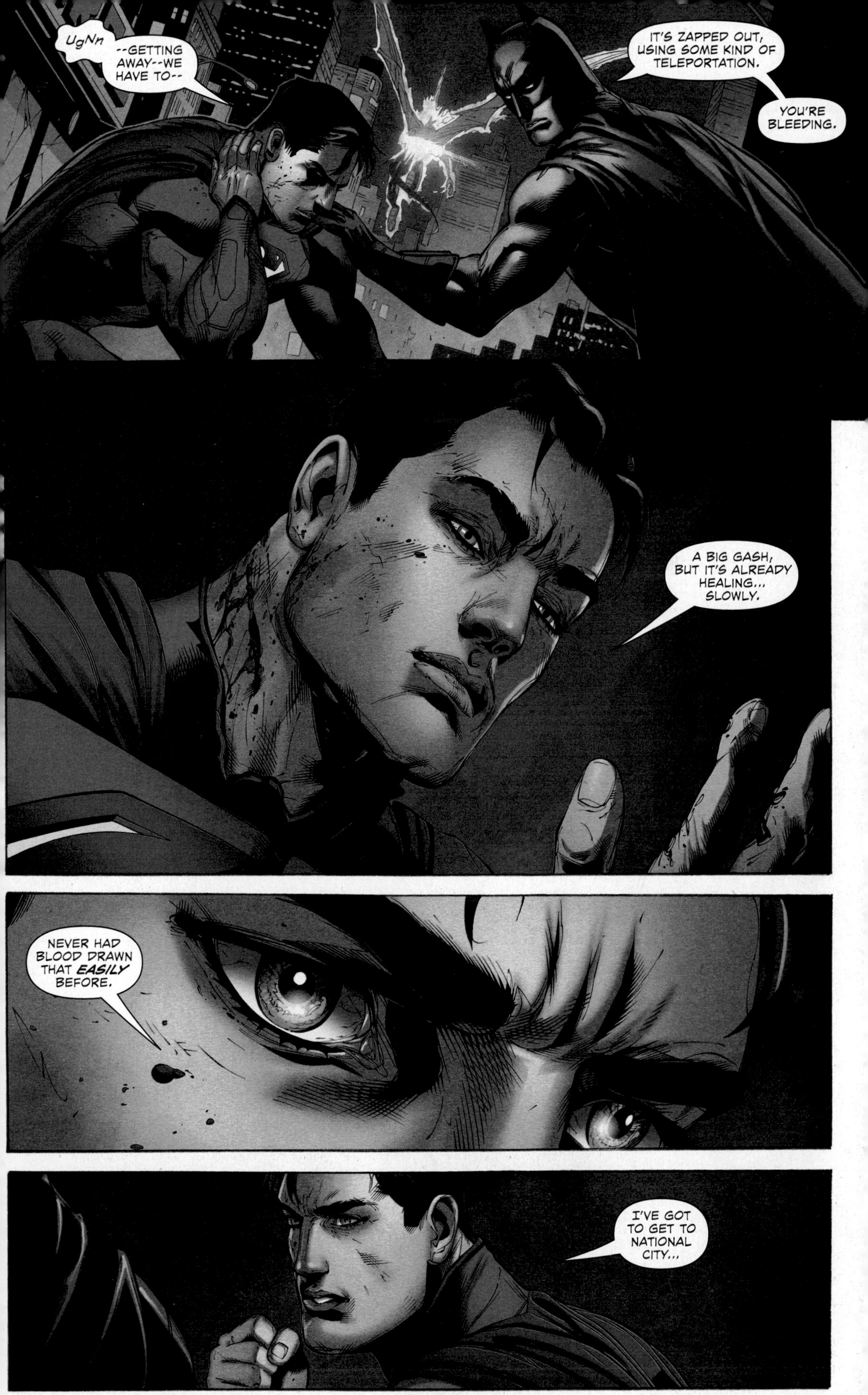
UgNn
--GETTING AWAY--WE HAVE TO--
IT'S ZAPPED OUT, USING SOME KIND OF TELEPORTATION.
YOU'RE BLEEDING.
A BIG GASH, BUT IT'S ALREADY HEALING... SLOWLY.
NEVER HAD BLOOD DRAWN THAT EASILY BEFORE.
I'VE GOT TO GET TO NATIONAL CITY...

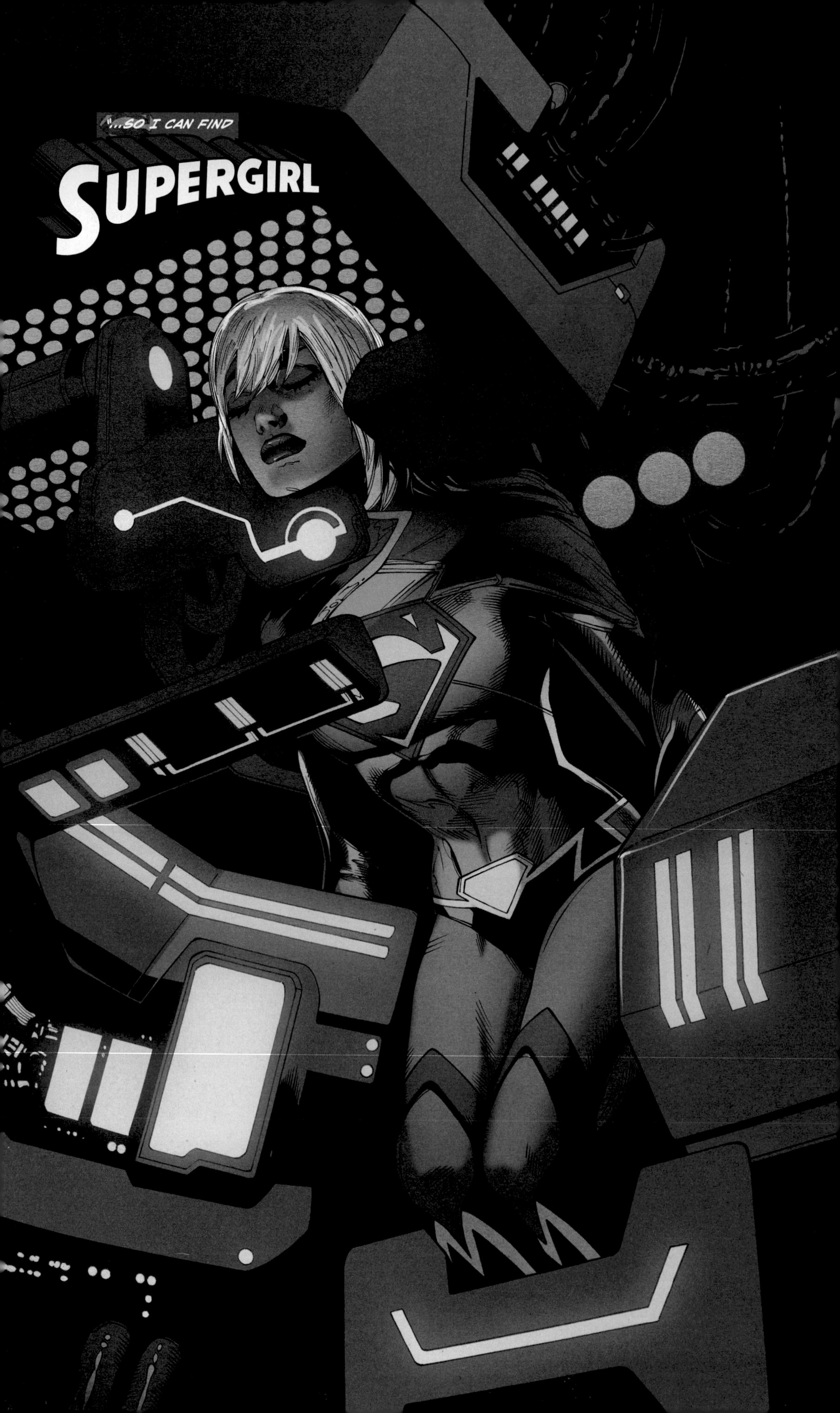
"...SO I CAN FIND
SUPERGIRL

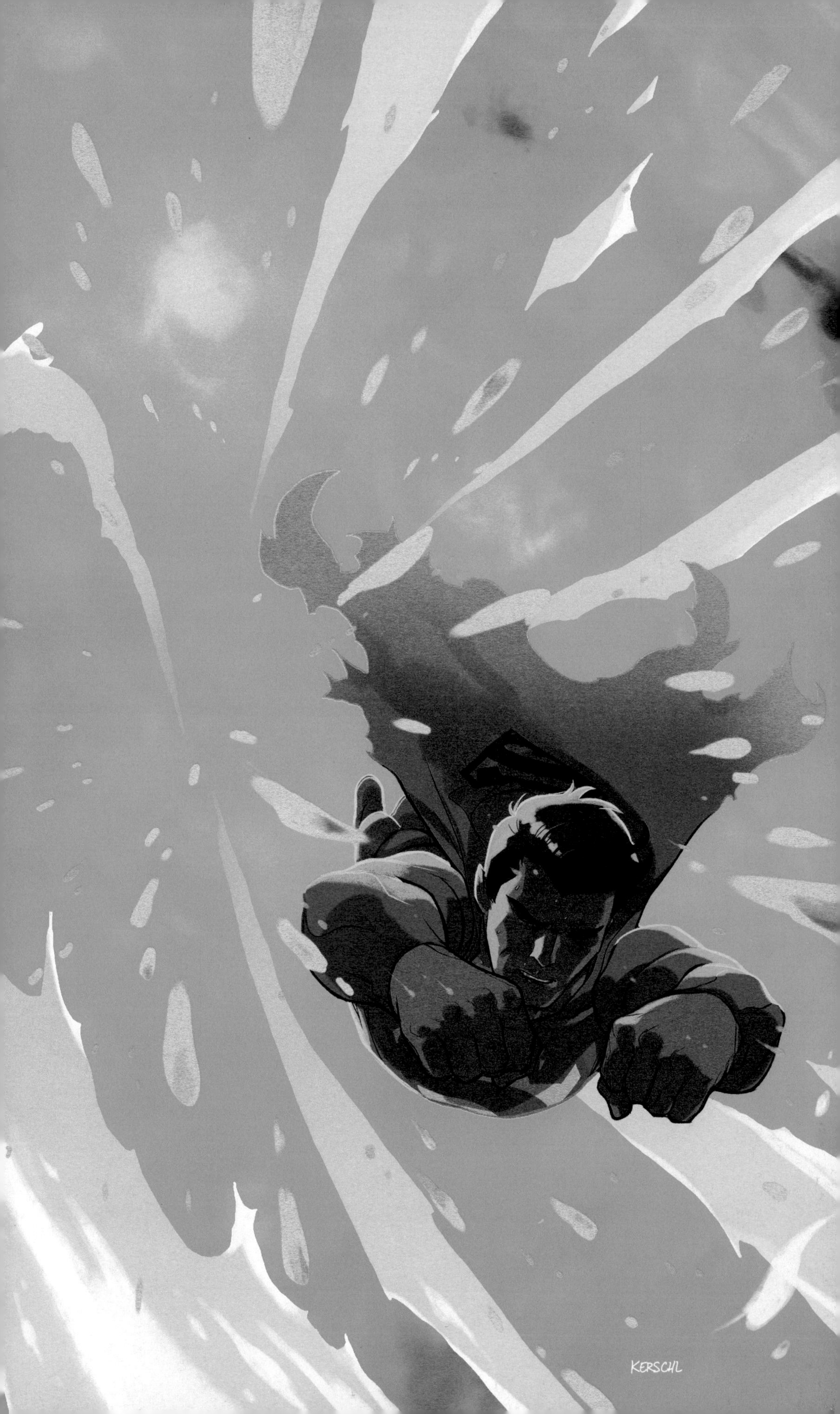
KERSCHL

THE FINAL DAYS OF SUPERMAN PART 3: DAZED AND CONFUSED

PETER J. TOMASI writer PAUL PELLETIER penciller SANDRA HOPE ARCHER inker TOMEU MOREY colorist ROB LEIGH letterer KARL KERSCHL cover

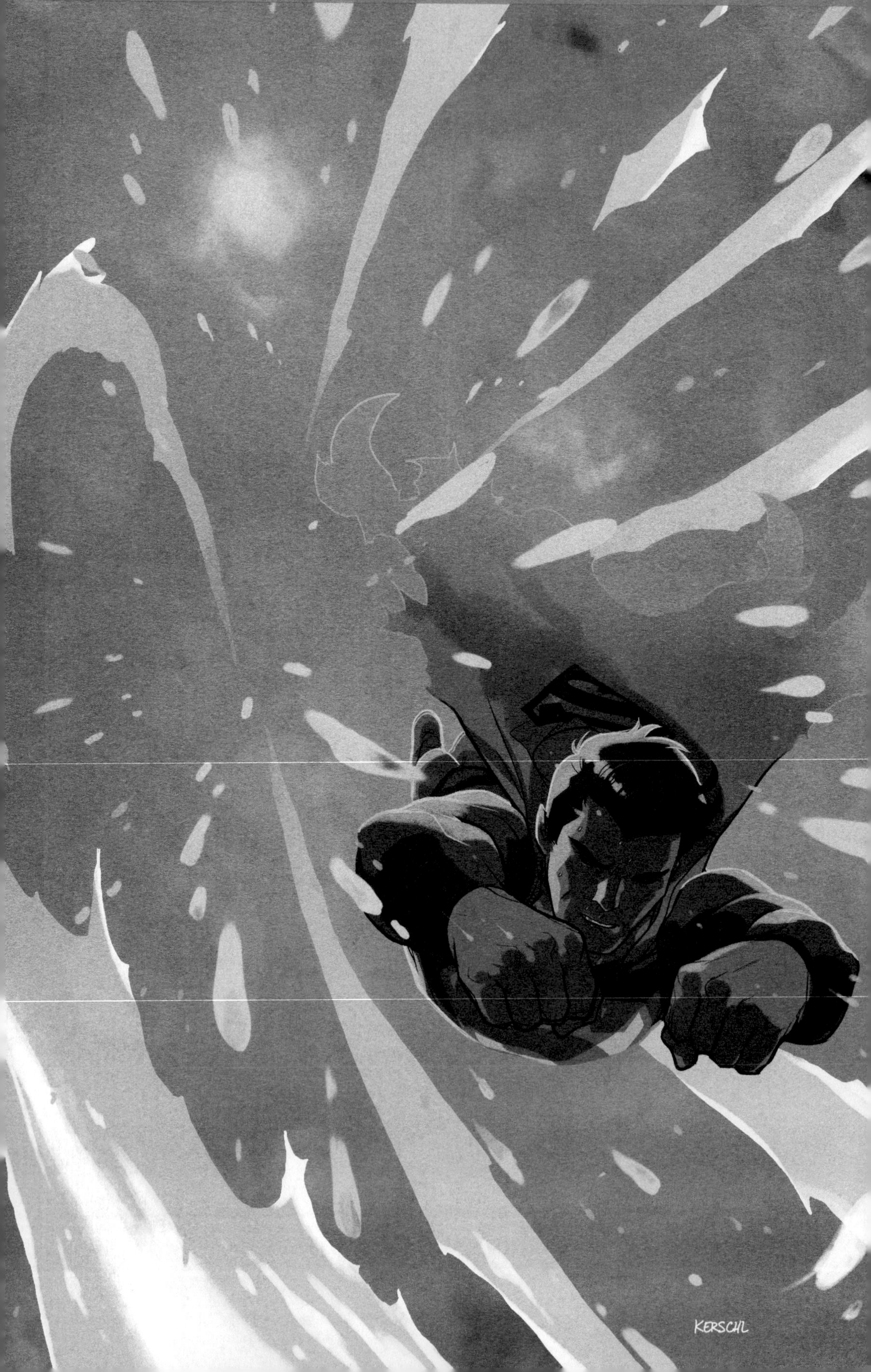
KERSCHL

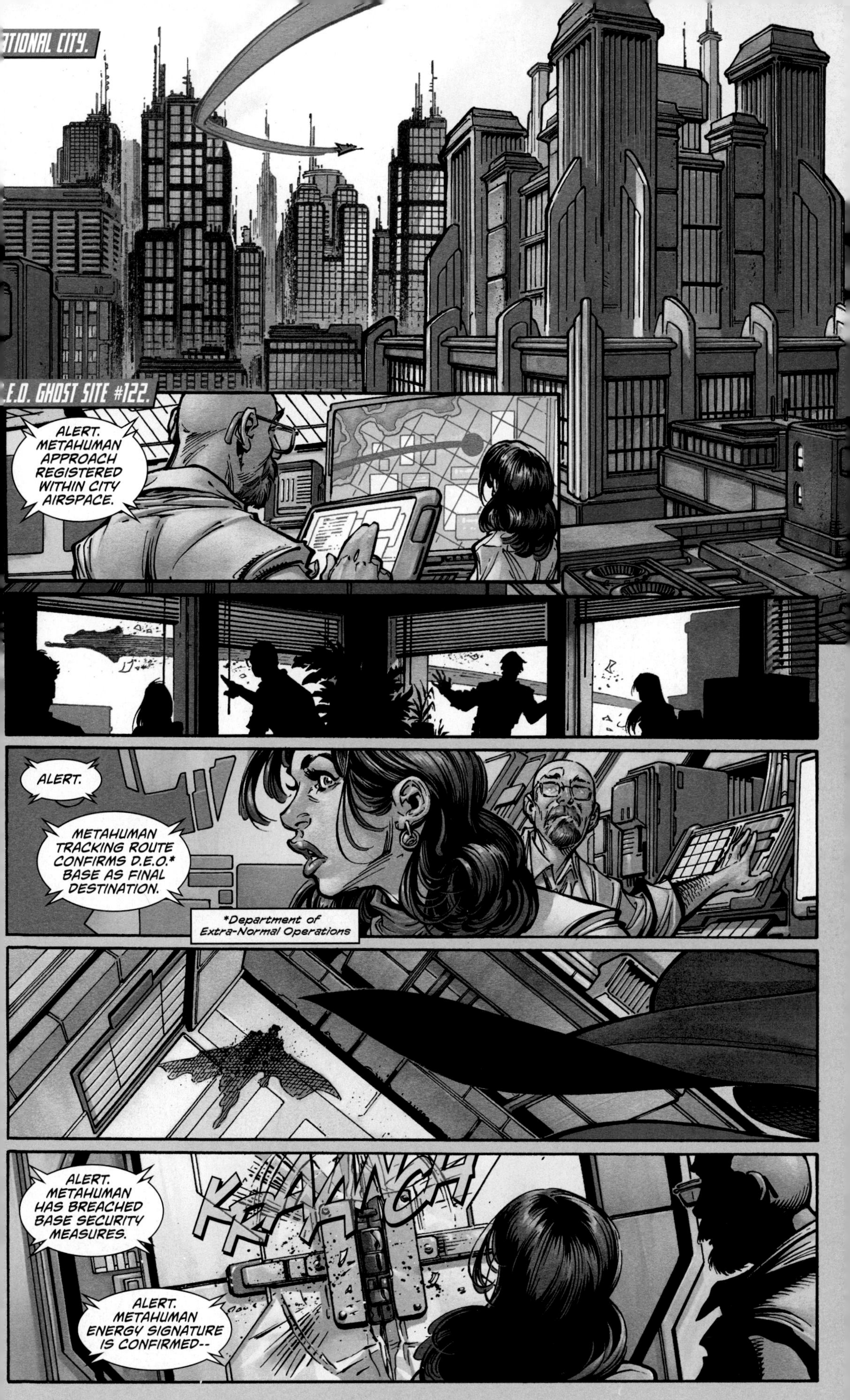
TIONAL CITY.
.E.O. GHOST SITE #122.
ALERT. METAHUMAN APPROACH REGISTERED WITHIN CITY AIRSPACE.
ALERT.
METAHUMAN TRACKING ROUTE CONFIRMS D.E.O.* BASE AS FINAL DESTINATION.
*Department of Extra-Normal Operations
ALERT. METAHUMAN HAS BREACHED BASE SECURITY MEASURES.
ALERT. METAHUMAN ENERGY SIGNATURE IS CONFIRMED--

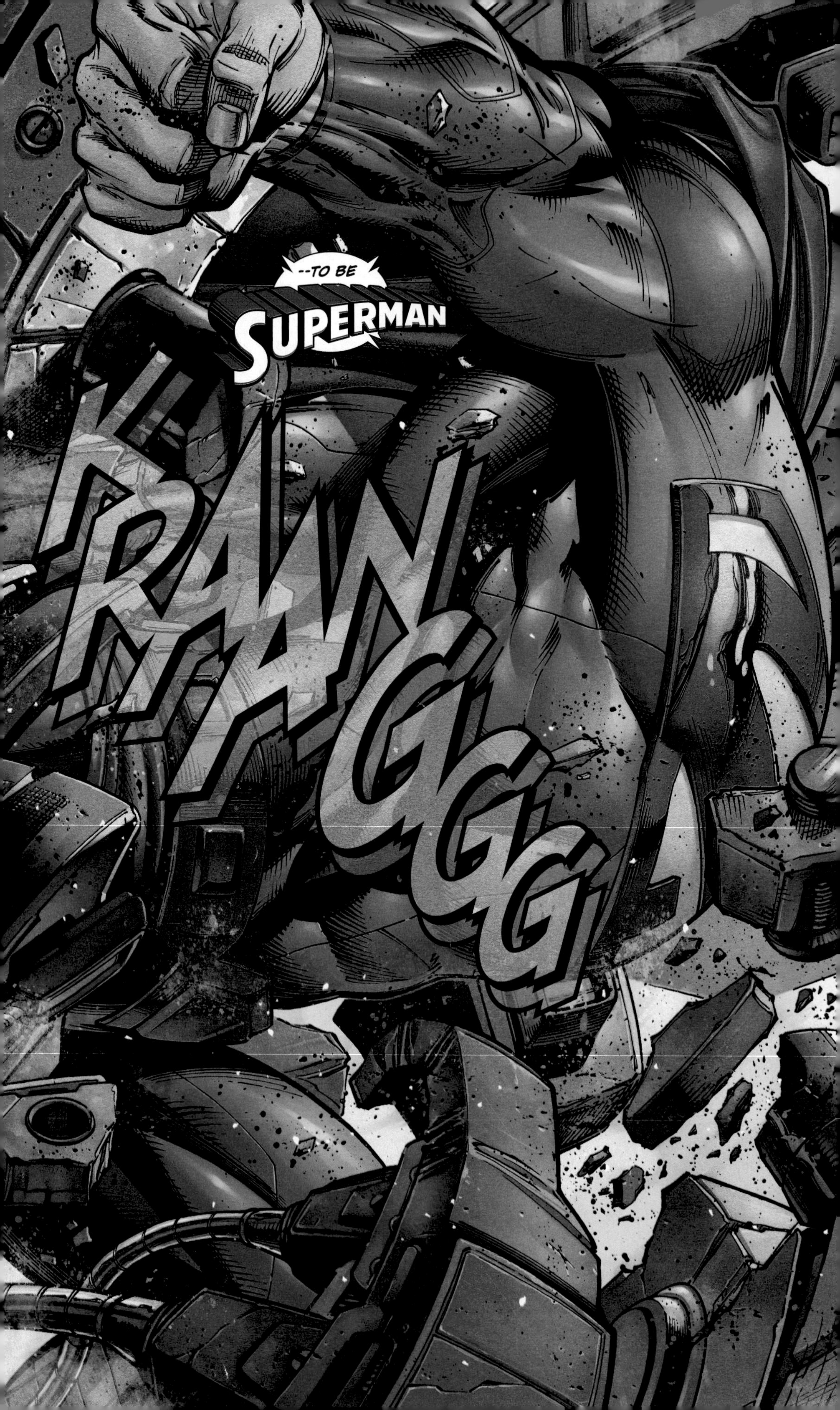

--TO BE
SUPERMAN
KRAKAGGG

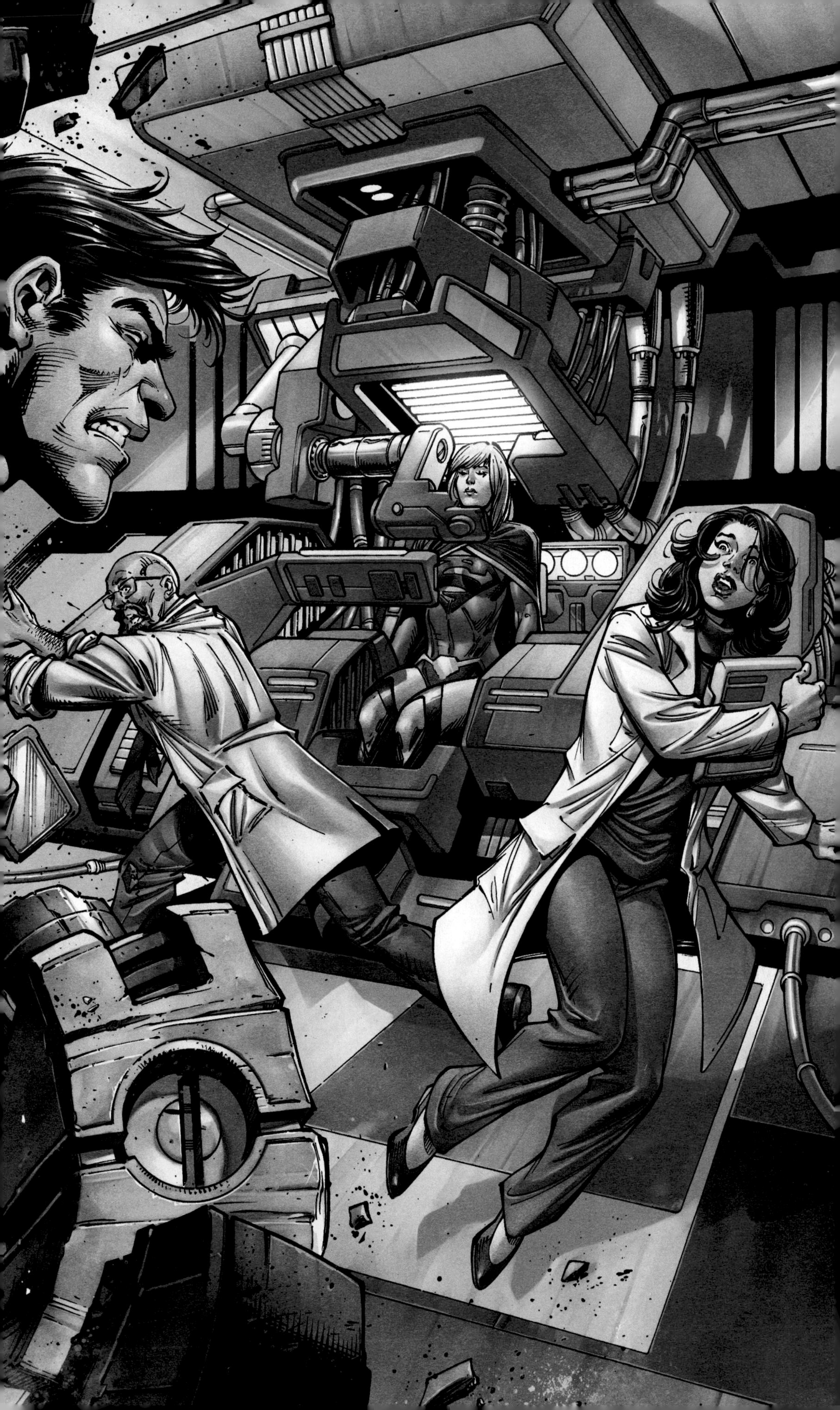

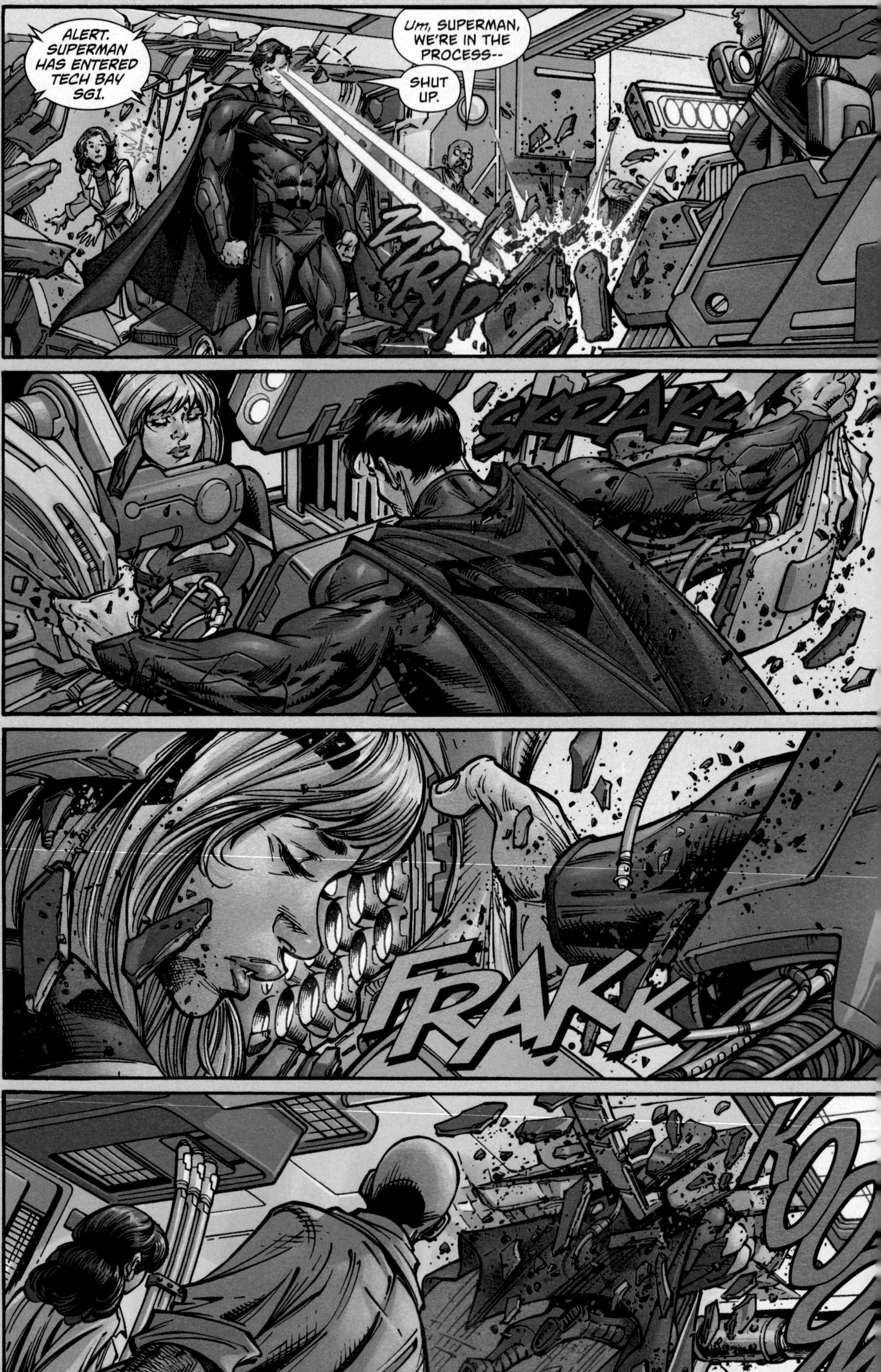
ALERT. SUPERMAN HAS ENTERED TECH BAY SG1.
Um, SUPERMAN, WE'RE IN THE PROCESS--
SHUT UP.
ZZWORAP
SKRAKK
FRAKK
KOOM

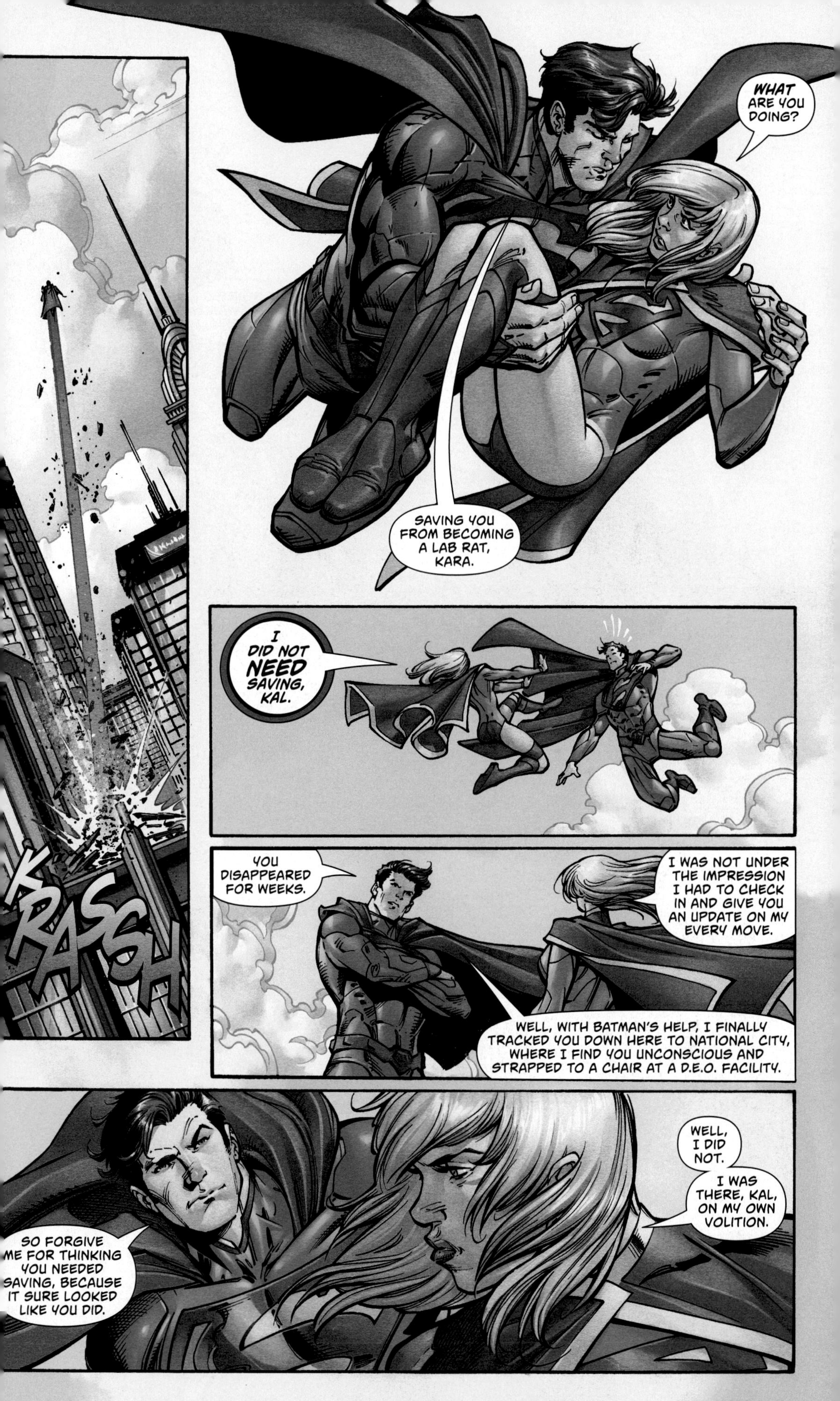

WHAT ARE YOU DOING?
SAVING YOU FROM BECOMING A LAB RAT, KARA.
KRASSH
I DID NOT NEED SAVING, KAL.
YOU DISAPPEARED FOR WEEKS.
I WAS NOT UNDER THE IMPRESSION I HAD TO CHECK IN AND GIVE YOU AN UPDATE ON MY EVERY MOVE.
WELL, WITH BATMAN'S HELP, I FINALLY TRACKED YOU DOWN HERE TO NATIONAL CITY, WHERE I FIND YOU UNCONSCIOUS AND STRAPPED TO A CHAIR AT A D.E.O. FACILITY.
SO FORGIVE ME FOR THINKING YOU NEEDED SAVING, BECAUSE IT SURE LOOKED LIKE YOU DID.
WELL, I DID NOT.
I WAS THERE, KAL, ON MY OWN VOLITION.

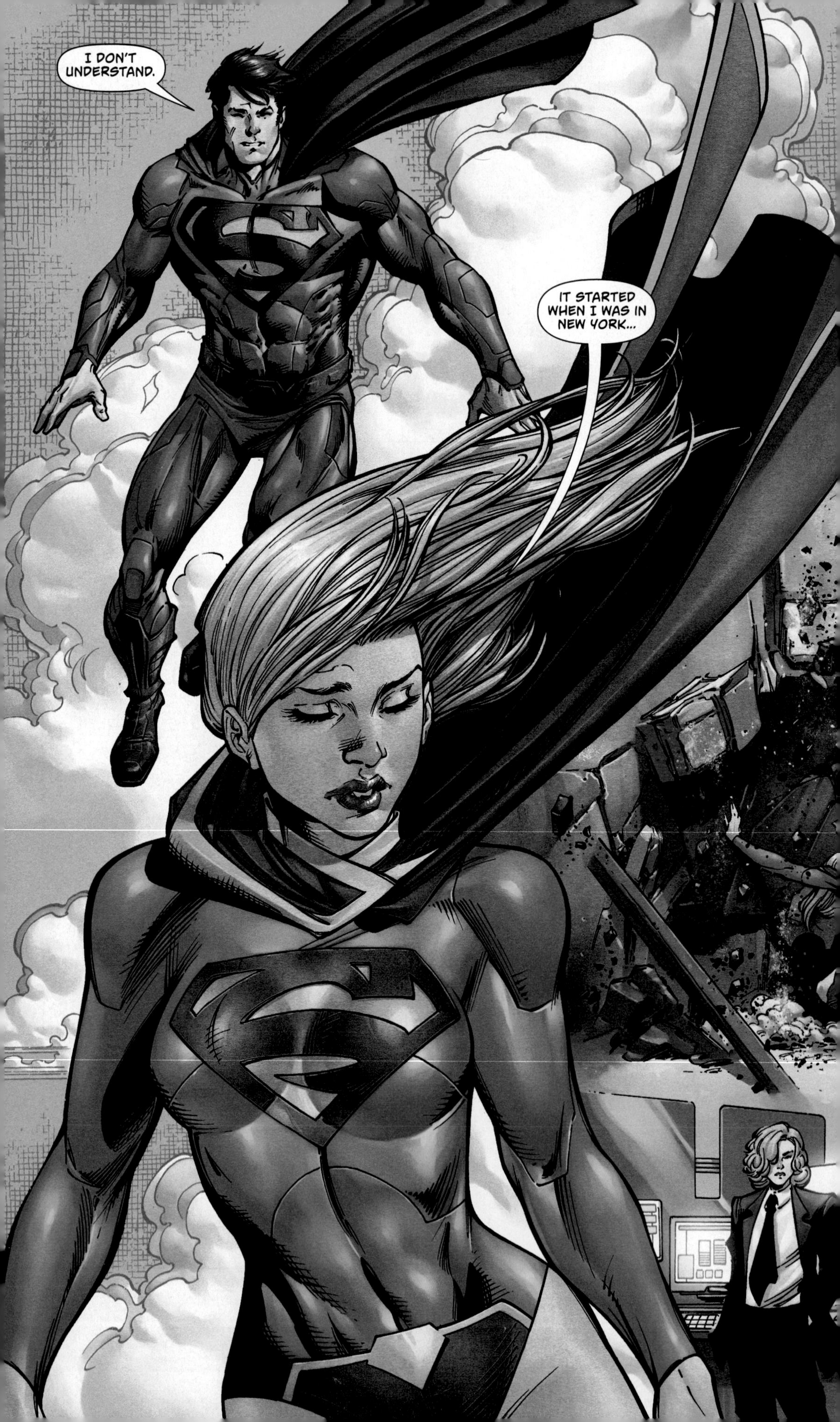
I DON'T UNDERSTAND.
IT STARTED WHEN I WAS IN NEW YORK...

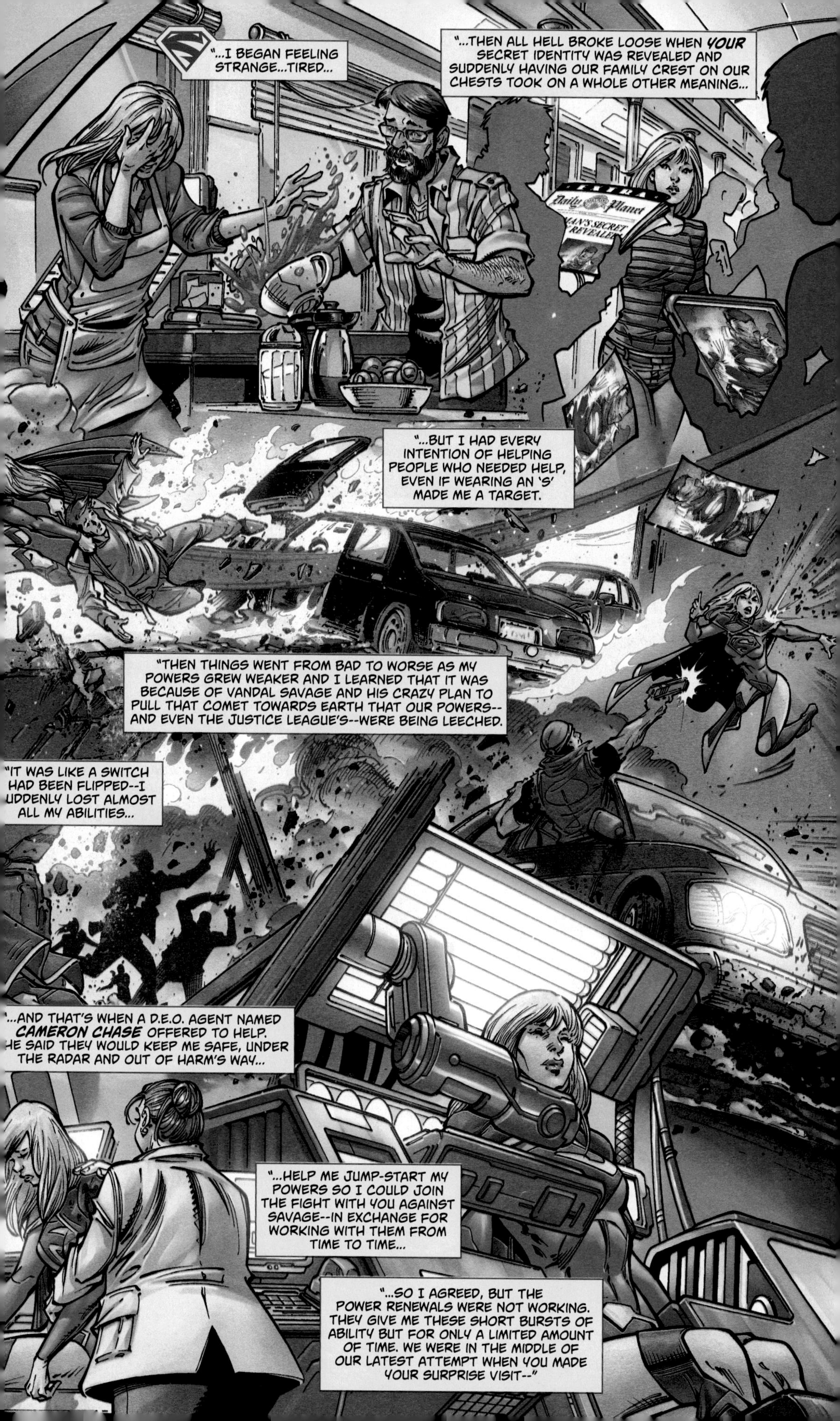
"...I BEGAN FEELING STRANGE...TIRED...
"...THEN ALL HELL BROKE LOOSE WHEN *YOUR* SECRET IDENTITY WAS REVEALED AND SUDDENLY HAVING OUR FAMILY CREST ON OUR CHESTS TOOK ON A WHOLE OTHER MEANING...
EXTRA
Daily Planet
MAN'S SECRET REVEALED
"...BUT I HAD EVERY INTENTION OF HELPING PEOPLE WHO NEEDED HELP, EVEN IF WEARING AN 'S' MADE ME A TARGET.
"THEN THINGS WENT FROM BAD TO WORSE AS MY POWERS GREW WEAKER AND I LEARNED THAT IT WAS BECAUSE OF VANDAL SAVAGE AND HIS CRAZY PLAN TO PULL THAT COMET TOWARDS EARTH THAT OUR POWERS--AND EVEN THE JUSTICE LEAGUE'S--WERE BEING LEECHED.
"IT WAS LIKE A SWITCH HAD BEEN FLIPPED--I SUDDENLY LOST ALMOST ALL MY ABILITIES...
"...AND THAT'S WHEN A D.E.O. AGENT NAMED ***CAMERON CHASE*** OFFERED TO HELP. SHE SAID THEY WOULD KEEP ME SAFE, UNDER THE RADAR AND OUT OF HARM'S WAY...
"...HELP ME JUMP-START MY POWERS SO I COULD JOIN THE FIGHT WITH YOU AGAINST SAVAGE--IN EXCHANGE FOR WORKING WITH THEM FROM TIME TO TIME...
"...SO I AGREED, BUT THE POWER RENEWALS WERE NOT WORKING. THEY GIVE ME THESE SHORT BURSTS OF ABILITY BUT FOR ONLY A LIMITED AMOUNT OF TIME. WE WERE IN THE MIDDLE OF OUR LATEST ATTEMPT WHEN YOU MADE YOUR SURPRISE VISIT--"

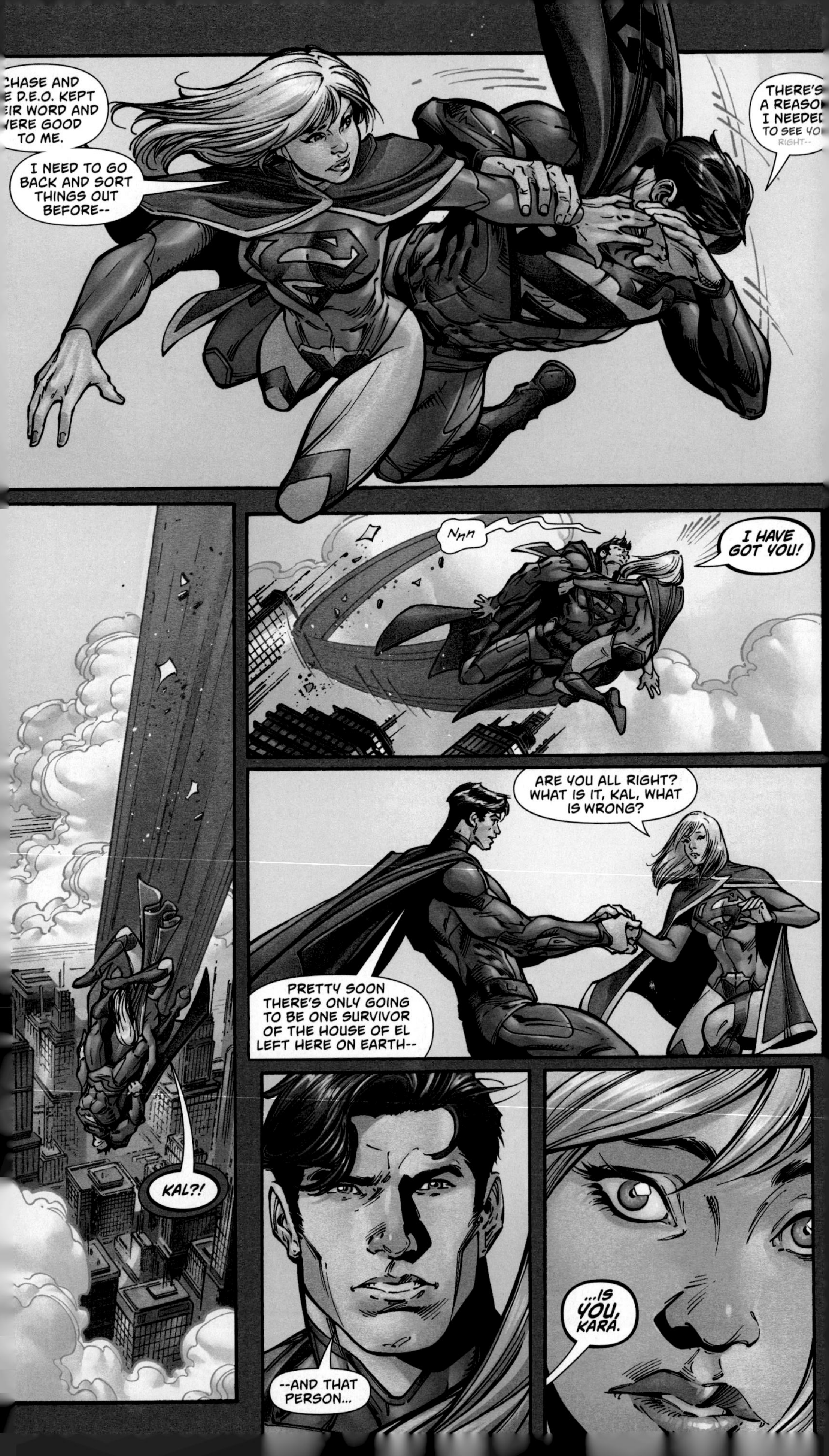
CHASE AND
E D.E.O. KEPT
EIR WORD AND
WERE GOOD
TO ME.
I NEED TO GO BACK AND SORT THINGS OUT BEFORE--
THERE'S A REASO I NEEDED TO SEE YO RIGHT--
Nnn
I HAVE GOT YOU!
KAL?!
ARE YOU ALL RIGHT? WHAT IS IT, KAL, WHAT IS WRONG?
PRETTY SOON THERE'S ONLY GOING TO BE ONE SURVIVOR OF THE HOUSE OF EL LEFT HERE ON EARTH--
--AND THAT PERSON...
...IS YOU, KARA.

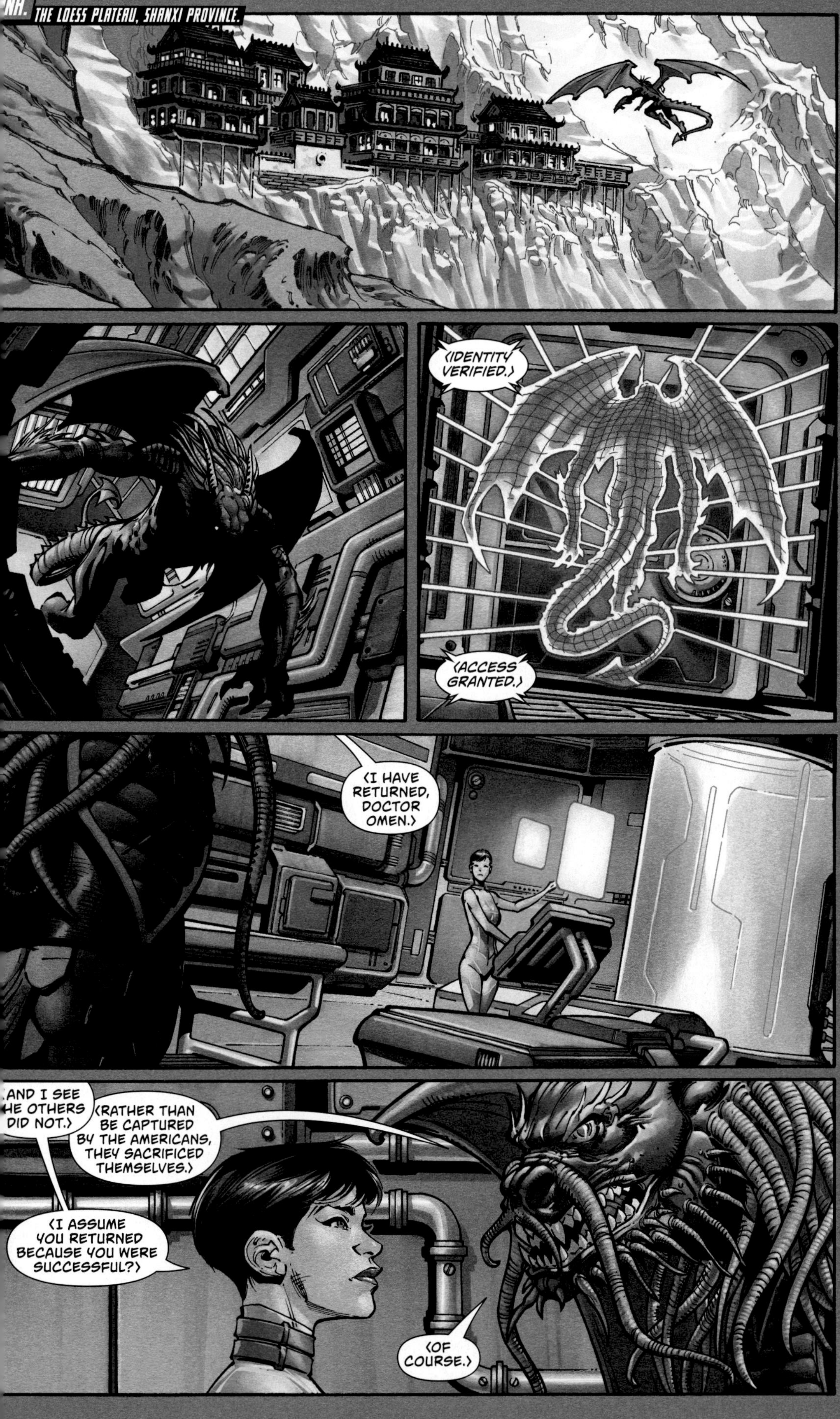
NA. THE LOESS PLATEAU, SHANXI PROVINCE.
‹IDENTITY VERIFIED.›
‹ACCESS GRANTED.›
‹I HAVE RETURNED, DOCTOR OMEN.›
‹AND I SEE THE OTHERS DID NOT.›
‹RATHER THAN BE CAPTURED BY THE AMERICANS, THEY SACRIFICED THEMSELVES.›
‹I ASSUME YOU RETURNED BECAUSE YOU WERE SUCCESSFUL?›
‹OF COURSE.›

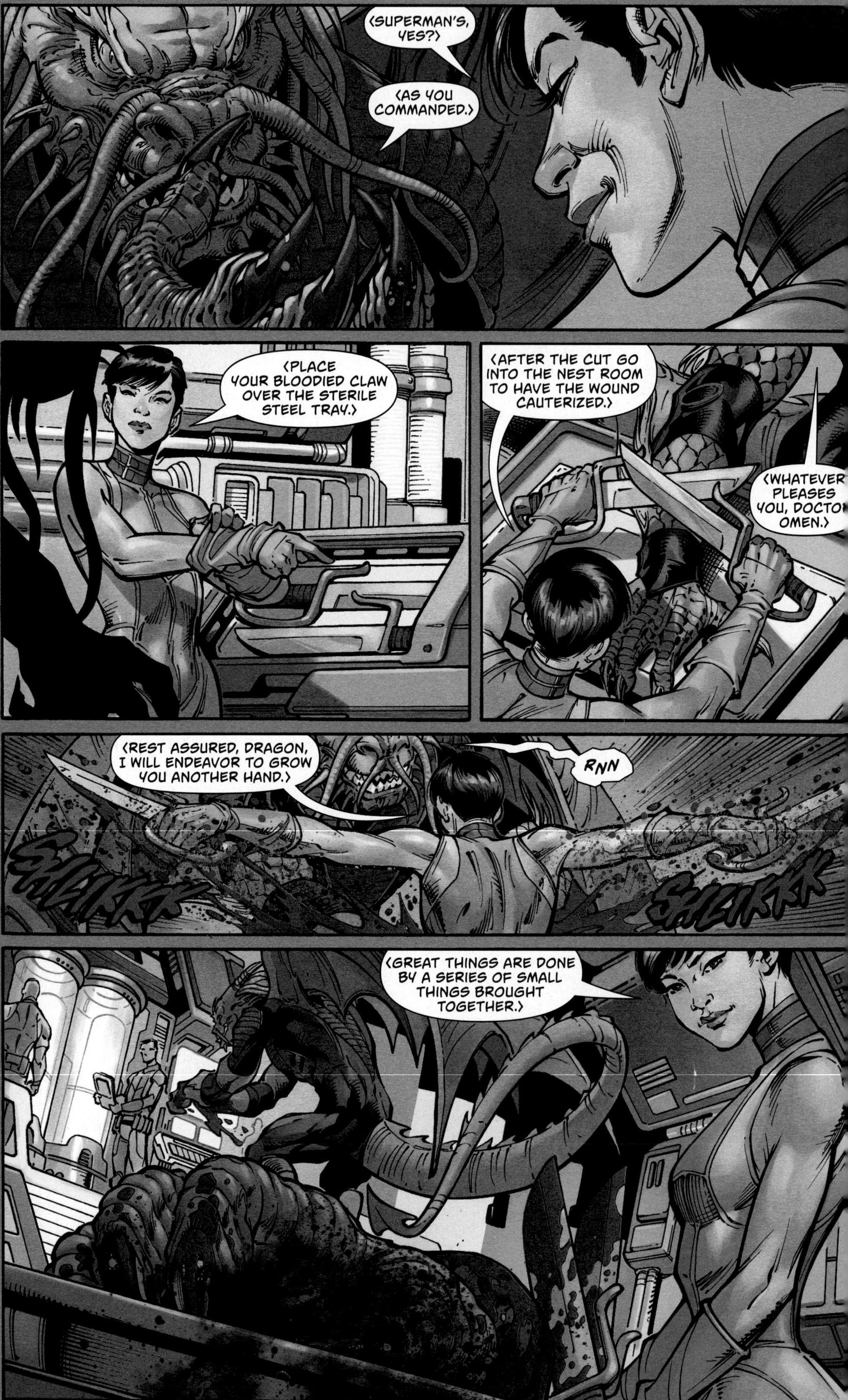

‹SUPERMAN'S, YES?›
‹AS YOU COMMANDED.›
‹PLACE YOUR BLOODIED CLAW OVER THE STERILE STEEL TRAY.›
‹AFTER THE CUT GO INTO THE NEST ROOM TO HAVE THE WOUND CAUTERIZED.›
‹WHATEVER PLEASES YOU, DOCTO OMEN.›
‹REST ASSURED, DRAGON, I WILL ENDEAVOR TO GROW YOU ANOTHER HAND.›
RNN
SHLIKKK
SHLIKKK
‹GREAT THINGS ARE DONE BY A SERIES OF SMALL THINGS BROUGHT TOGETHER.›

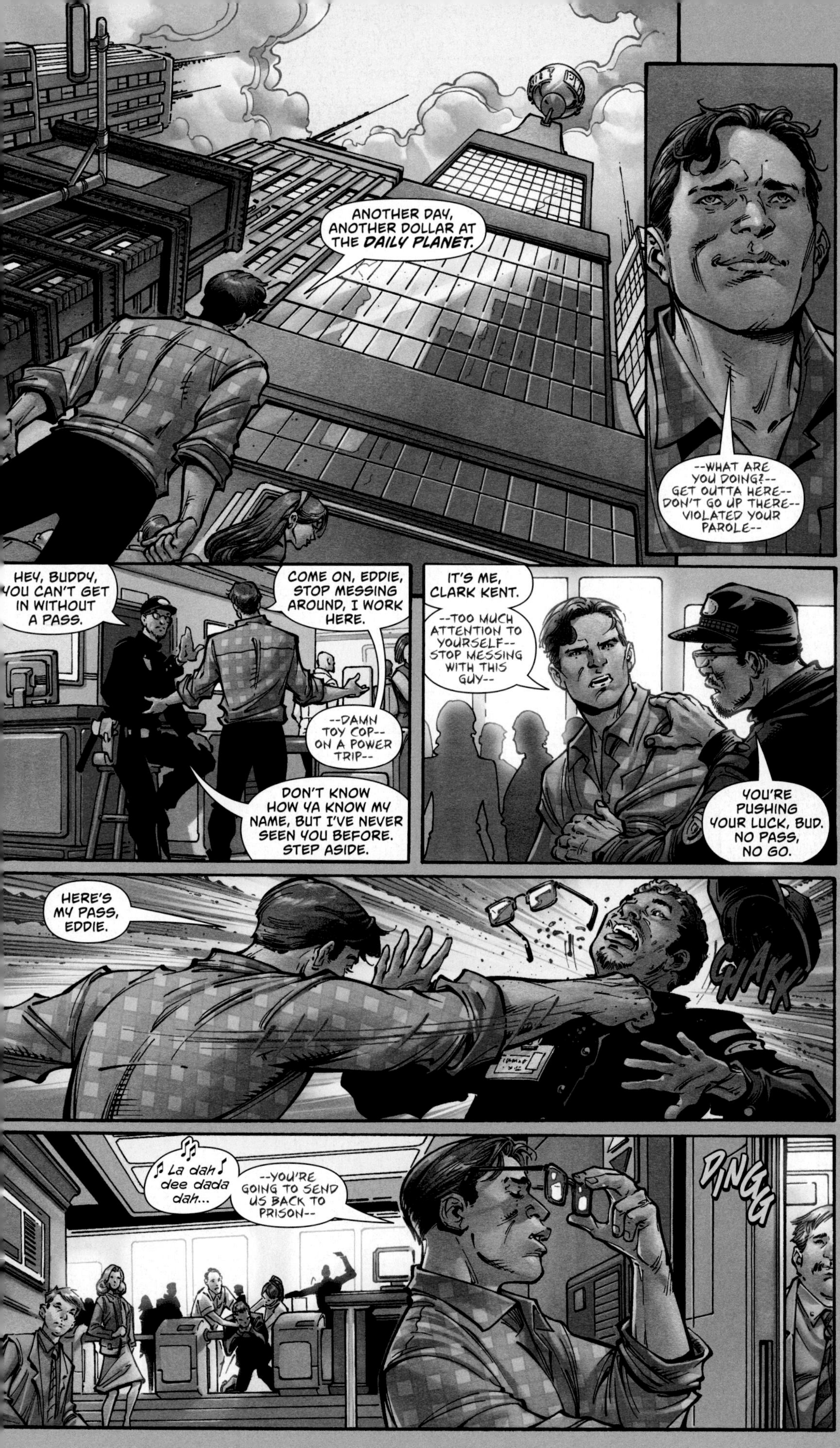
ANOTHER DAY, ANOTHER DOLLAR AT THE *DAILY PLANET*.
--WHAT ARE YOU DOING?-- GET OUTTA HERE-- DON'T GO UP THERE-- VIOLATED YOUR PAROLE--
HEY, BUDDY, YOU CAN'T GET IN WITHOUT A PASS.
COME ON, EDDIE, STOP MESSING AROUND, I WORK HERE.
--DAMN TOY COP-- ON A POWER TRIP--
DON'T KNOW HOW YA KNOW MY NAME, BUT I'VE NEVER SEEN YOU BEFORE. STEP ASIDE.
IT'S ME, CLARK KENT.
--TOO MUCH ATTENTION TO YOURSELF-- STOP MESSING WITH THIS GUY--
YOU'RE PUSHING YOUR LUCK, BUD. NO PASS, NO GO.
HERE'S MY PASS, EDDIE.
CHAKK
♫ La dah ♪ dee dada dah...
--YOU'RE GOING TO SEND US BACK TO PRISON--
DINGG

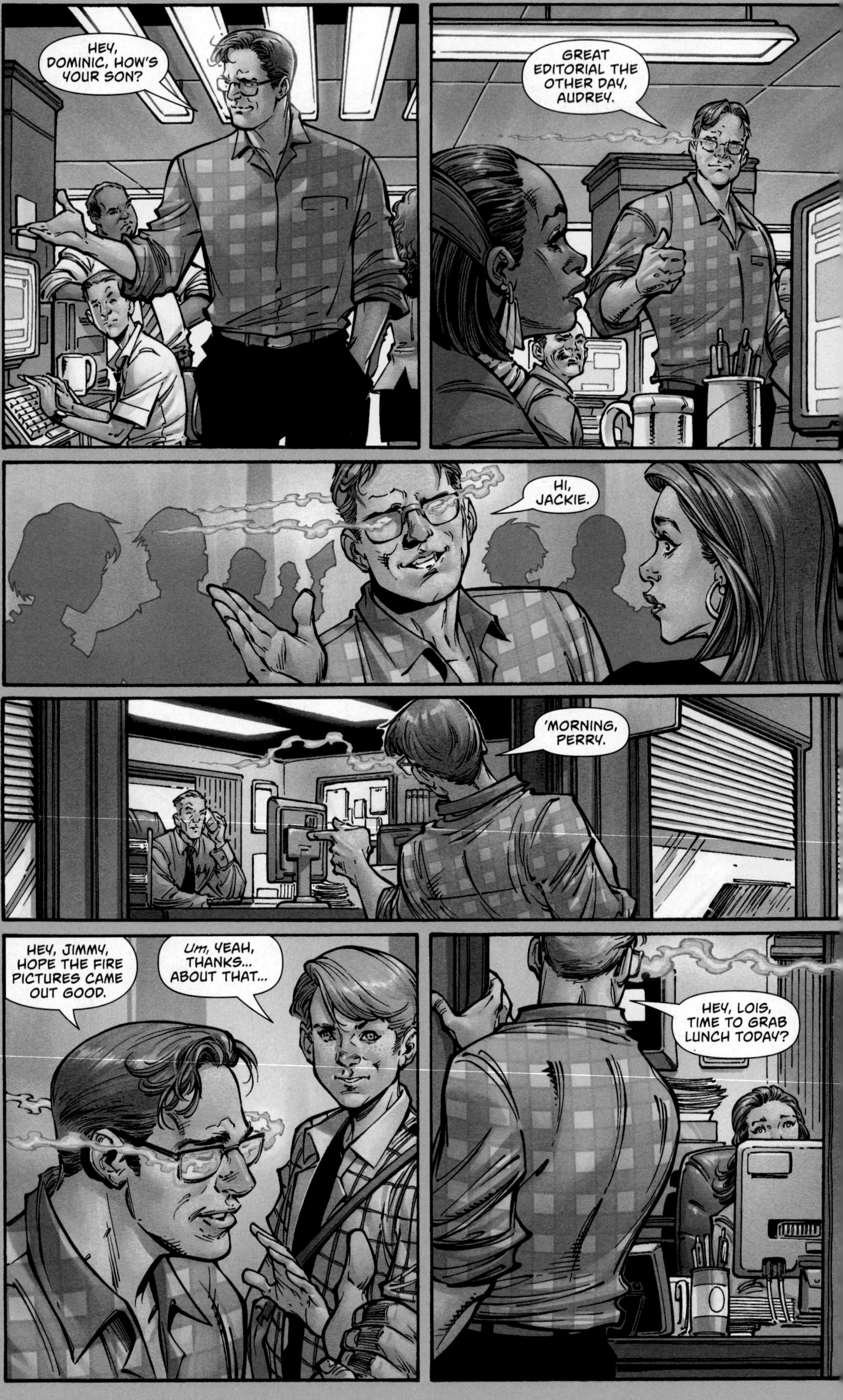
HEY, DOMINIC, HOW'S YOUR SON?
GREAT EDITORIAL THE OTHER DAY, AUDREY.
HI, JACKIE.
'MORNING, PERRY.
HEY, JIMMY, HOPE THE FIRE PICTURES CAME OUT GOOD.
Um, YEAH, THANKS... ABOUT THAT...
HEY, LOIS, TIME TO GRAB LUNCH TODAY?

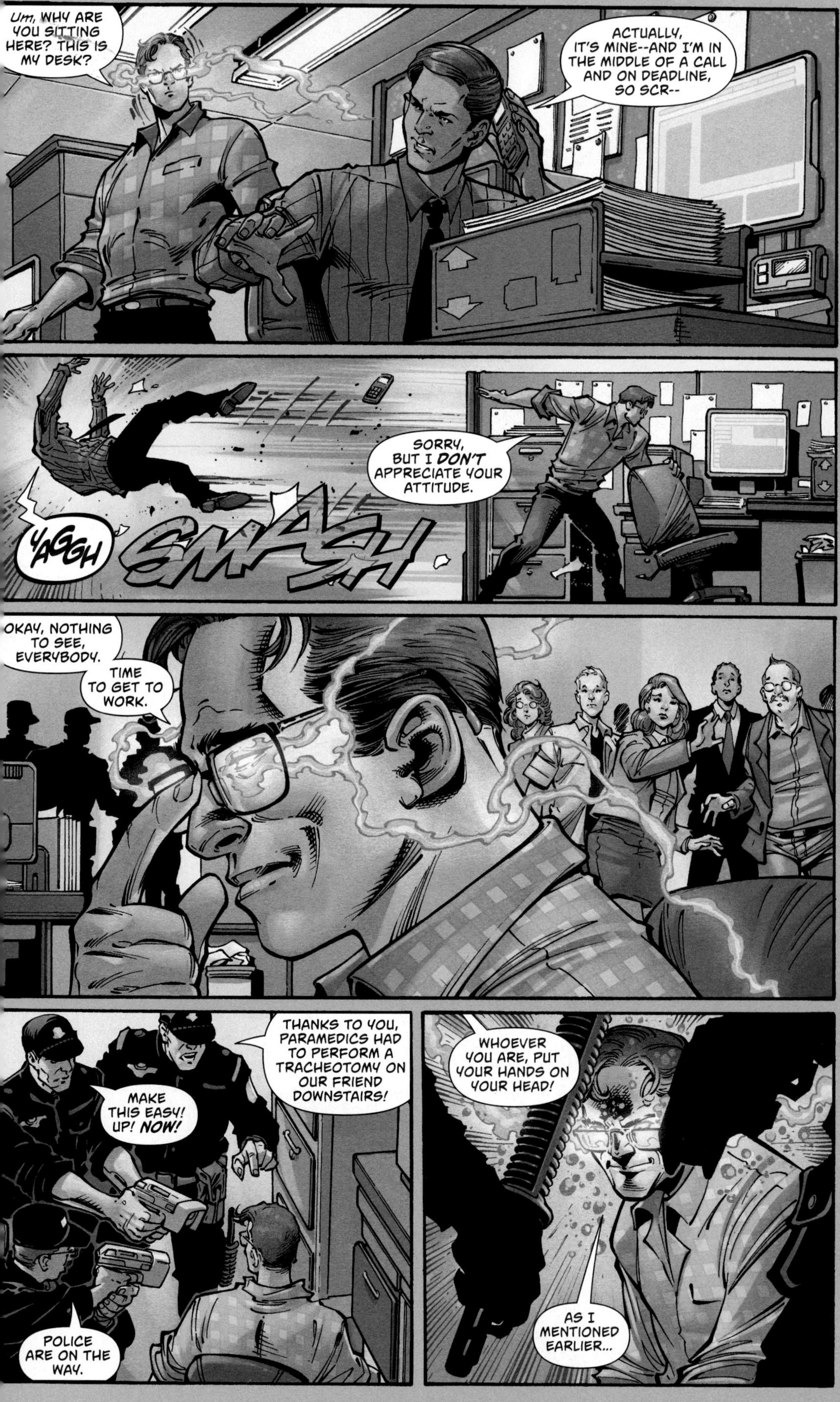
Um, WHY ARE YOU SITTING HERE? THIS IS MY DESK?
ACTUALLY, IT'S MINE--AND I'M IN THE MIDDLE OF A CALL AND ON DEADLINE, SO SCR--
YAGGH
SMASH
SORRY, BUT I DON'T APPRECIATE YOUR ATTITUDE.
OKAY, NOTHING TO SEE, EVERYBODY.
TIME TO GET TO WORK.
THANKS TO YOU, PARAMEDICS HAD TO PERFORM A TRACHEOTOMY ON OUR FRIEND DOWNSTAIRS!
MAKE THIS EASY! UP! NOW!
POLICE ARE ON THE WAY.
WHOEVER YOU ARE, PUT YOUR HANDS ON YOUR HEAD!
AS I MENTIONED EARLIER...

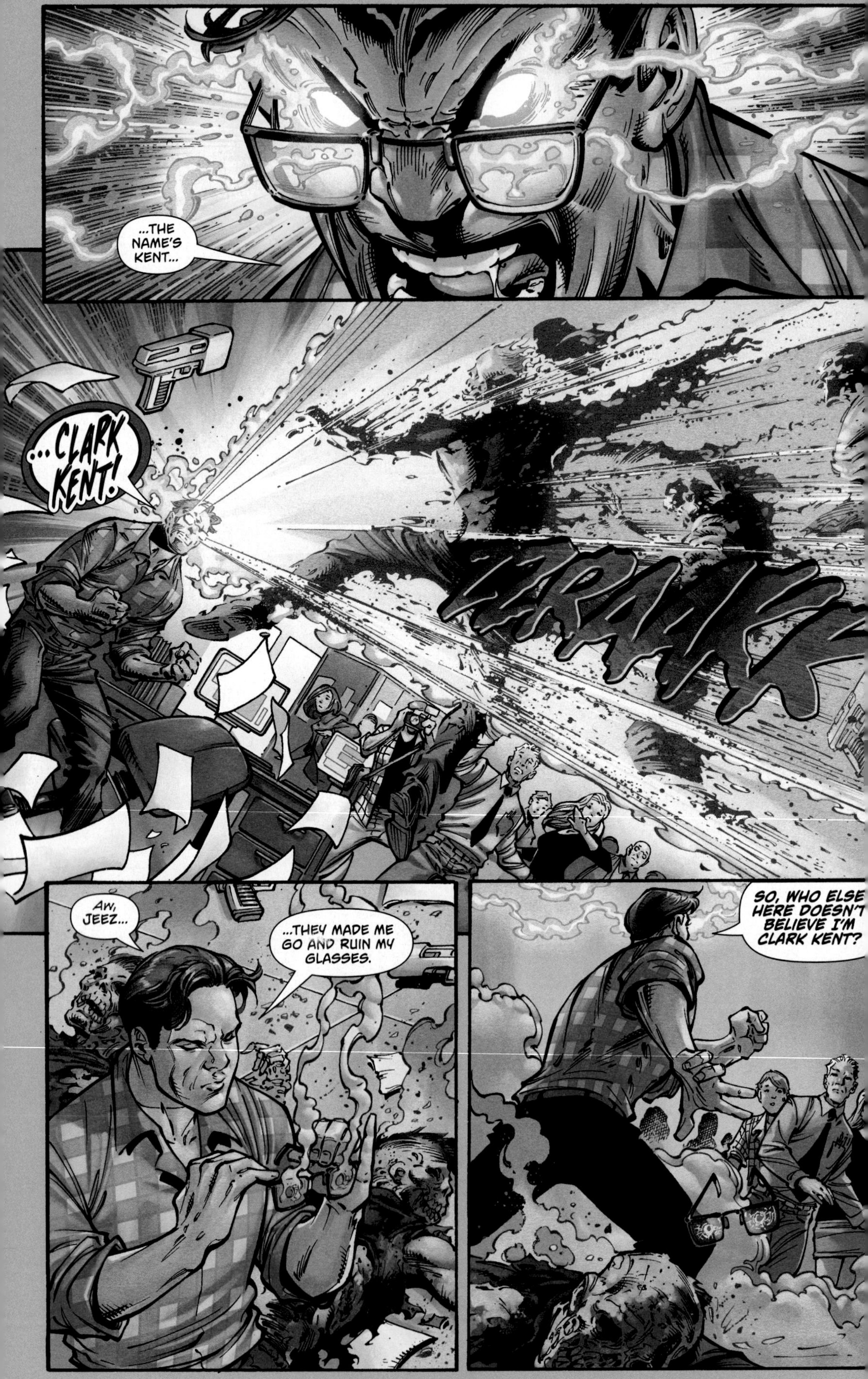
...THE NAME'S KENT...
...CLARK KENT!
Aw, JEEZ...
...THEY MADE ME GO AND RUIN MY GLASSES.
SO, WHO ELSE HERE DOESN'T BELIEVE I'M CLARK KENT?

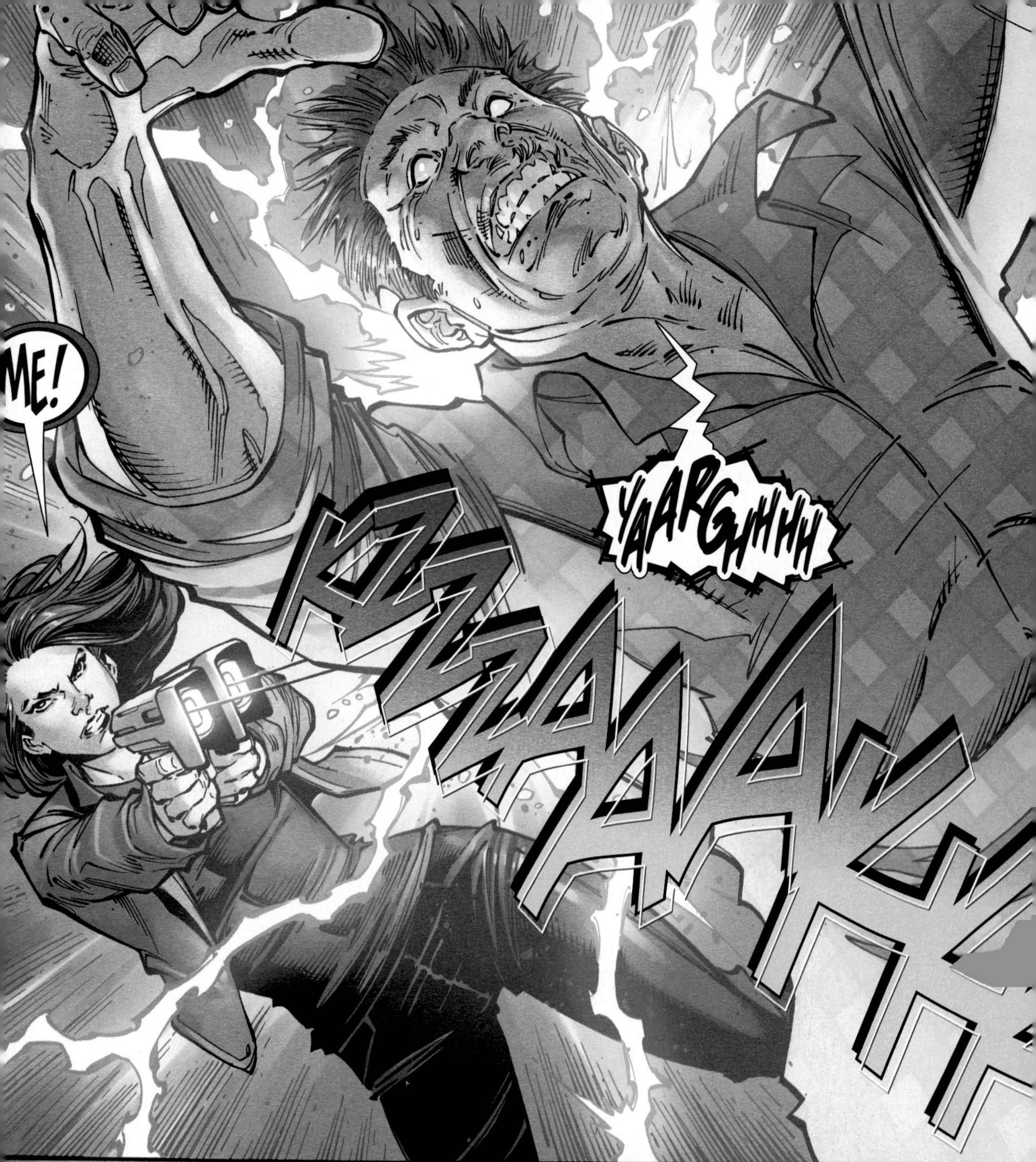
ME!
YAARGHHHH
KZZZAAAAAK!

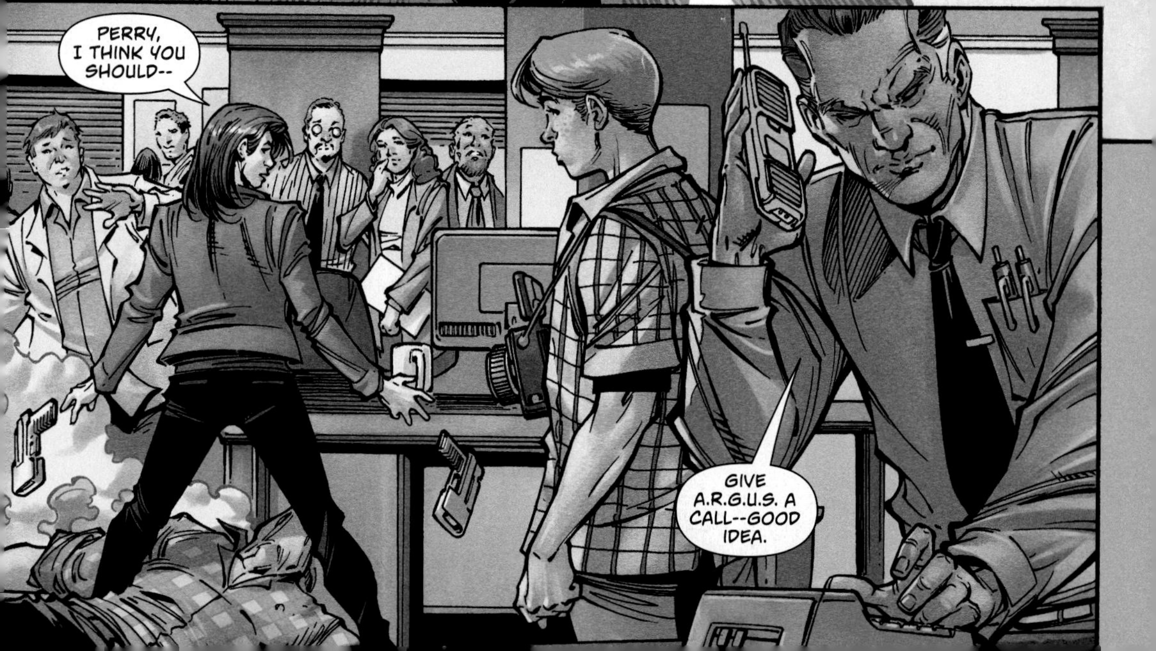
PERRY, I THINK YOU SHOULD--
GIVE A.R.G.U.S. A CALL--GOOD IDEA.

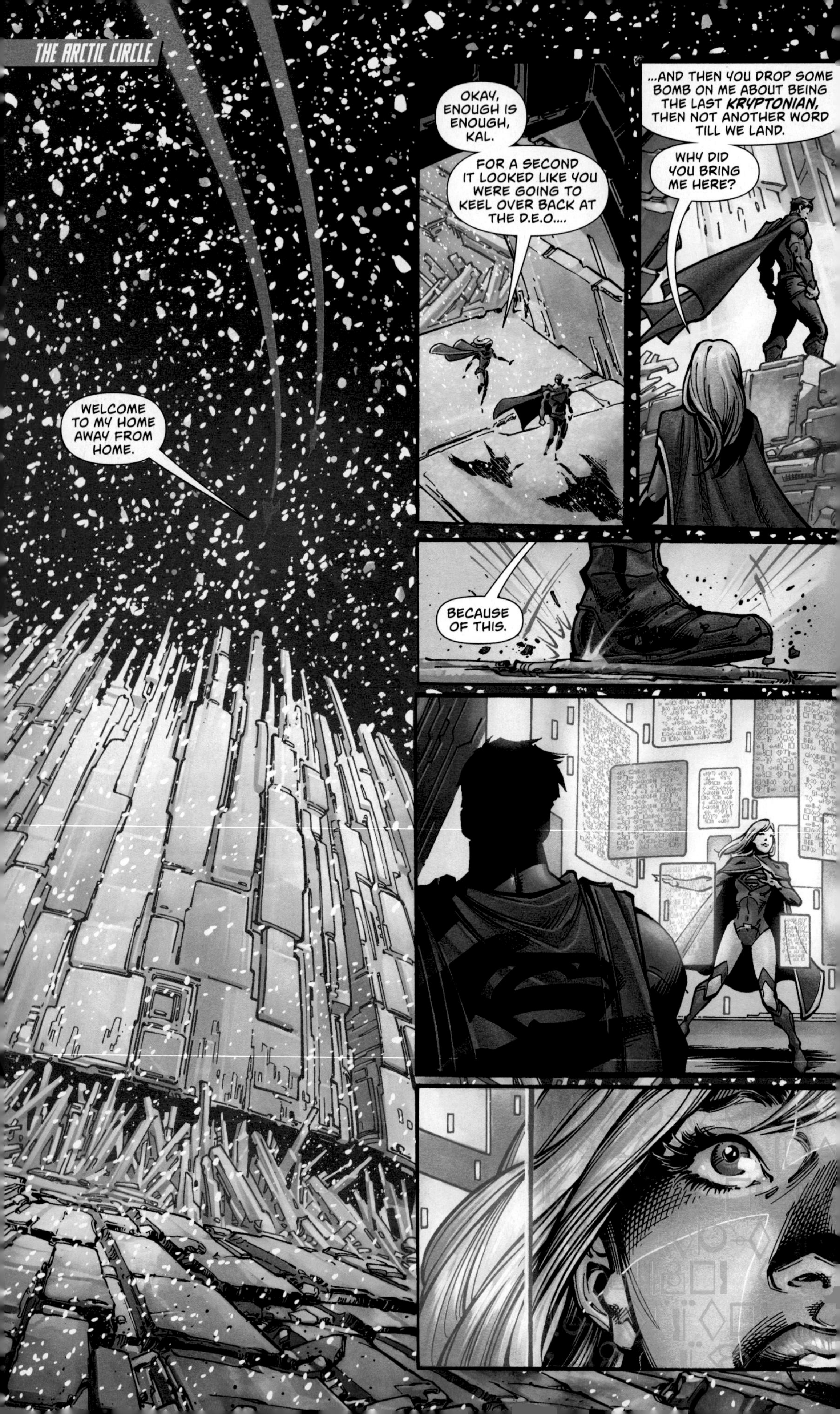

THE ARCTIC CIRCLE.
WELCOME TO MY HOME AWAY FROM HOME.
OKAY, ENOUGH IS ENOUGH, KAL.
FOR A SECOND IT LOOKED LIKE YOU WERE GOING TO KEEL OVER BACK AT THE D.E.O....
...AND THEN YOU DROP SOME BOMB ON ME ABOUT BEING THE LAST *KRYPTONIAN,* THEN NOT ANOTHER WORD TILL WE LAND.
WHY DID YOU BRING ME HERE?
BECAUSE OF THIS.

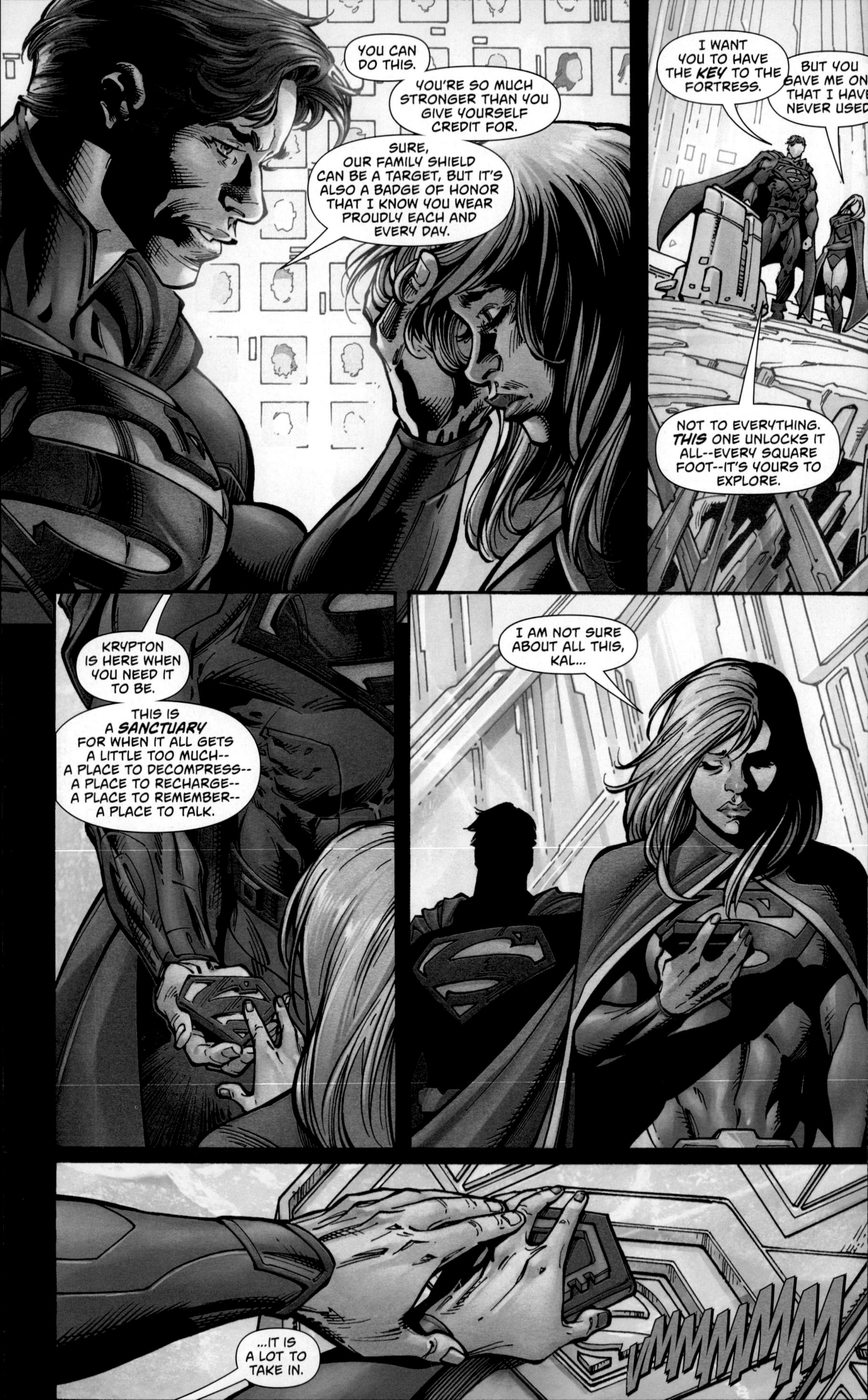
YOU CAN DO THIS.
YOU'RE SO MUCH STRONGER THAN YOU GIVE YOURSELF CREDIT FOR.
SURE, OUR FAMILY SHIELD CAN BE A TARGET, BUT IT'S ALSO A BADGE OF HONOR THAT I KNOW YOU WEAR PROUDLY EACH AND EVERY DAY.
I WANT YOU TO HAVE THE ***KEY*** TO THE FORTRESS.
BUT YOU GAVE ME ON THAT I HAVE NEVER USED
NOT TO EVERYTHING. ***THIS*** ONE UNLOCKS IT ALL--EVERY SQUARE FOOT--IT'S YOURS TO EXPLORE.
KRYPTON IS HERE WHEN YOU NEED IT TO BE.
THIS IS A ***SANCTUARY*** FOR WHEN IT ALL GETS A LITTLE TOO MUCH-- A PLACE TO DECOMPRESS-- A PLACE TO RECHARGE-- A PLACE TO REMEMBER-- A PLACE TO TALK.
I AM NOT SURE ABOUT ALL THIS, KAL...
...IT IS A LOT TO TAKE IN.

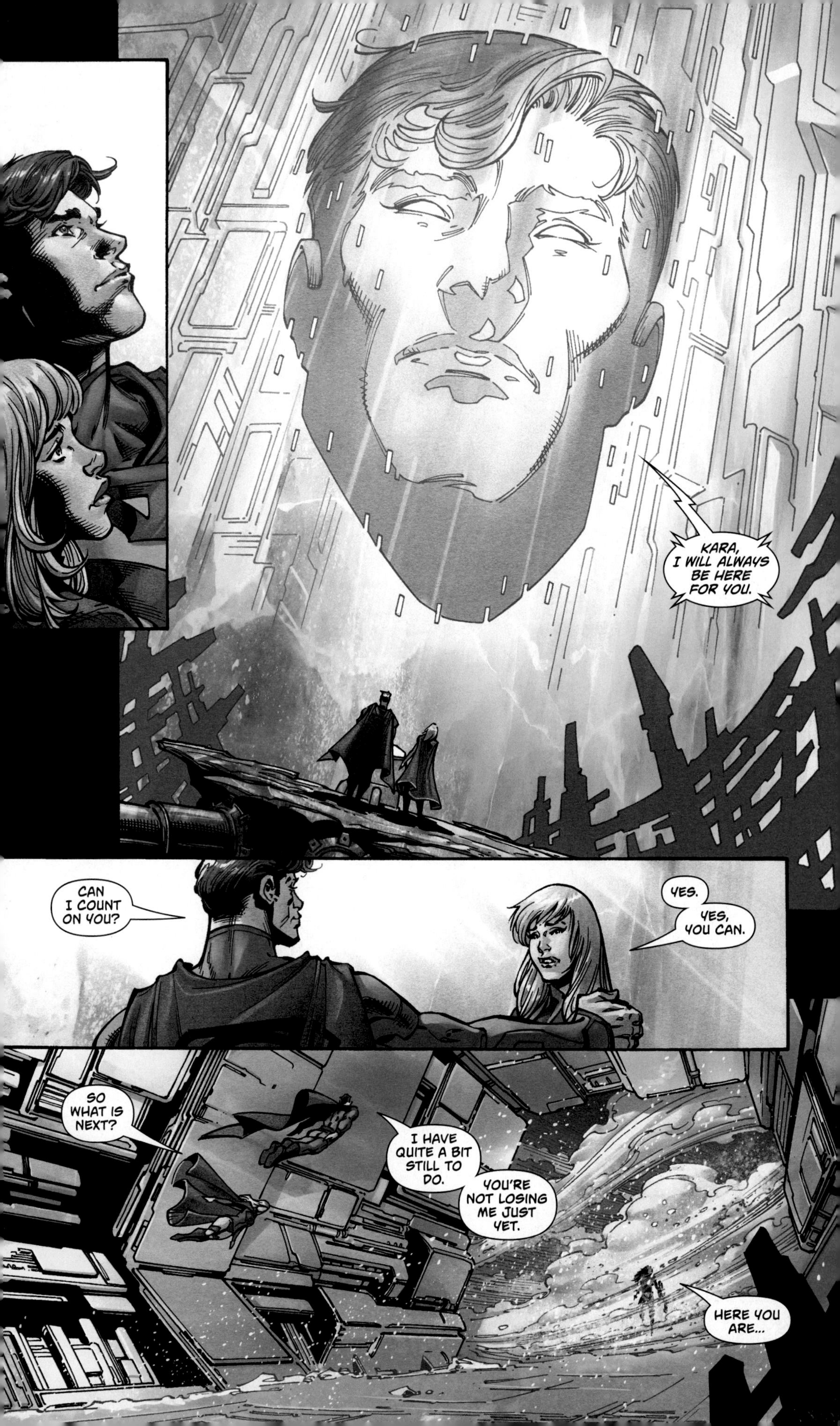
KARA, I WILL ALWAYS BE HERE FOR YOU.
CAN I COUNT ON YOU?
YES.
YES, YOU CAN.
SO WHAT IS NEXT?
I HAVE QUITE A BIT STILL TO DO.
YOU'RE NOT LOSING ME JUST YET.
HERE YOU ARE...

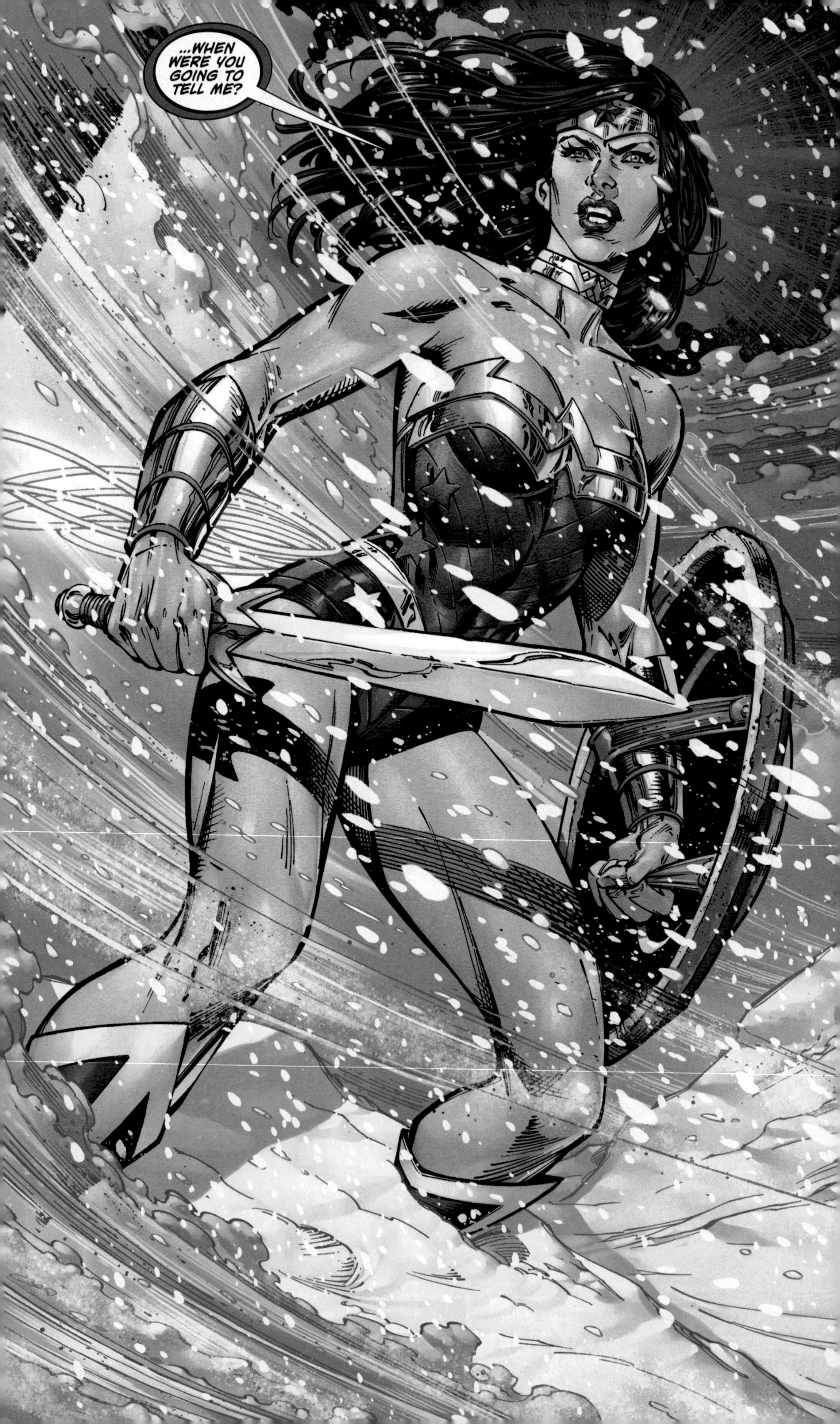
...WHEN WERE YOU GOING TO TELL ME?

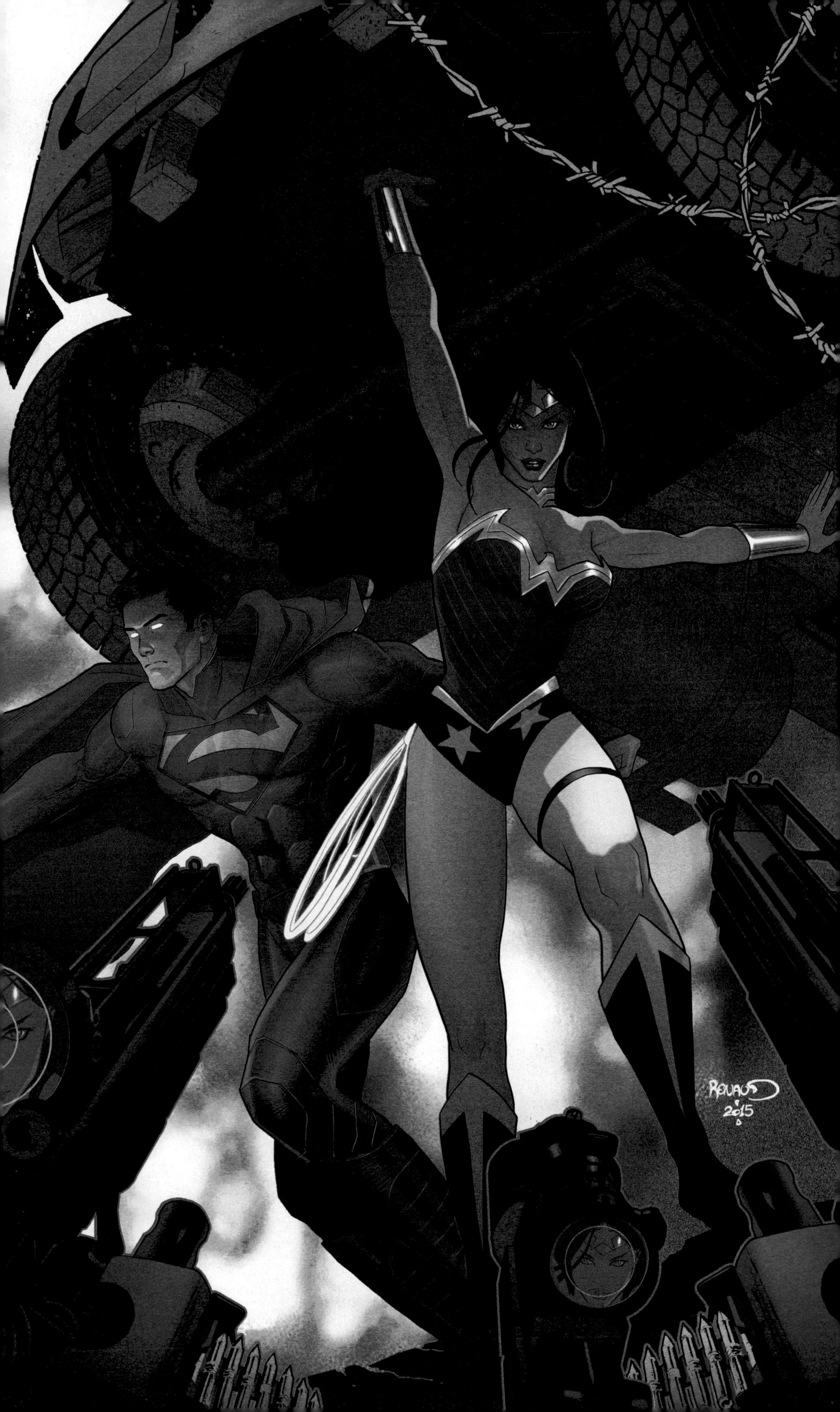

THE FINAL DAYS OF SUPERMAN PART 4: LAST KISS

PETER J. TOMASI writer ED BENES artist SANDRA HOPE ARCHER inker ALEX SINCLAIR colorist ROB LEIGH letterer PAUL RENAUD cover

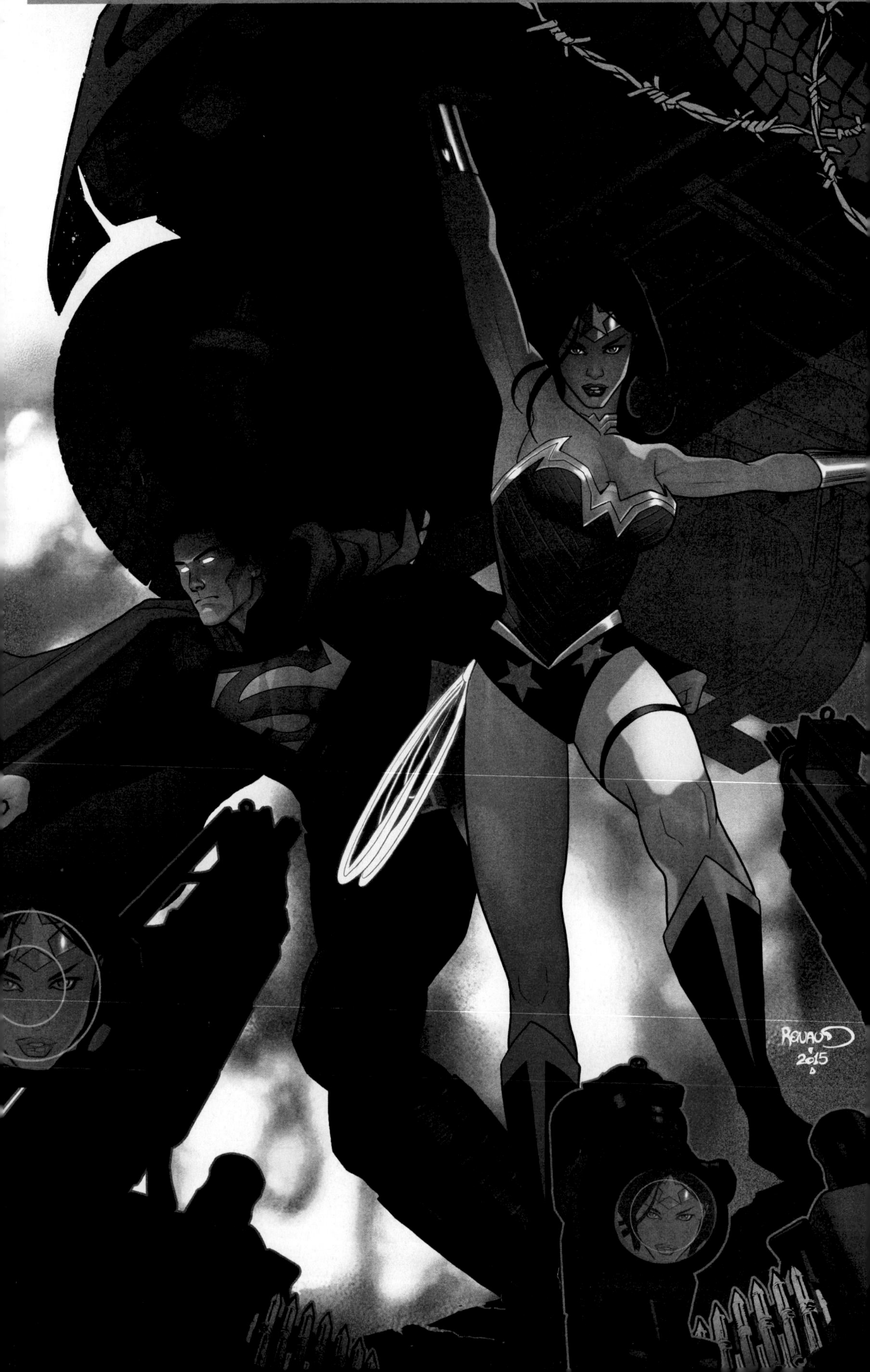

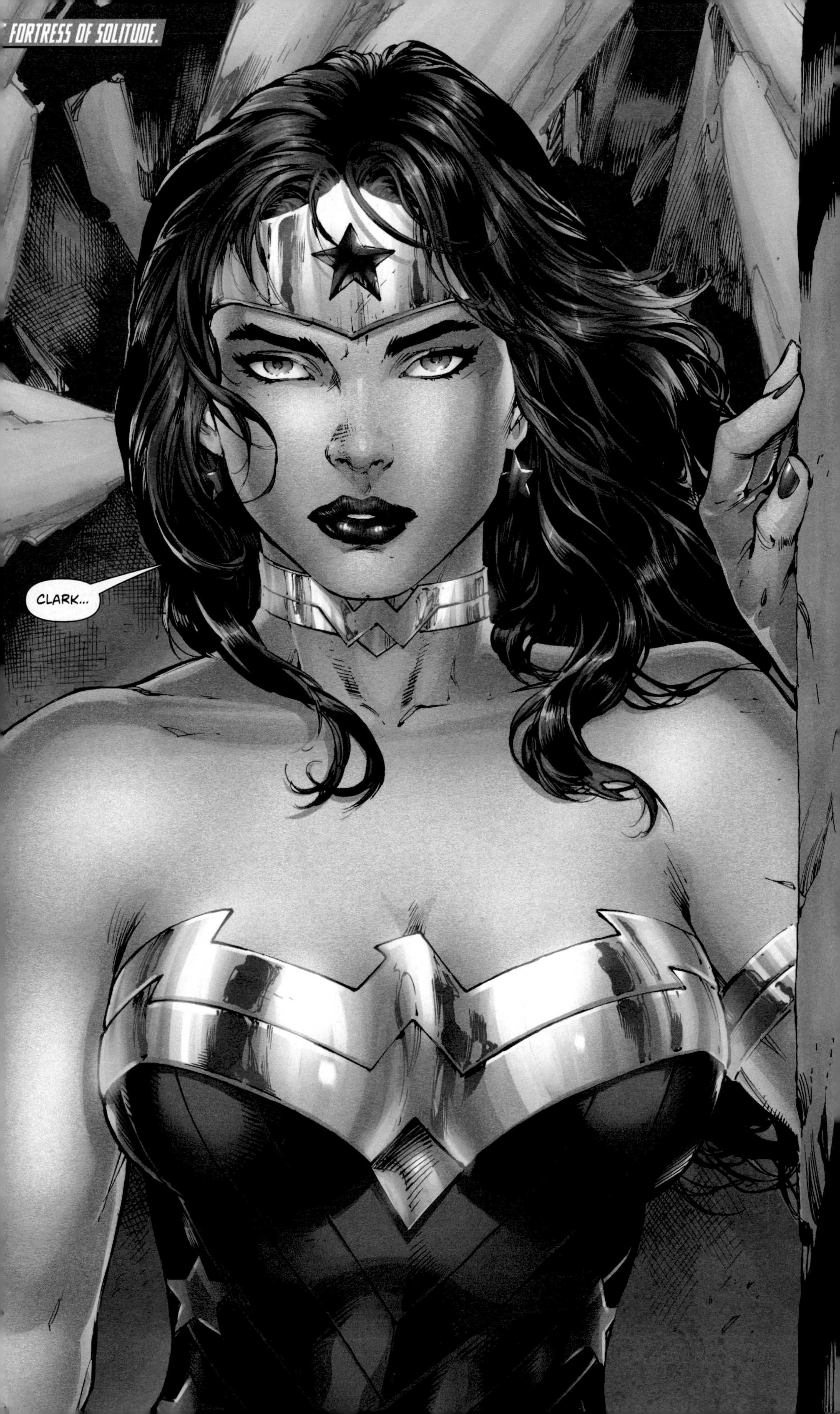
FORTRESS OF SOLITUDE.
CLARK...

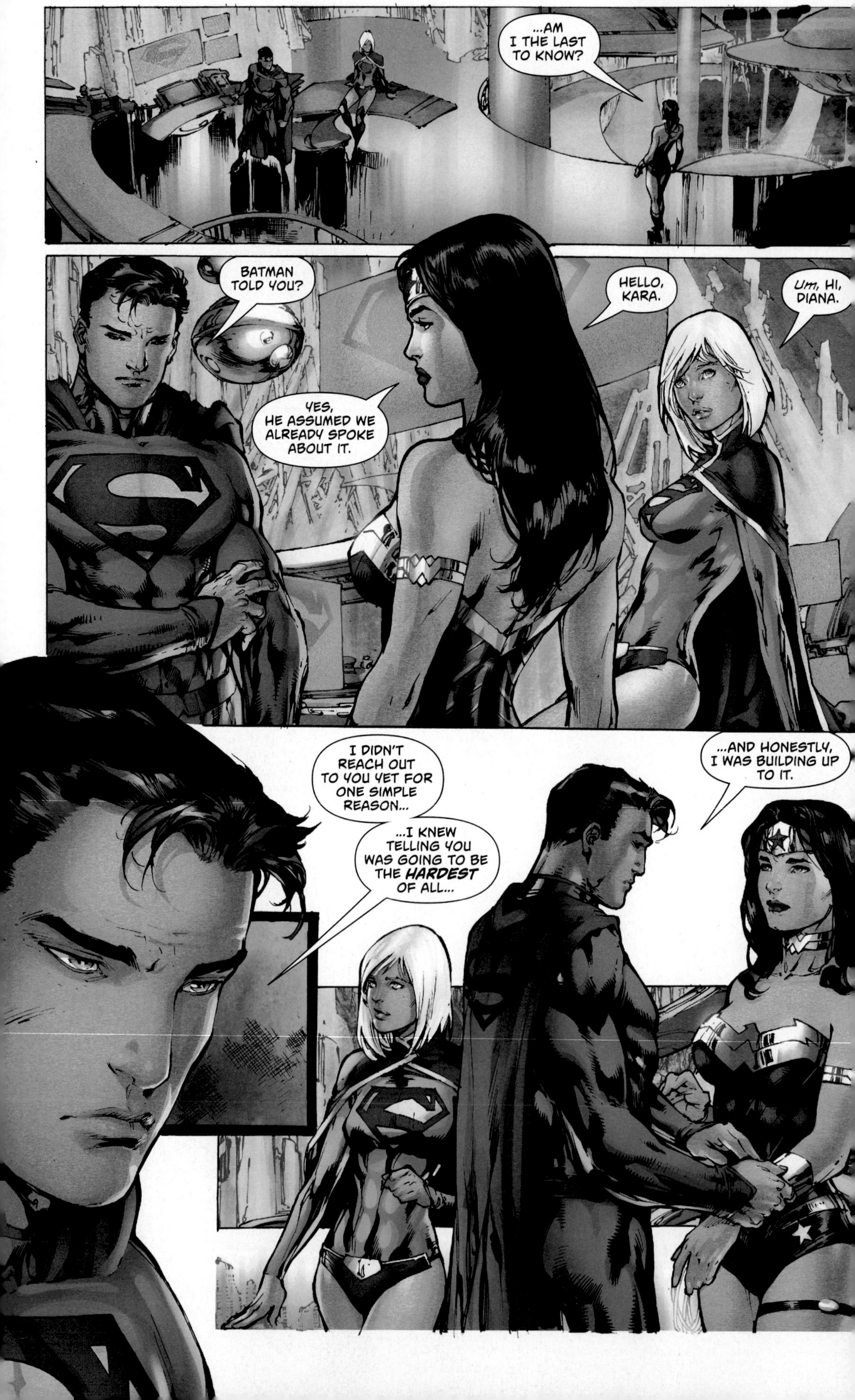
...AM I THE LAST TO KNOW?
BATMAN TOLD YOU?
YES, HE ASSUMED WE ALREADY SPOKE ABOUT IT.
HELLO, KARA.
UM, HI, DIANA.
I DIDN'T REACH OUT TO YOU YET FOR ONE SIMPLE REASON...
...I KNEW TELLING YOU WAS GOING TO BE THE *HARDEST* OF ALL...
...AND HONESTLY, I WAS BUILDING UP TO IT.

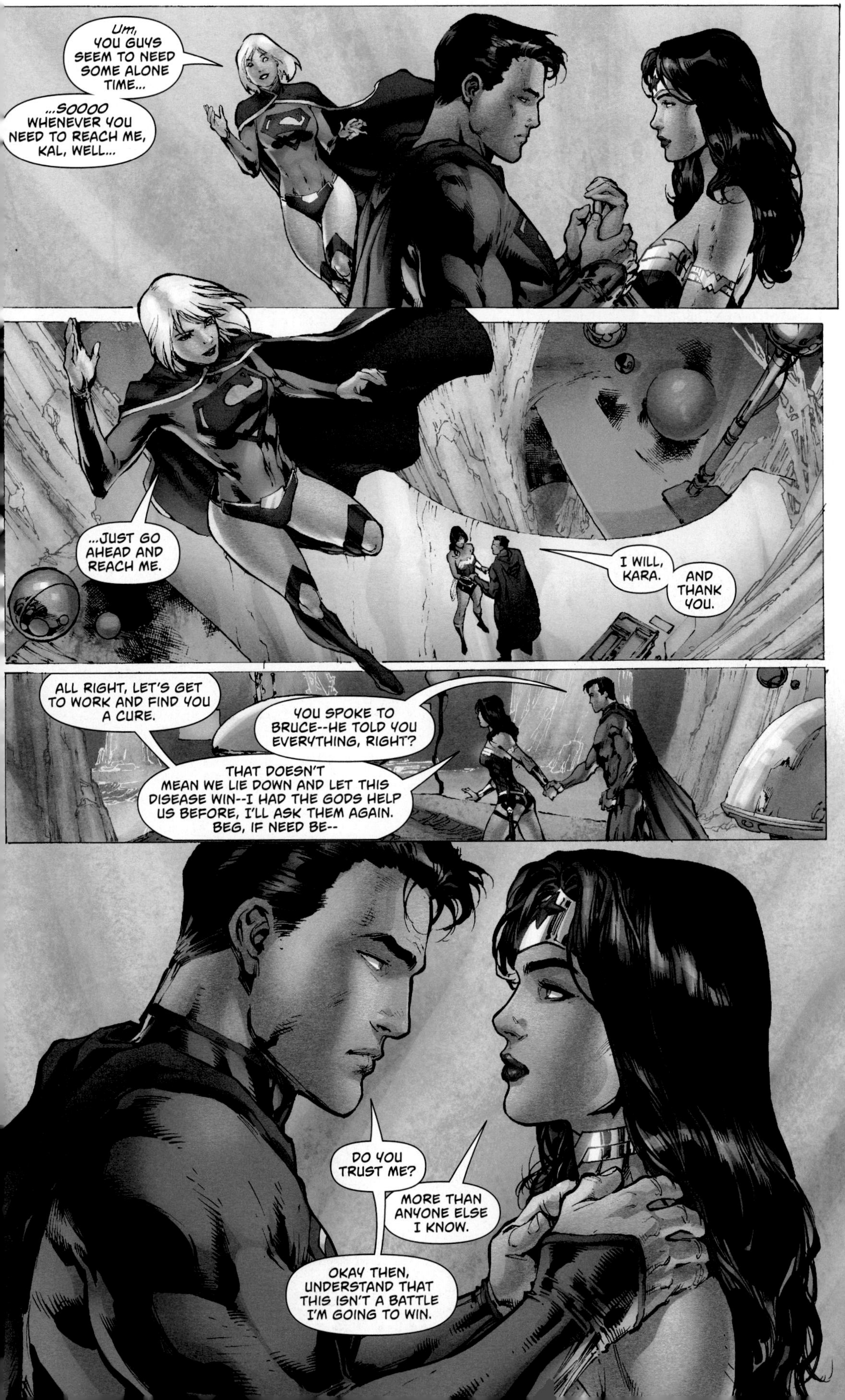
UM, YOU GUYS SEEM TO NEED SOME ALONE TIME...
...SOOOO WHENEVER YOU NEED TO REACH ME, KAL, WELL...
...JUST GO AHEAD AND REACH ME.
I WILL, KARA.
AND THANK YOU.
ALL RIGHT, LET'S GET TO WORK AND FIND YOU A CURE.
YOU SPOKE TO BRUCE--HE TOLD YOU EVERYTHING, RIGHT?
THAT DOESN'T MEAN WE LIE DOWN AND LET THIS DISEASE WIN--I HAD THE GODS HELP US BEFORE, I'LL ASK THEM AGAIN. BEG, IF NEED BE--
DO YOU TRUST ME?
MORE THAN ANYONE ELSE I KNOW.
OKAY THEN, UNDERSTAND THAT THIS ISN'T A BATTLE I'M GOING TO WIN.

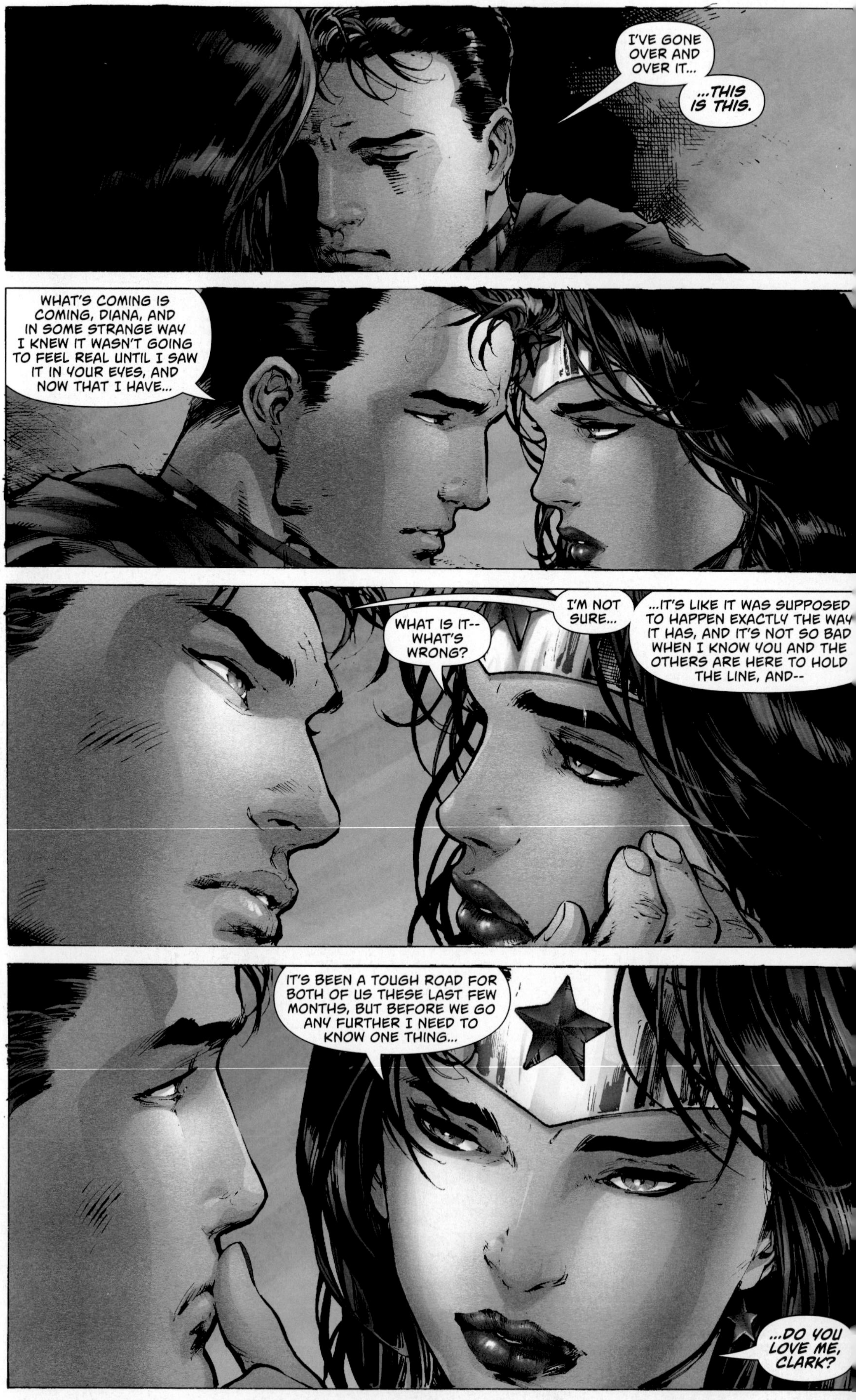
I'VE GONE OVER AND OVER IT...
...THIS IS THIS.
WHAT'S COMING IS COMING, DIANA, AND IN SOME STRANGE WAY I KNEW IT WASN'T GOING TO FEEL REAL UNTIL I SAW IT IN YOUR EYES, AND NOW THAT I HAVE...
WHAT IS IT-- WHAT'S WRONG?
I'M NOT SURE...
...IT'S LIKE IT WAS SUPPOSED TO HAPPEN EXACTLY THE WAY IT HAS, AND IT'S NOT SO BAD WHEN I KNOW YOU AND THE OTHERS ARE HERE TO HOLD THE LINE, AND--
IT'S BEEN A TOUGH ROAD FOR BOTH OF US THESE LAST FEW MONTHS, BUT BEFORE WE GO ANY FURTHER I NEED TO KNOW ONE THING...
...DO YOU LOVE ME, CLARK?

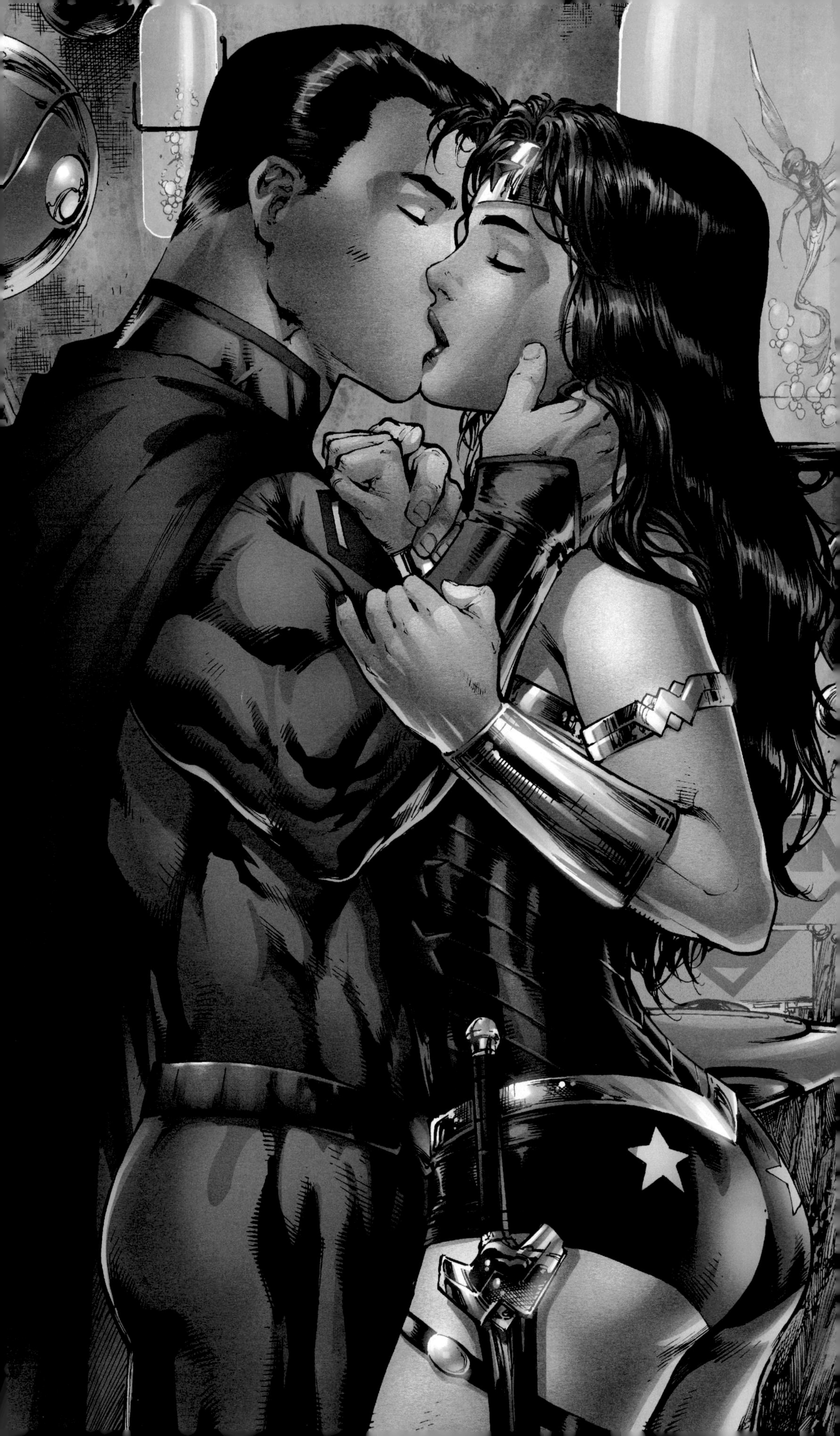

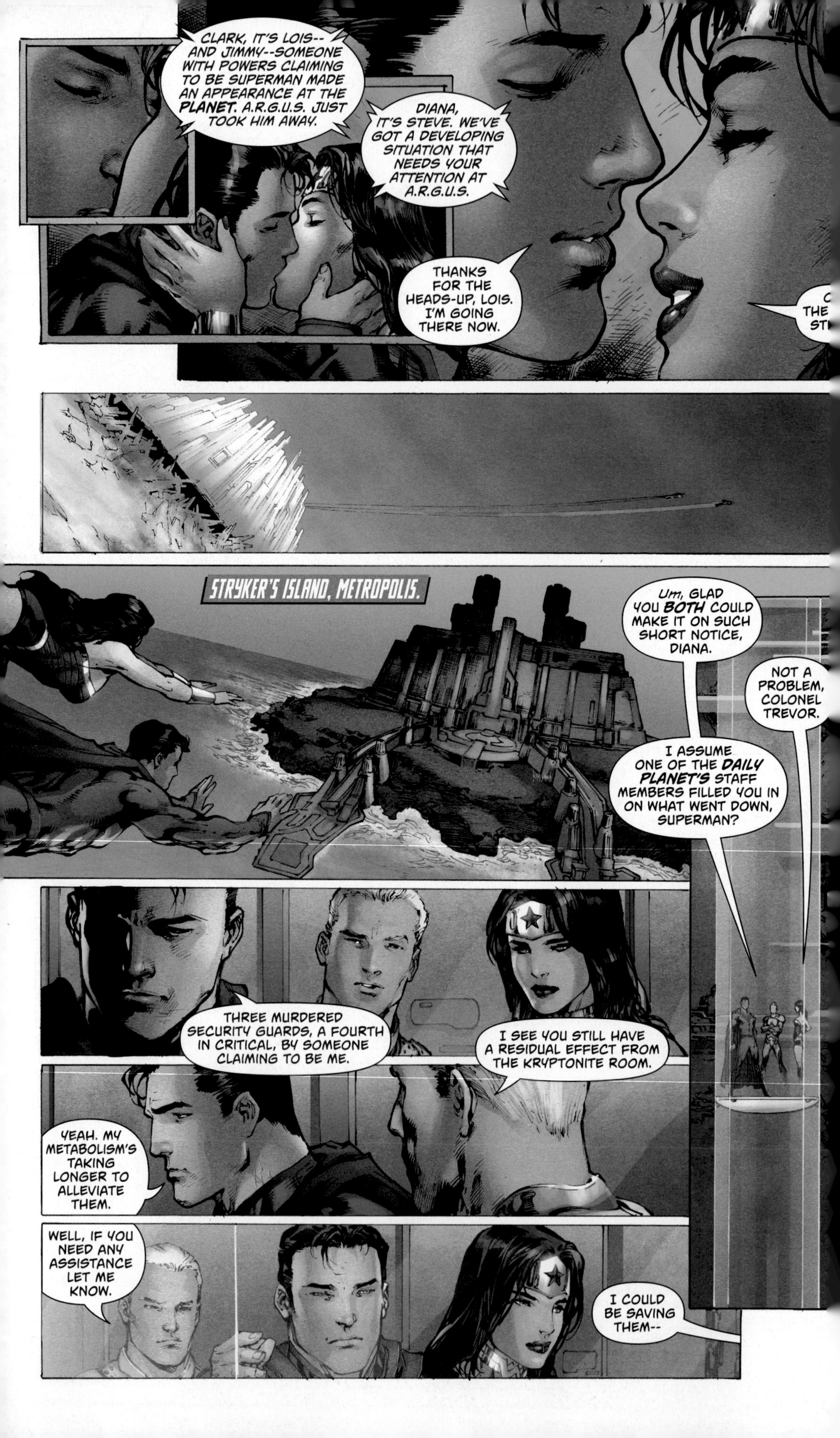
CLARK, IT'S LOIS--AND JIMMY--SOMEONE WITH POWERS CLAIMING TO BE SUPERMAN MADE AN APPEARANCE AT THE PLANET. A.R.G.U.S. JUST TOOK HIM AWAY.
DIANA, IT'S STEVE. WE'VE GOT A DEVELOPING SITUATION THAT NEEDS YOUR ATTENTION AT A.R.G.U.S.
THANKS FOR THE HEADS-UP, LOIS. I'M GOING THERE NOW.
STRYKER'S ISLAND, METROPOLIS.
Um, GLAD YOU BOTH COULD MAKE IT ON SUCH SHORT NOTICE, DIANA.
NOT A PROBLEM, COLONEL TREVOR.
I ASSUME ONE OF THE DAILY PLANET'S STAFF MEMBERS FILLED YOU IN ON WHAT WENT DOWN, SUPERMAN?
THREE MURDERED SECURITY GUARDS, A FOURTH IN CRITICAL, BY SOMEONE CLAIMING TO BE ME.
I SEE YOU STILL HAVE A RESIDUAL EFFECT FROM THE KRYPTONITE ROOM.
YEAH. MY METABOLISM'S TAKING LONGER TO ALLEVIATE THEM.
WELL, IF YOU NEED ANY ASSISTANCE LET ME KNOW.
I COULD BE SAVING THEM--

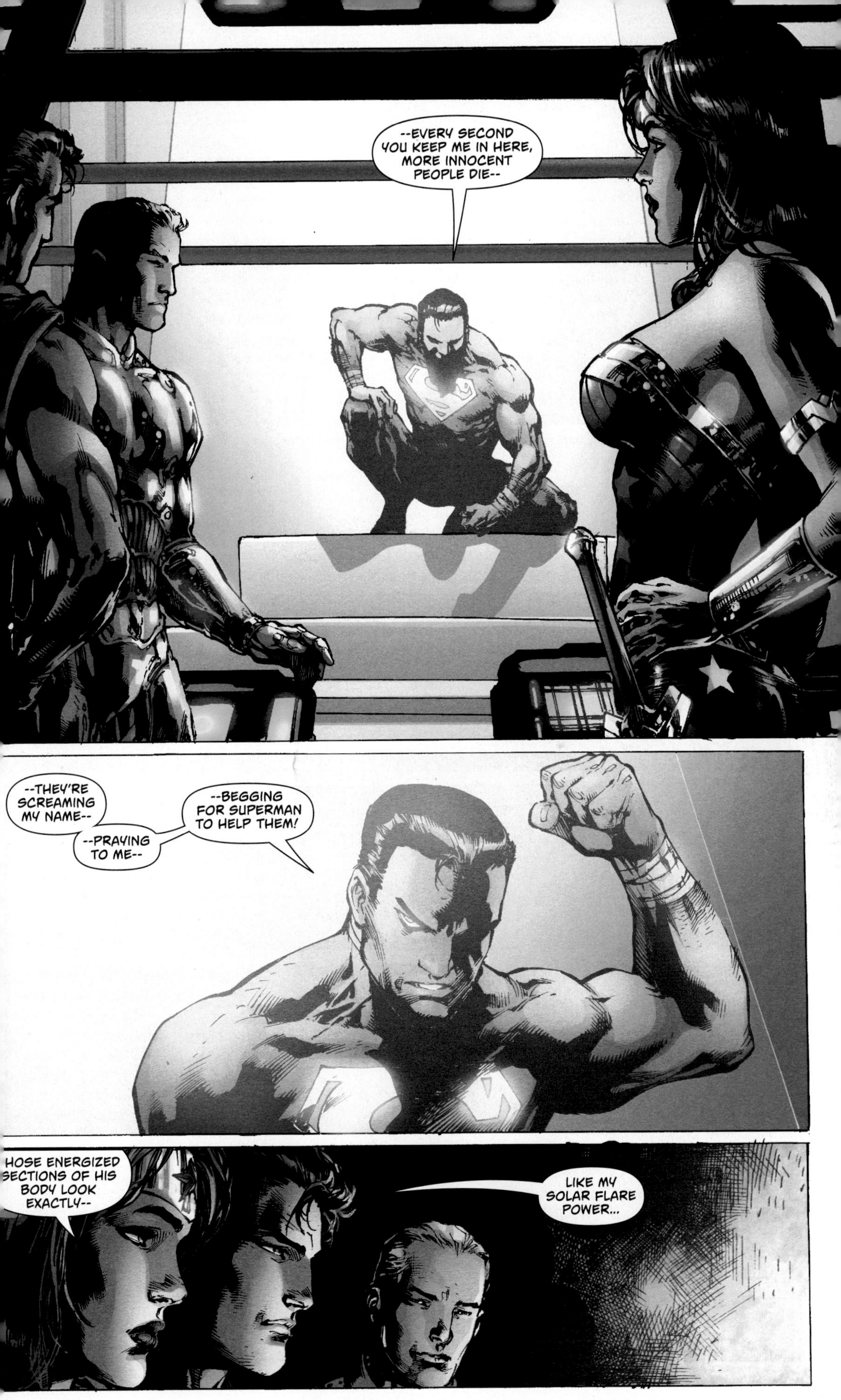
--EVERY SECOND YOU KEEP ME IN HERE, MORE INNOCENT PEOPLE DIE--
--THEY'RE SCREAMING MY NAME--
--PRAYING TO ME--
--BEGGING FOR SUPERMAN TO HELP THEM!
HOSE ENERGIZED SECTIONS OF HIS BODY LOOK EXACTLY--
LIKE MY SOLAR FLARE POWER...

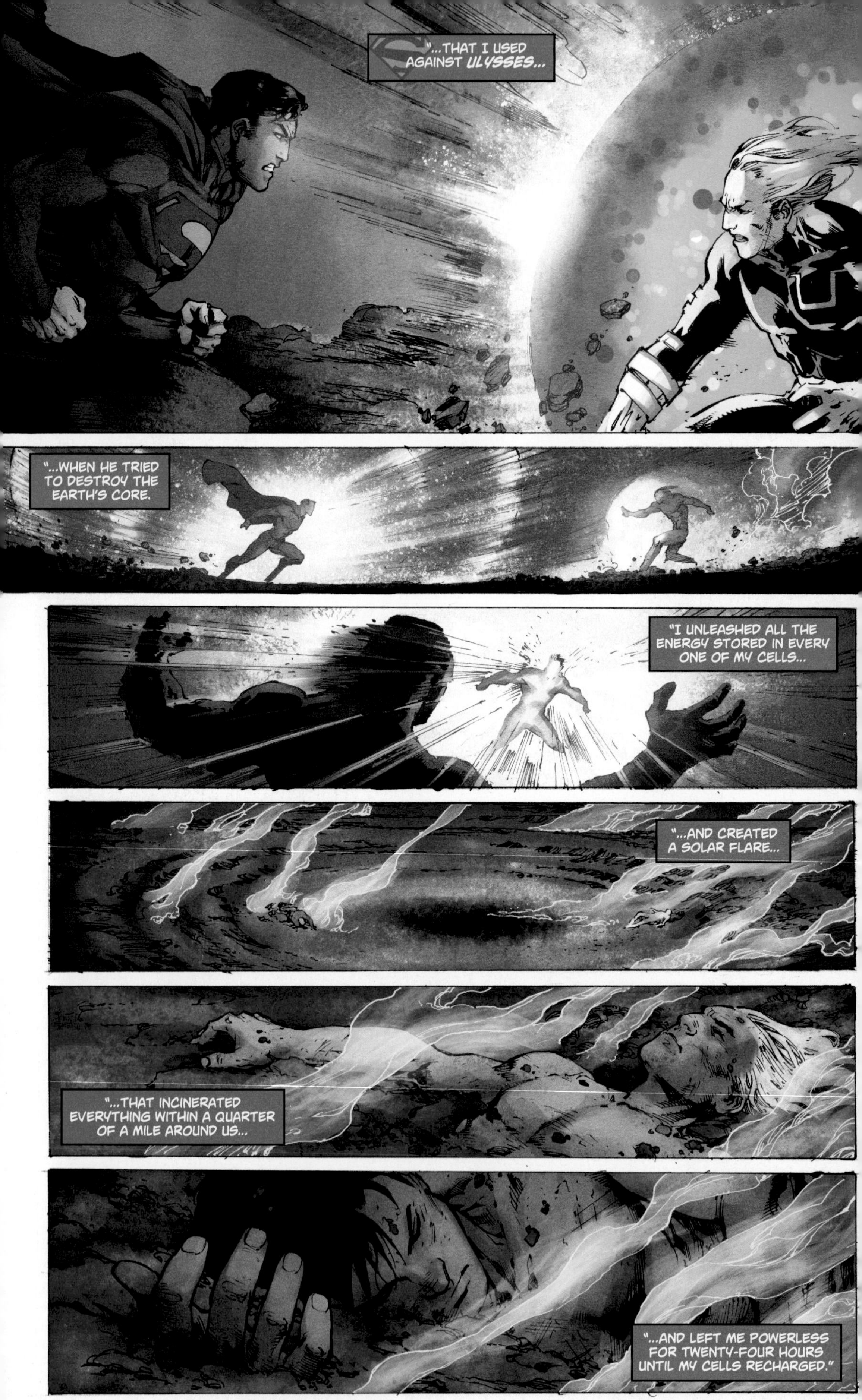
"...THAT I USED AGAINST ULYSSES...
"...WHEN HE TRIED TO DESTROY THE EARTH'S CORE.
"I UNLEASHED ALL THE ENERGY STORED IN EVERY ONE OF MY CELLS...
"...AND CREATED A SOLAR FLARE...
"...THAT INCINERATED EVERYTHING WITHIN A QUARTER OF A MILE AROUND US...
"...AND LEFT ME POWERLESS FOR TWENTY-FOUR HOURS UNTIL MY CELLS RECHARGED."

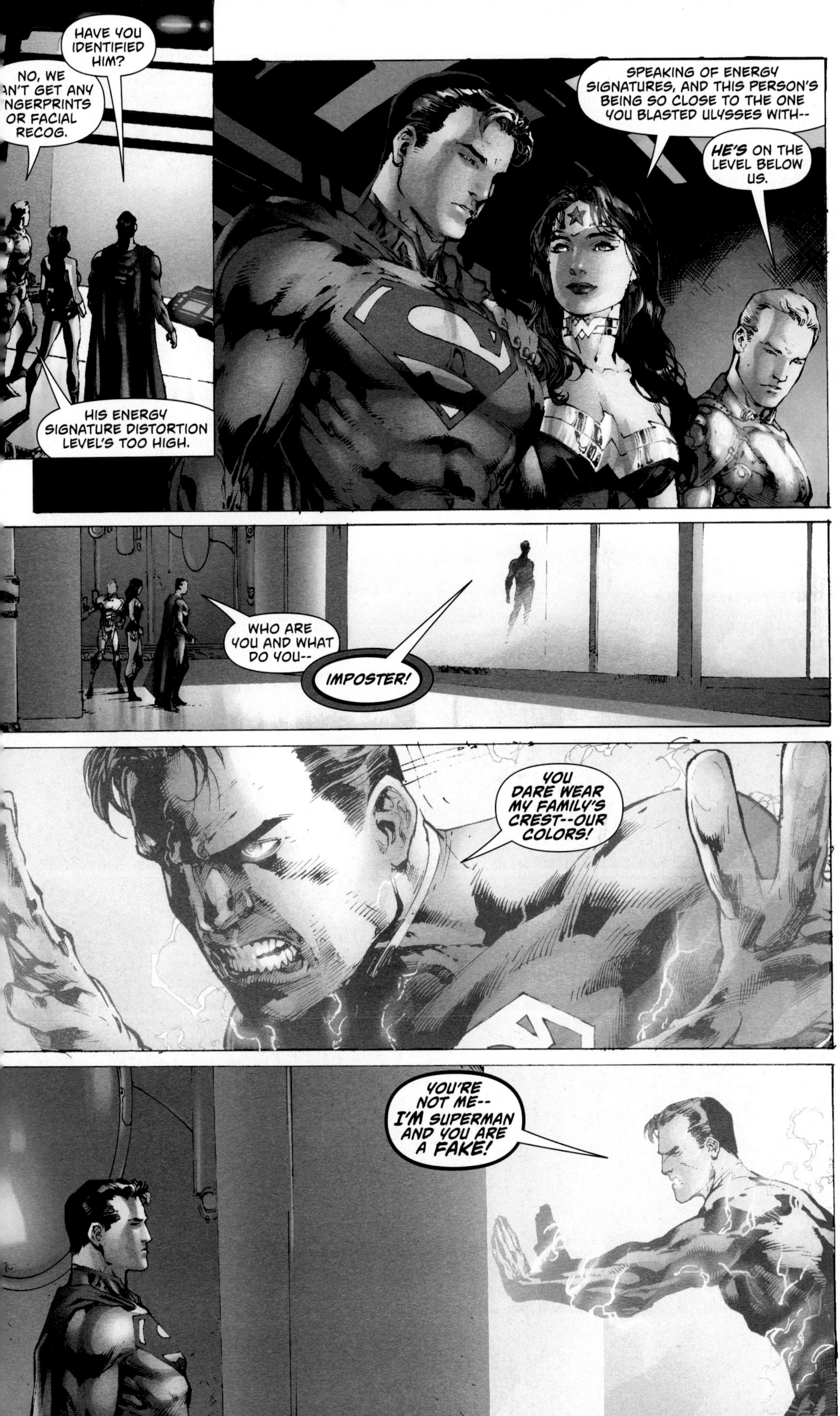
HAVE YOU IDENTIFIED HIM?
NO, WE [C]AN'T GET ANY [FI]NGERPRINTS OR FACIAL RECOG.
HIS ENERGY SIGNATURE DISTORTION LEVEL'S TOO HIGH.
SPEAKING OF ENERGY SIGNATURES, AND THIS PERSON'S BEING SO CLOSE TO THE ONE YOU BLASTED ULYSSES WITH--
HE'S ON THE LEVEL BELOW US.
WHO ARE YOU AND WHAT DO YOU--
IMPOSTER!
YOU DARE WEAR MY FAMILY'S CREST--OUR COLORS!
YOU'RE NOT ME-- I'M SUPERMAN AND YOU ARE A FAKE!

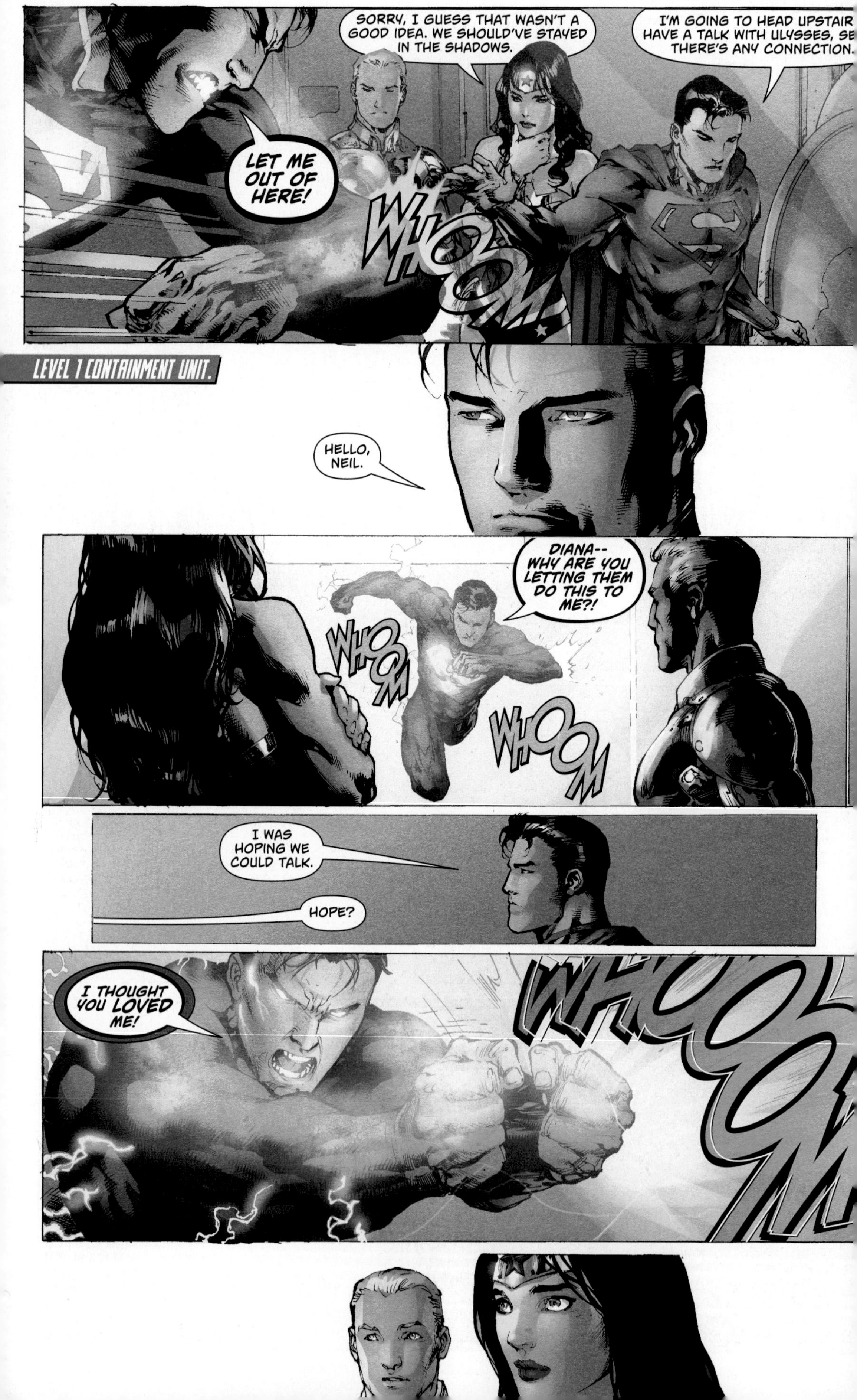
SORRY, I GUESS THAT WASN'T A GOOD IDEA. WE SHOULD'VE STAYED IN THE SHADOWS.
I'M GOING TO HEAD UPSTAIR HAVE A TALK WITH ULYSSES, SE THERE'S ANY CONNECTION.
LET ME OUT OF HERE!
WHOOM
LEVEL 1 CONTAINMENT UNIT.
HELLO, NEIL.
DIANA-- WHY ARE YOU LETTING THEM DO THIS TO ME?!
WHOOM
WHOOM
I WAS HOPING WE COULD TALK.
HOPE?
I THOUGHT YOU LOVED ME!

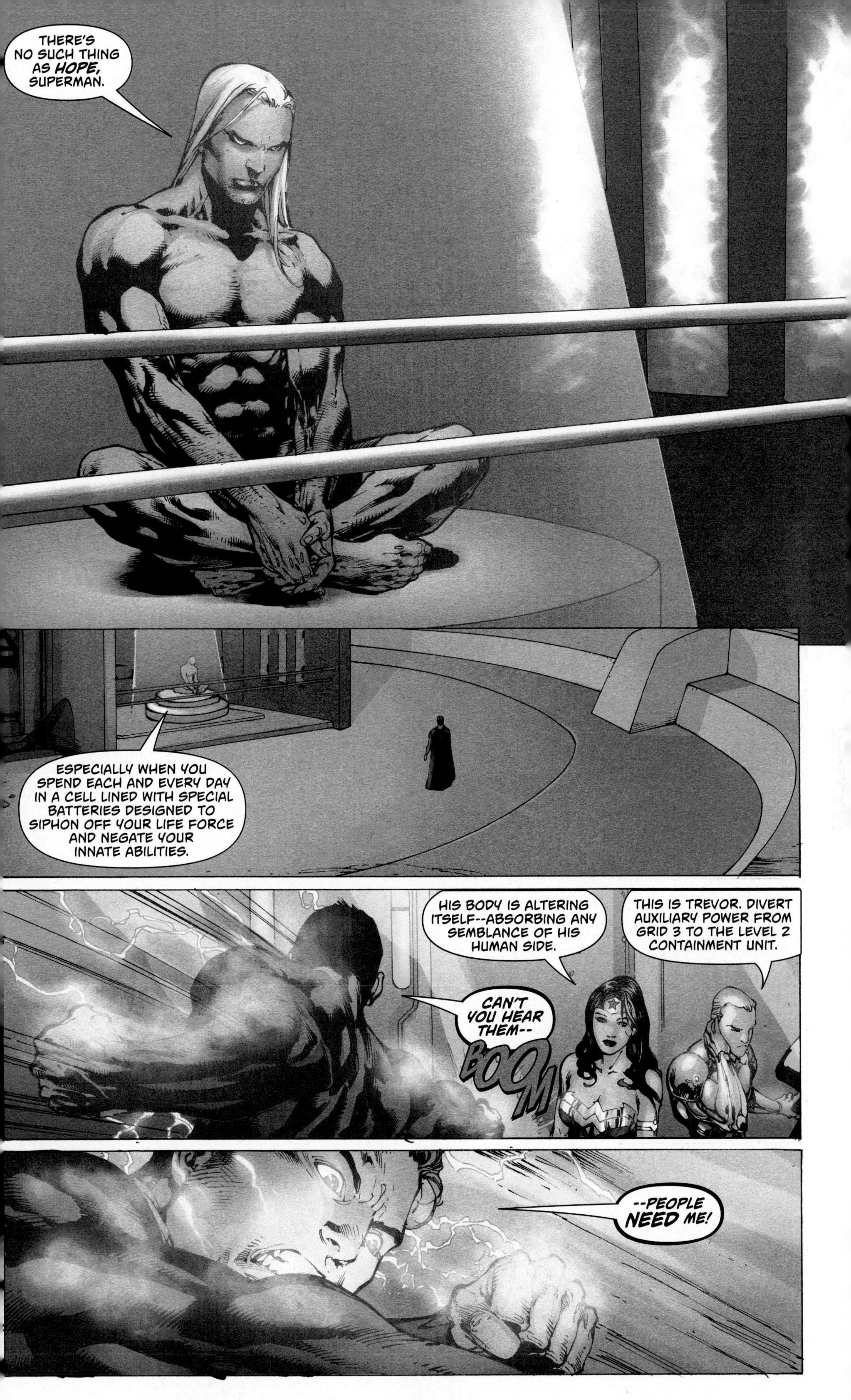
THERE'S NO SUCH THING AS *HOPE,* SUPERMAN.
ESPECIALLY WHEN YOU SPEND EACH AND EVERY DAY IN A CELL LINED WITH SPECIAL BATTERIES DESIGNED TO SIPHON OFF YOUR LIFE FORCE AND NEGATE YOUR INNATE ABILITIES.
HIS BODY IS ALTERING ITSELF--ABSORBING ANY SEMBLANCE OF HIS HUMAN SIDE.
THIS IS TREVOR. DIVERT AUXILIARY POWER FROM GRID 3 TO THE LEVEL 2 CONTAINMENT UNIT.
CAN'T YOU HEAR THEM--
BOOM
--PEOPLE **NEED** ME!

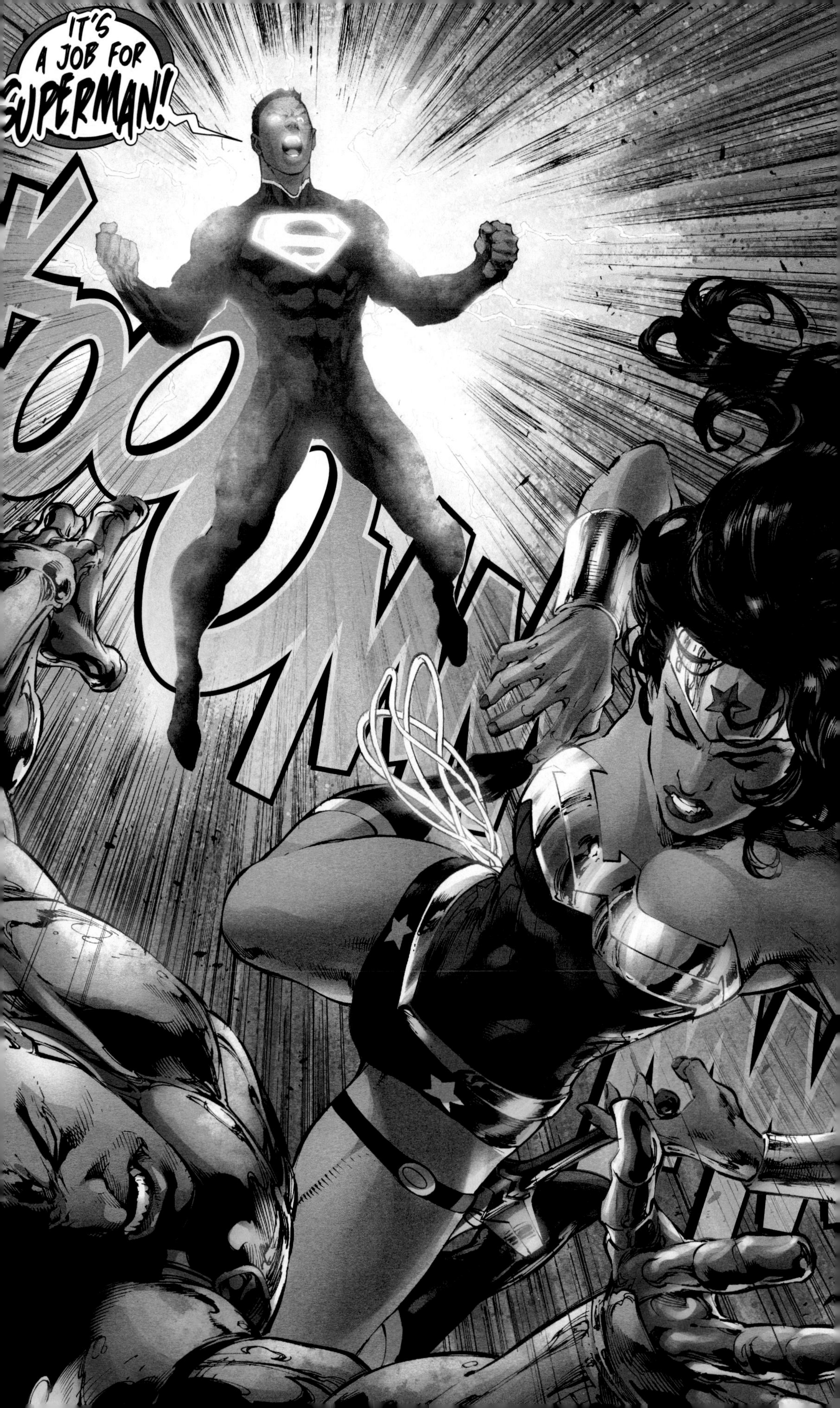
IT'S A JOB FOR SUPERMAN!

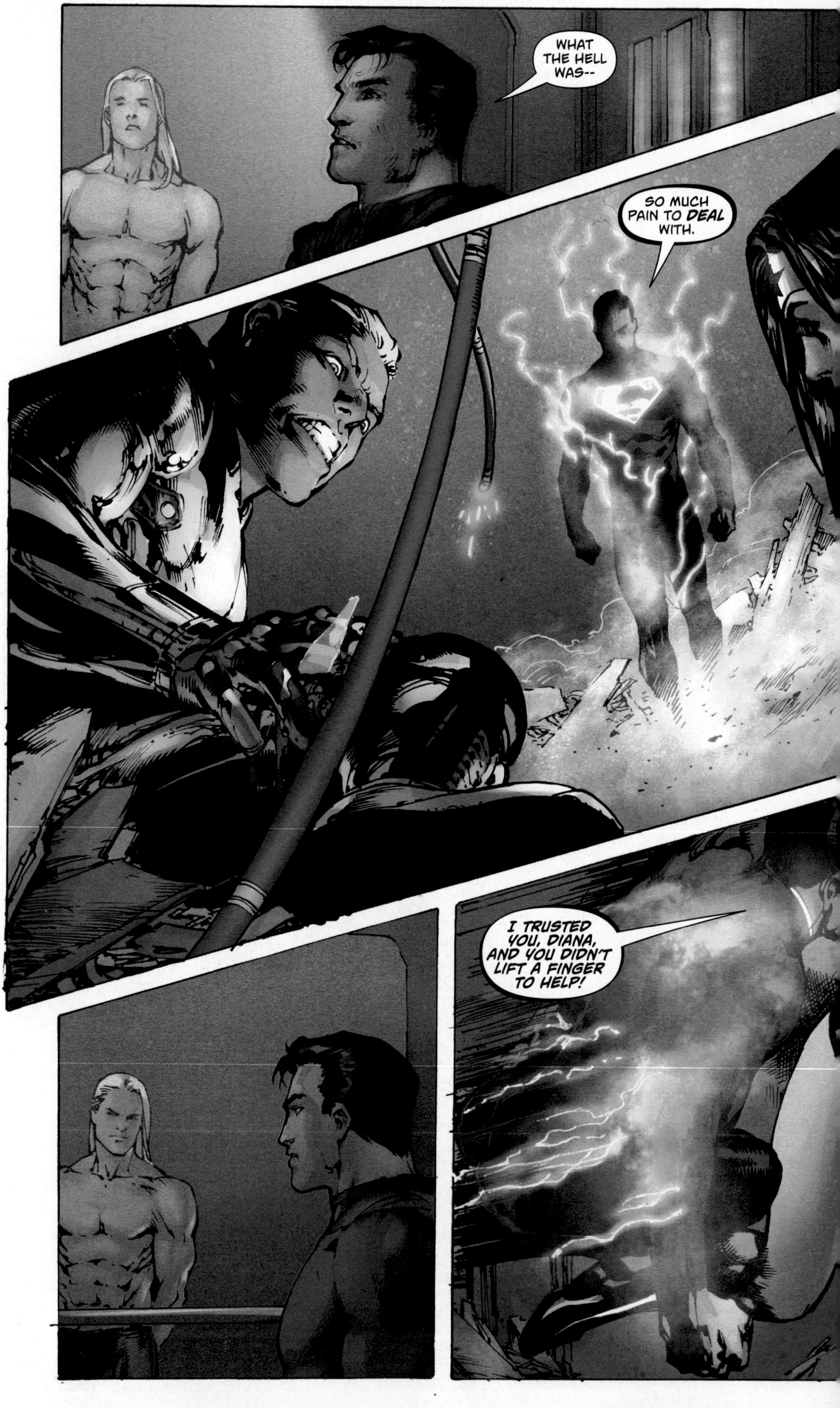
WHAT THE HELL WAS--
SO MUCH PAIN TO DEAL WITH.
I TRUSTED YOU, DIANA, AND YOU DIDN'T LIFT A FINGER TO HELP!

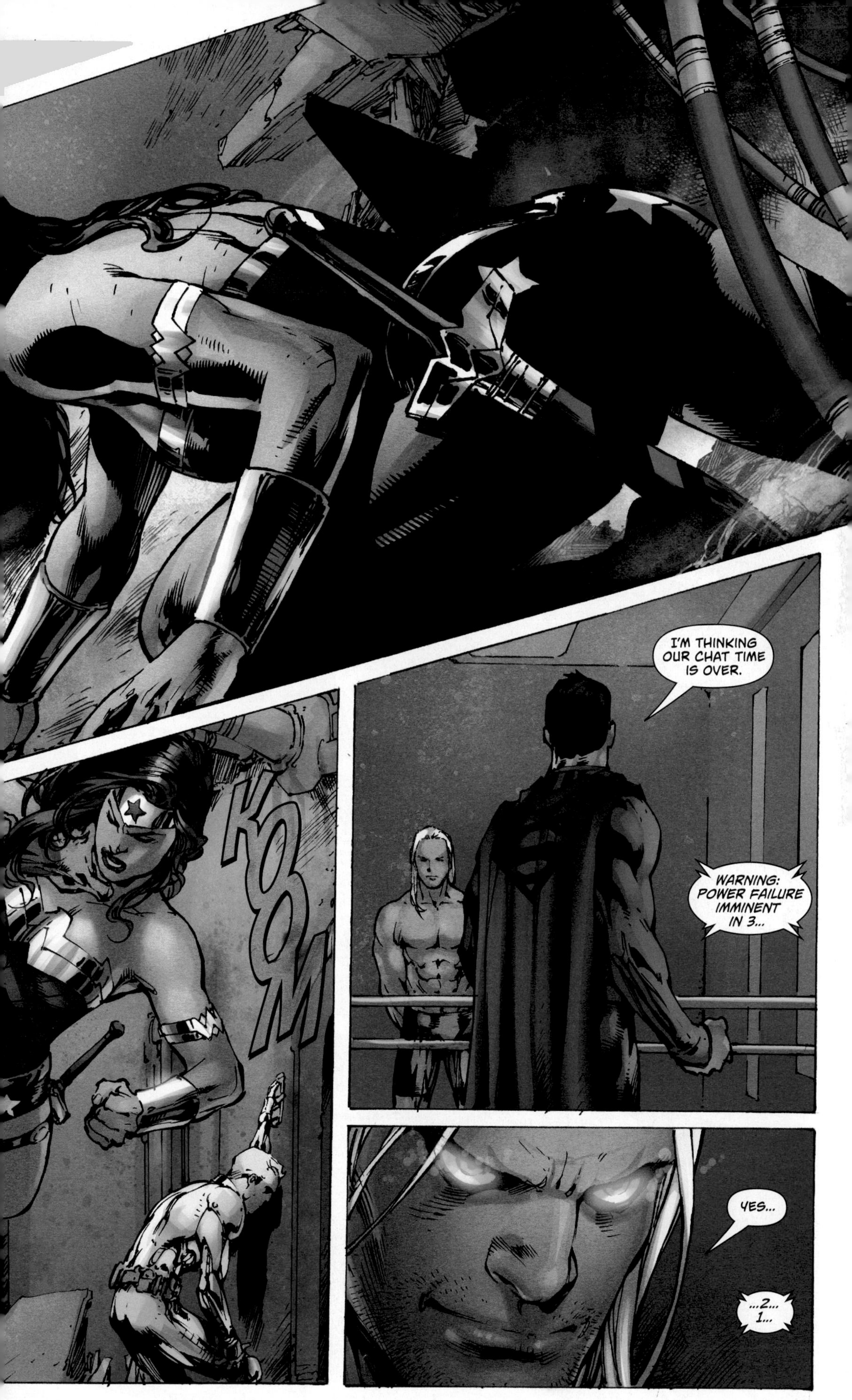
I'M THINKING OUR CHAT TIME IS OVER.
KOOM
WARNING: POWER FAILURE IMMINENT IN 3...
YES...
...2... 1...

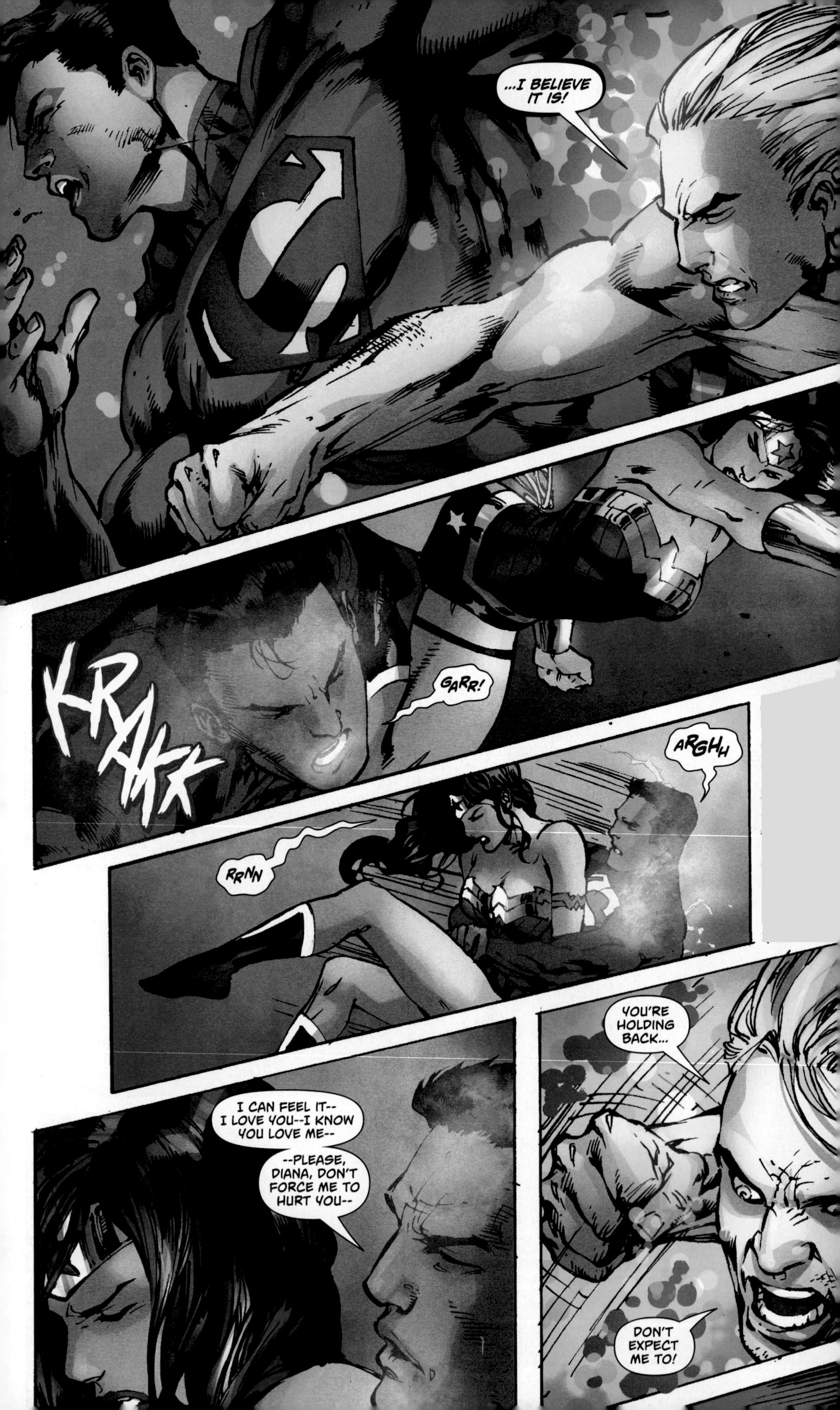
...I BELIEVE IT IS!
KRAKK
GARR!
ARGHH
RRNN
YOU'RE HOLDING BACK...
I CAN FEEL IT-- I LOVE YOU--I KNOW YOU LOVE ME--
--PLEASE, DIANA, DON'T FORCE ME TO HURT YOU--
DON'T EXPECT ME TO!

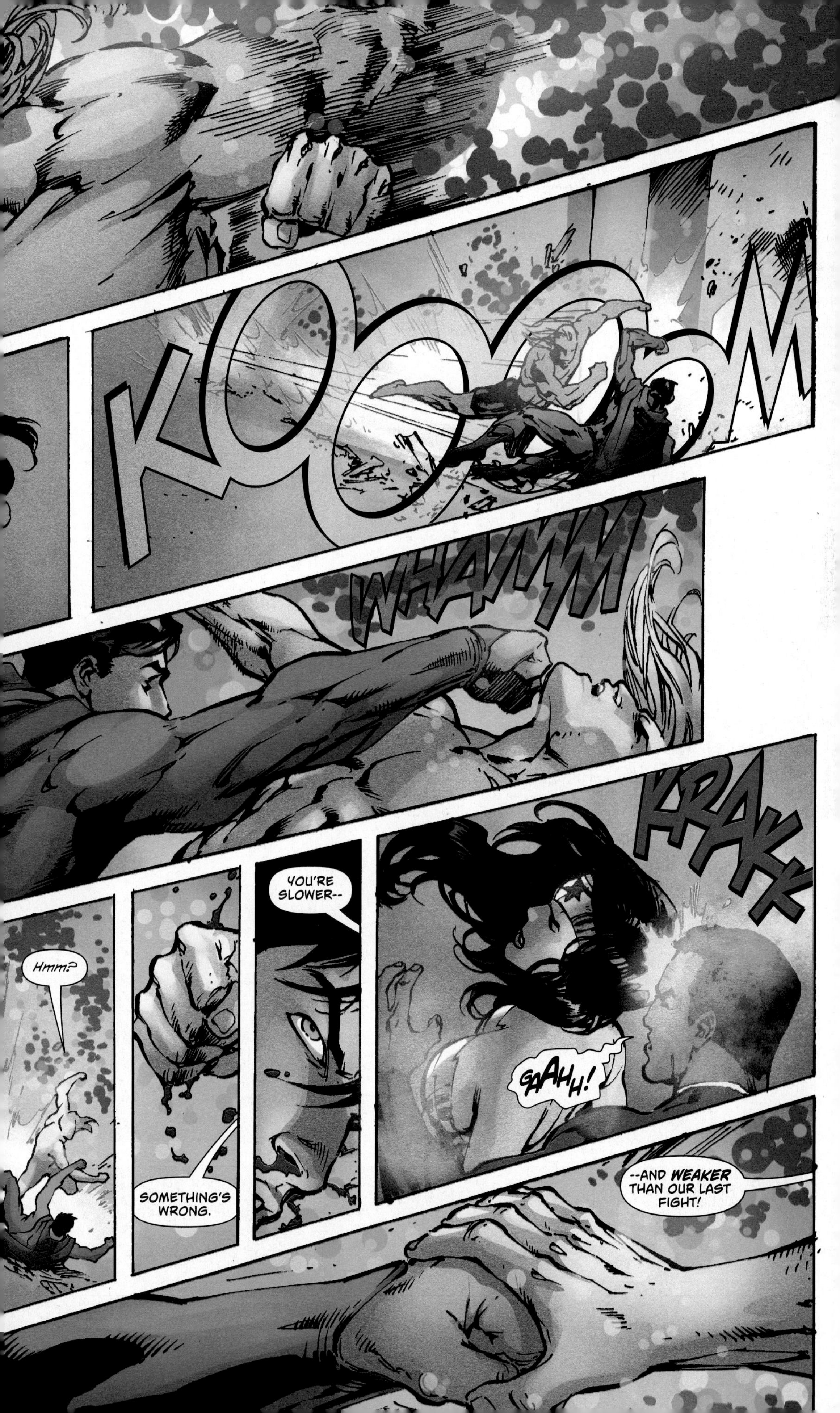
KOOOOM
WHAMM
KRAKK
GAAHH!
Hmm?
SOMETHING'S WRONG.
YOU'RE SLOWER--
--AND WEAKER THAN OUR LAST FIGHT!

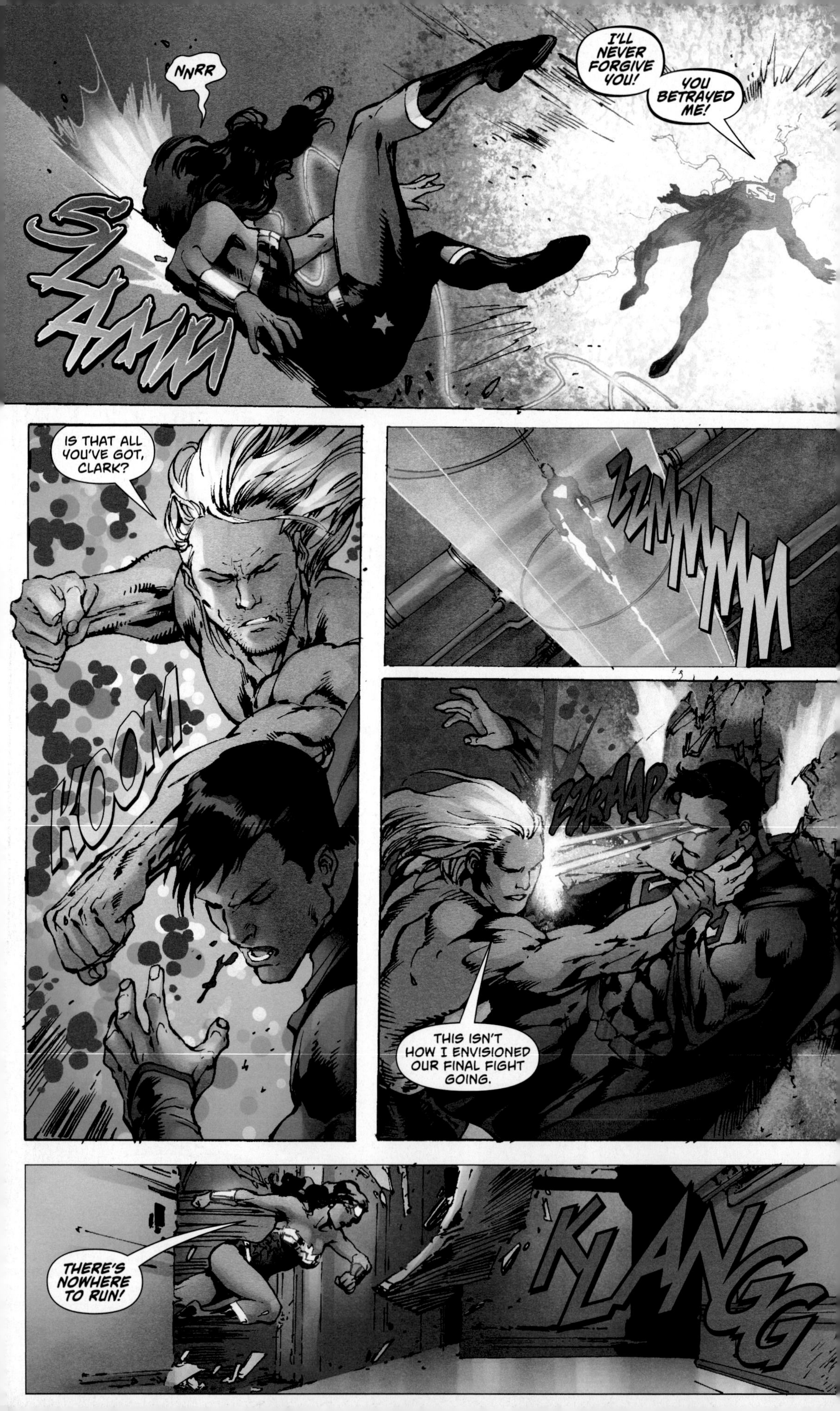
NNRR
SZAMM
I'LL NEVER FORGIVE YOU!
YOU BETRAYED ME!
IS THAT ALL YOU'VE GOT, CLARK?
KOOM
ZZMMMMM
ZZRAAAP
THIS ISN'T HOW I ENVISIONED OUR FINAL FIGHT GOING.
THERE'S NOWHERE TO RUN!
KLANGG

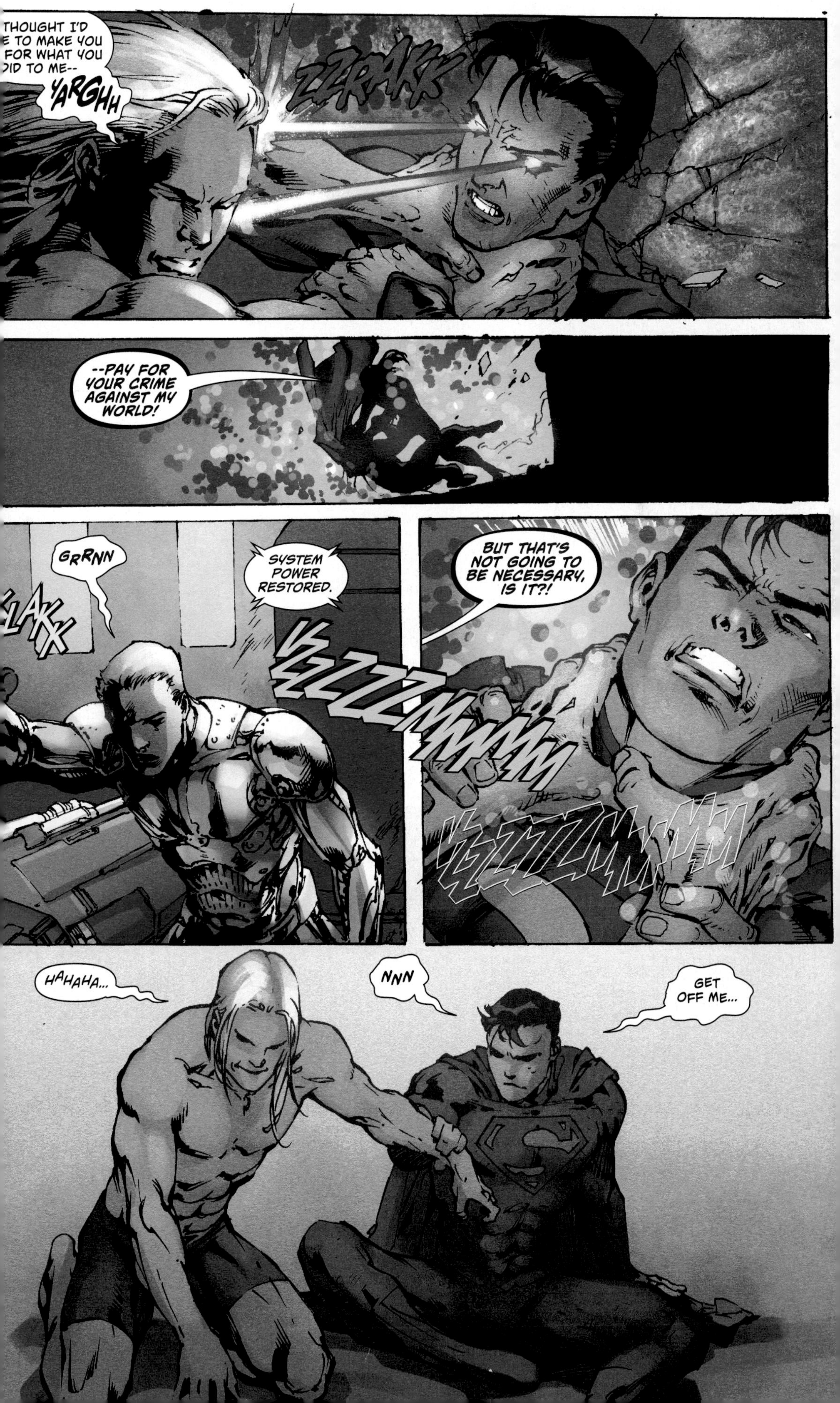
THOUGHT I'D
E TO MAKE YOU
FOR WHAT YOU
DID TO ME--
YARGHH
ZZRAKK
--PAY FOR YOUR CRIME AGAINST MY WORLD!
GRRNN
KLAKK
SYSTEM POWER RESTORED.
VZZZZMMMMM
BUT THAT'S NOT GOING TO BE NECESSARY, IS IT?!
VZZZZMMMMM
HAHAHA...
NNN
GET OFF ME...

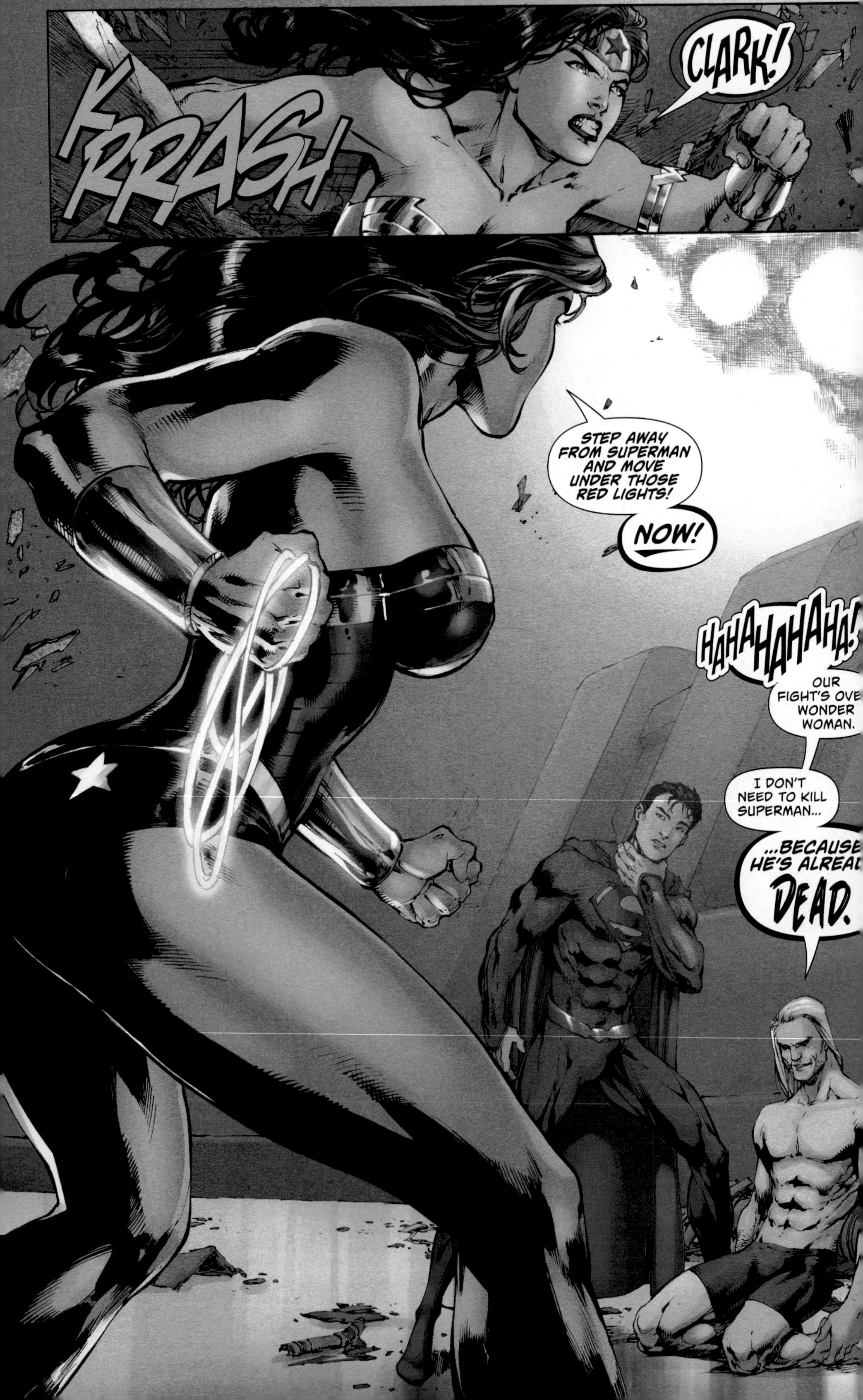
KRRASH
CLARK!
STEP AWAY FROM SUPERMAN AND MOVE UNDER THOSE RED LIGHTS!
NOW!
HAHAHAHAHAHA!
OUR FIGHT'S OVE WONDER WOMAN.
I DON'T NEED TO KILL SUPERMAN...
...BECAUSE HE'S ALREA DEAD.

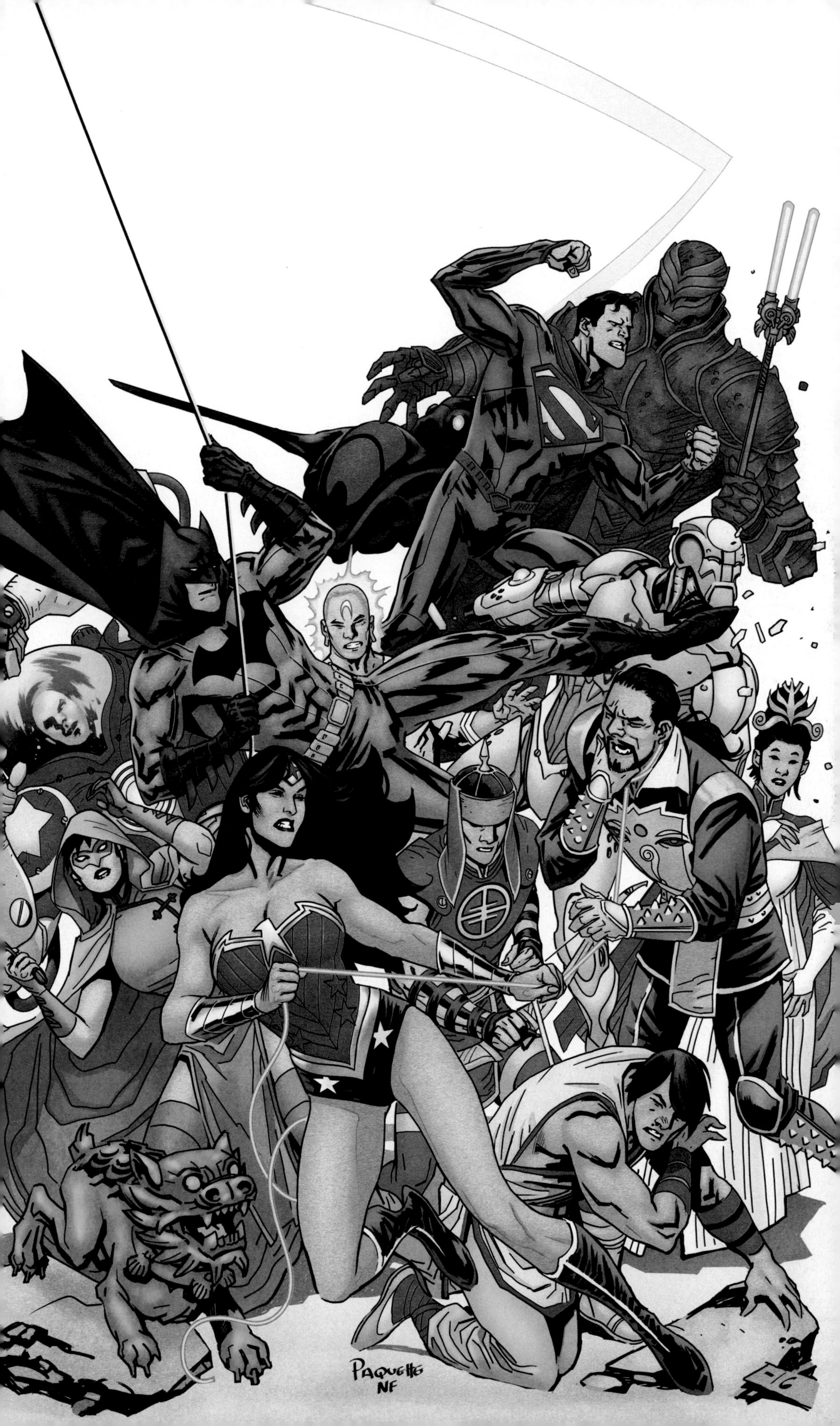
PAQUETTE
NF

THE FINAL DAYS OF SUPERMAN PART 5: OMEN OF DEATH

PETER J. TOMASI writer **DOUG MAHNKE** penciller **JAIME MENDOZA CHRISTIAN ALAMY JOHN LIVESAY TOM NGUYEN** inkers
WIL QUINTANA colorist **ROB LEIGH** letterer **YANICK PAQUETTE NATHAN FAIRBAIRN** cover

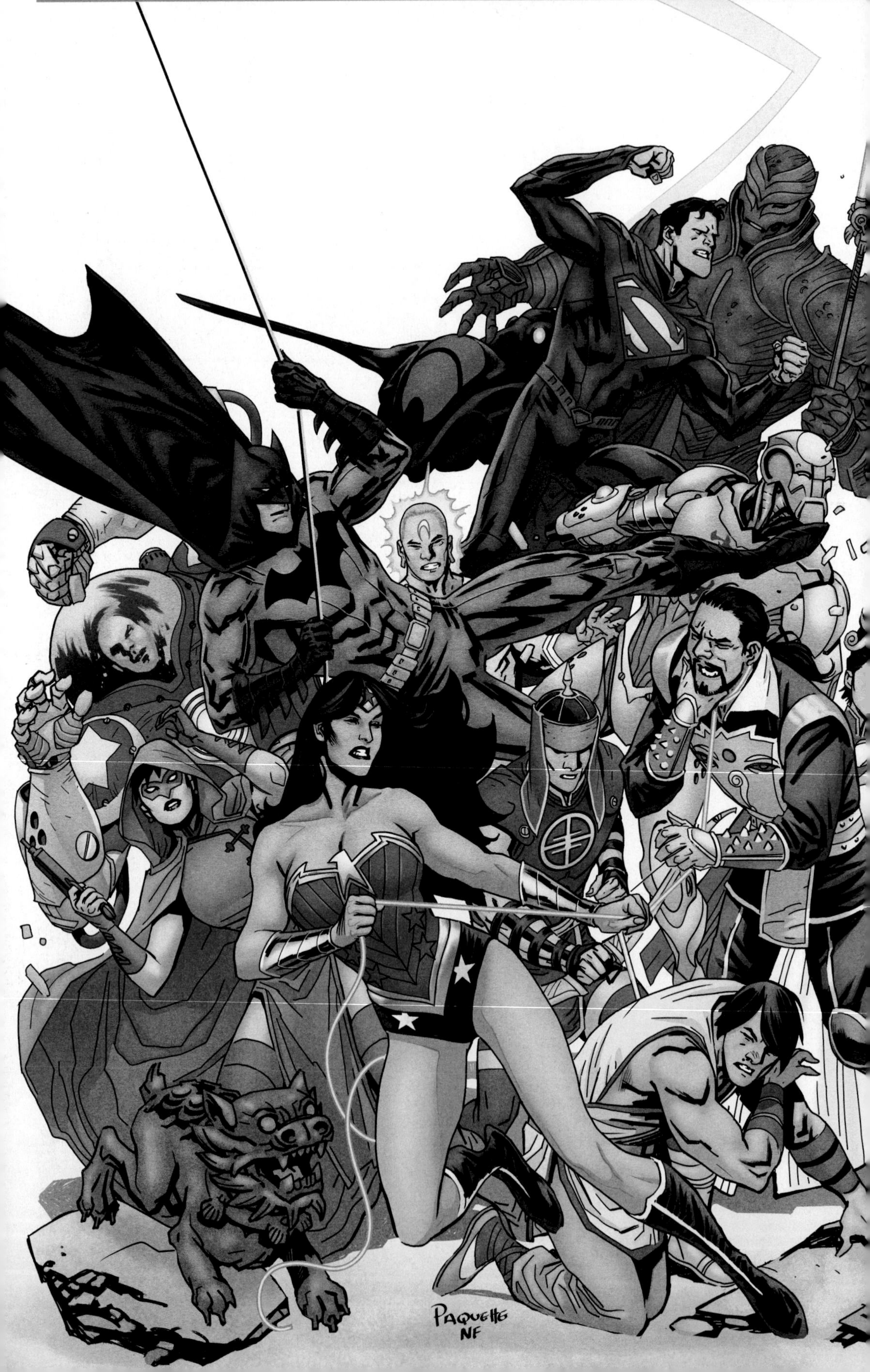
PAQUETTE
NF

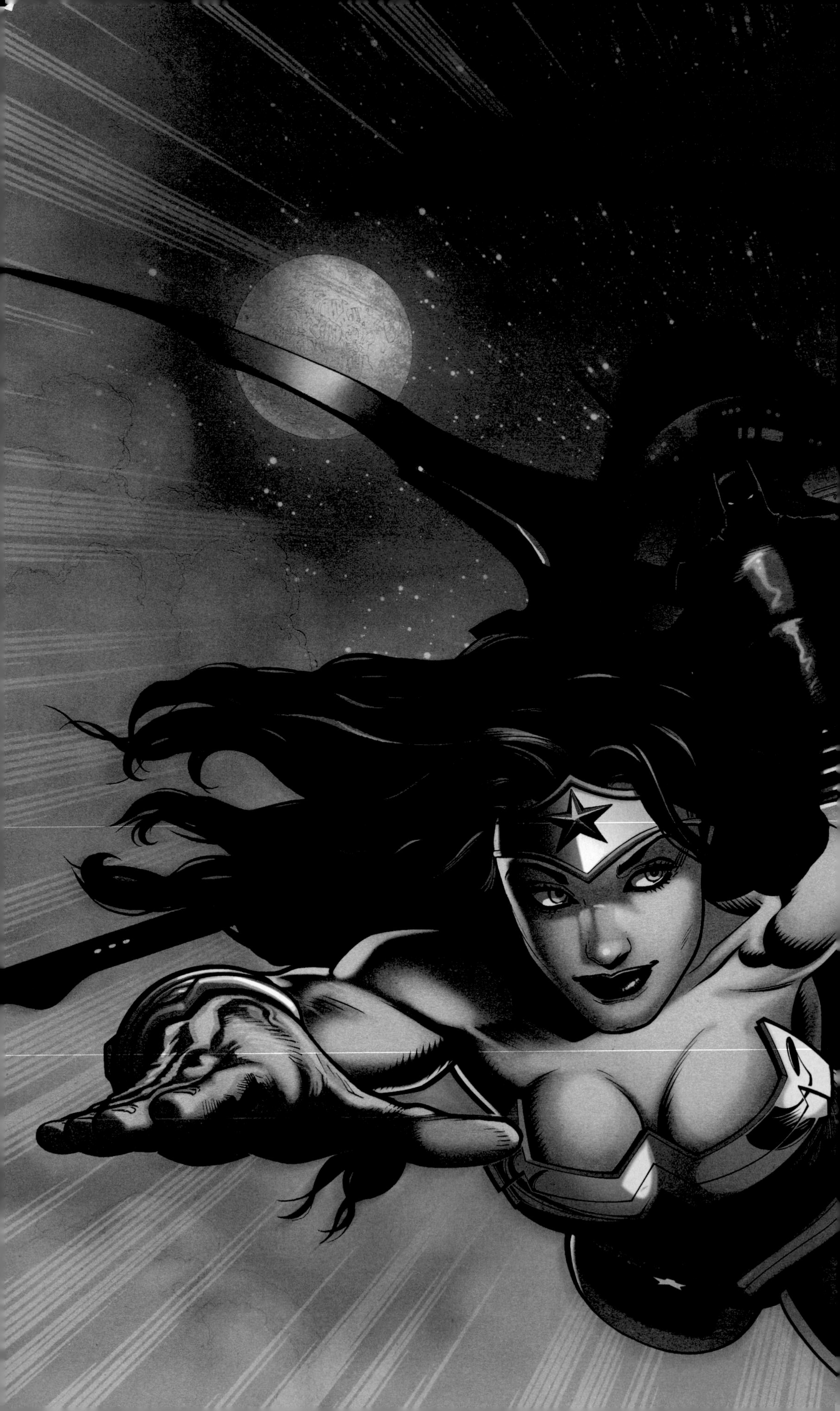

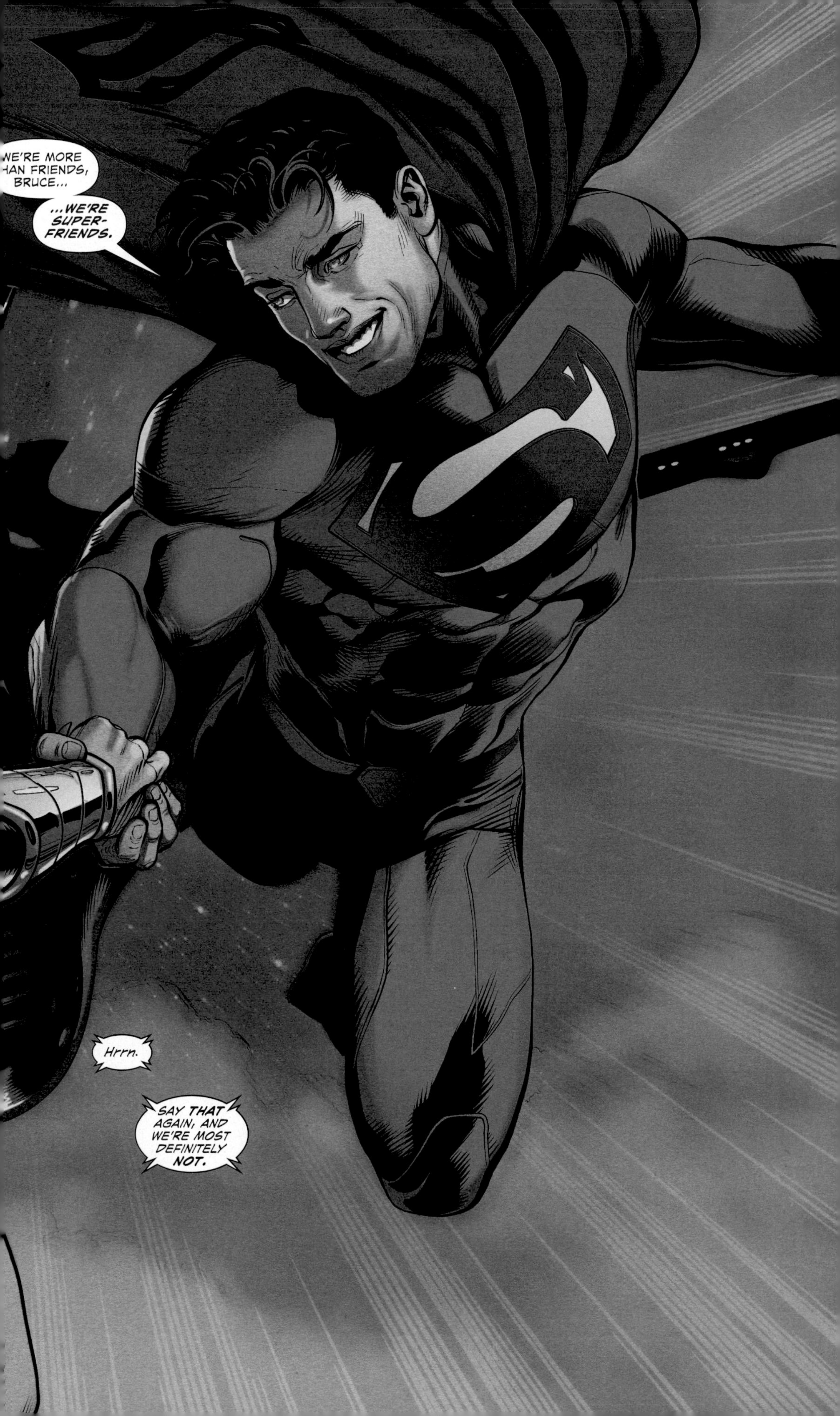
WE'RE MORE
HAN FRIENDS,
BRUCE...
...WE'RE SUPER-FRIENDS.
Hrrn.
SAY THAT AGAIN, AND WE'RE MOST DEFINITELY NOT.

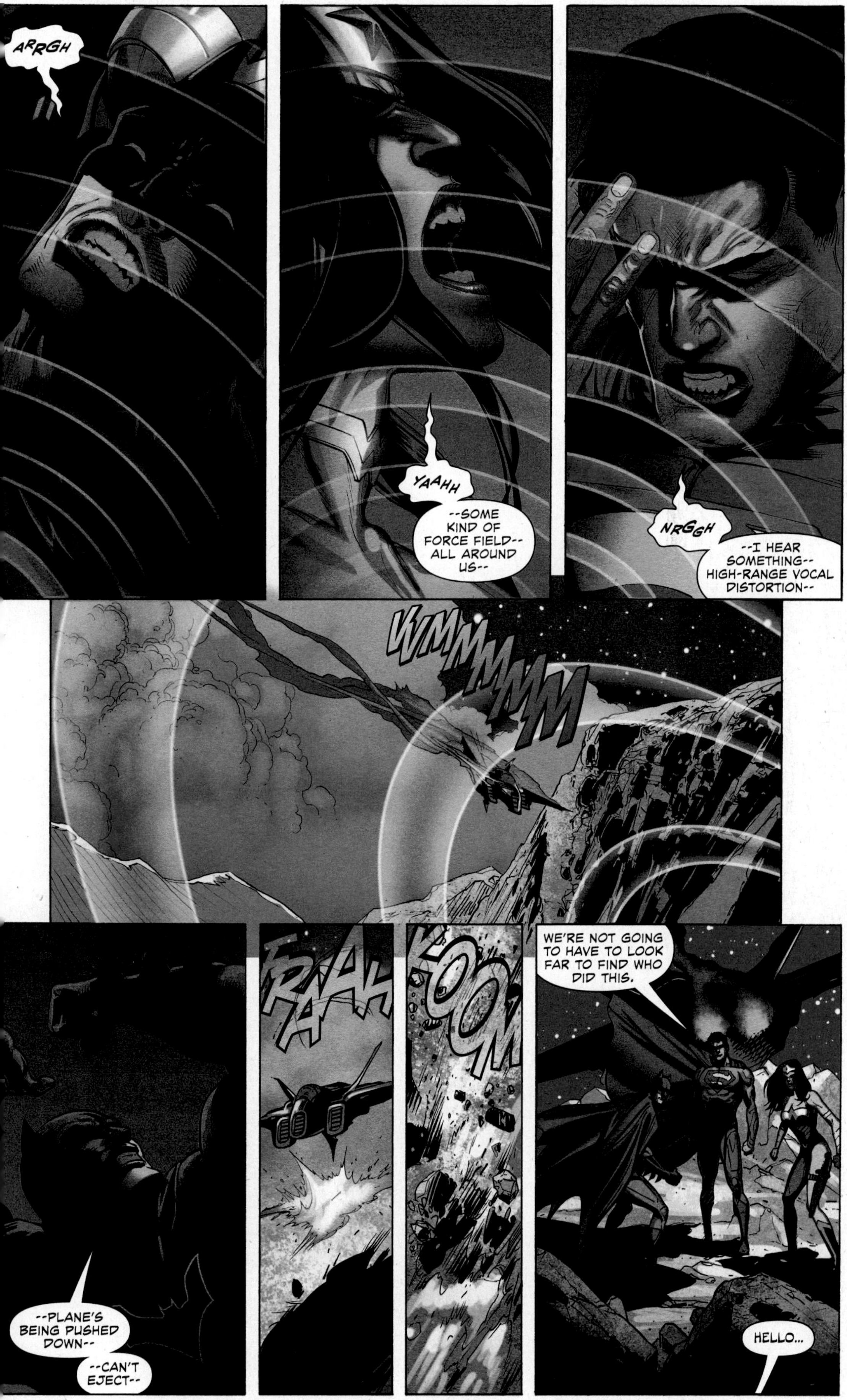
ARRGH
YAAHH
--SOME KIND OF FORCE FIELD-- ALL AROUND US--
NRGGH
--I HEAR SOMETHING-- HIGH-RANGE VOCAL DISTORTION--
WMMMMMM
--PLANE'S BEING PUSHED DOWN--
--CAN'T EJECT--
FRAAK
KOOOM
WE'RE NOT GOING TO HAVE TO LOOK FAR TO FIND WHO DID THIS.
HELLO...

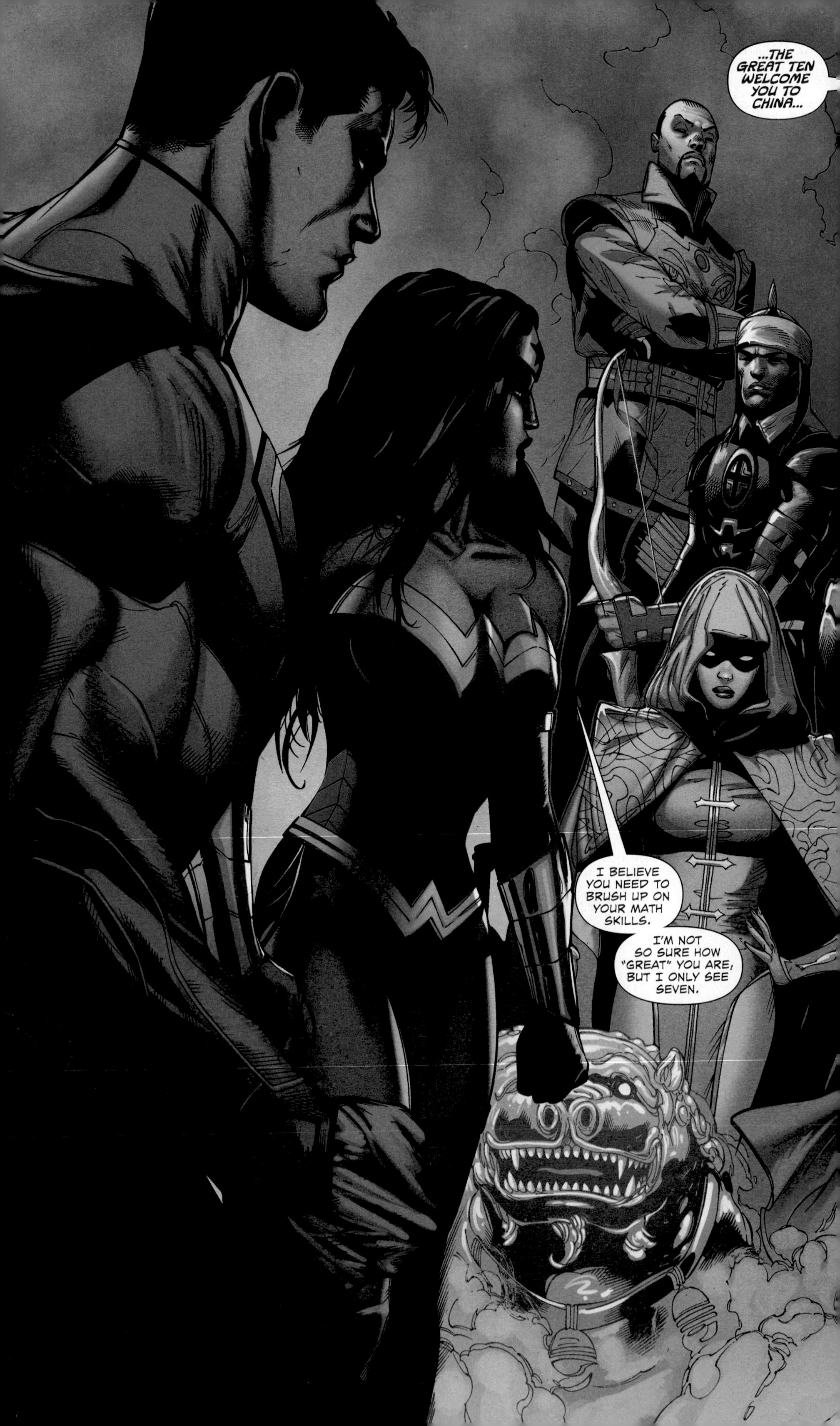
...THE GREAT TEN WELCOME YOU TO CHINA...
I BELIEVE YOU NEED TO BRUSH UP ON YOUR MATH SKILLS.
I'M NOT SO SURE HOW "GREAT" YOU ARE, BUT I ONLY SEE SEVEN.

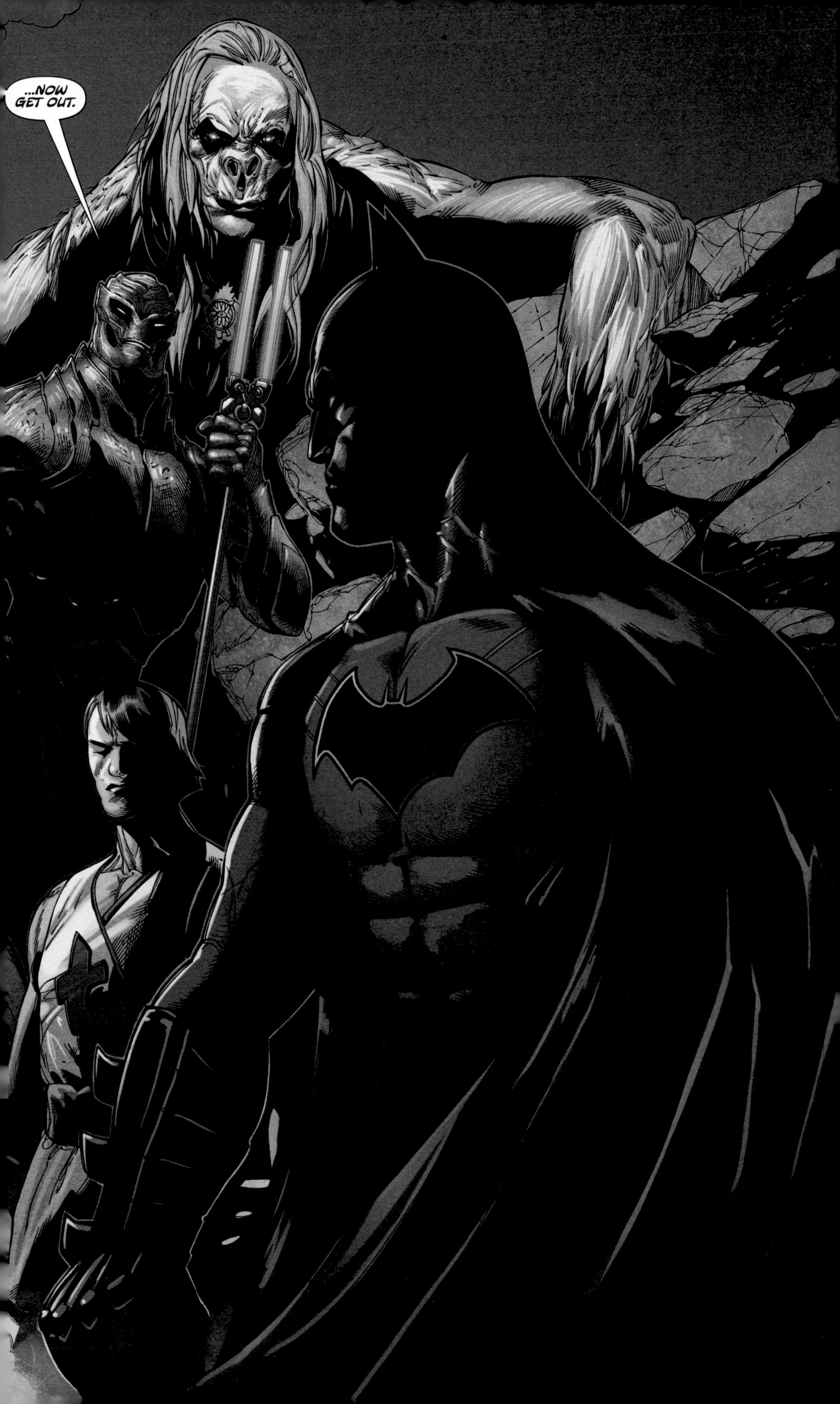
...NOW GET OUT.

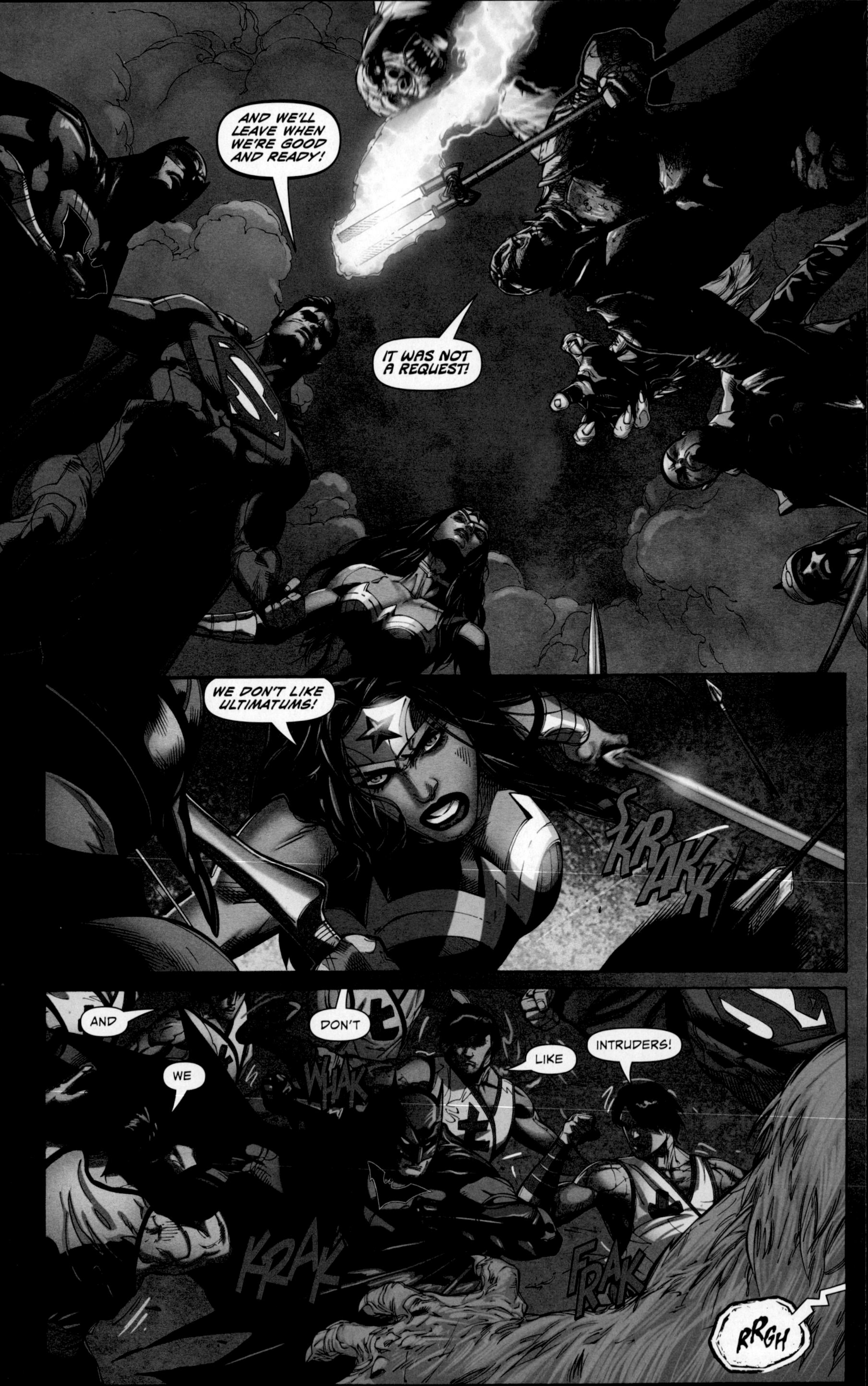
AND WE'LL LEAVE WHEN WE'RE GOOD AND READY!
IT WAS NOT A REQUEST!
WE DON'T LIKE ULTIMATUMS!
KRAKK
AND
WE
DON'T
WHAK
LIKE
INTRUDERS!
KRAK
FRAK
RRGH

WE HAVE QUESTIONS!

HGNN

SKRAKK

DON'T

EXPECT

ANSWERS!

KRAK RAK RAK KRAK KRAK

NARGH

ZZRAK

YETI, SHOW THE AMERICAN WHAT WE THINK OF HIS TEMERITY!

GRRGGH

BRAGHH

AND YOUR LACK OF HOSPITALITY!

KOOM

MY VOCAL DISTORTION CAN ONLY TEMPORARILY PARALYZE HER, GHOST FOX!

THAT'S WHY IT'S TIME FOR--

NNGG

--THE JADE LION TO MAKE HER ACQUAINTANCE!

GRRFF

RRROOAAAR

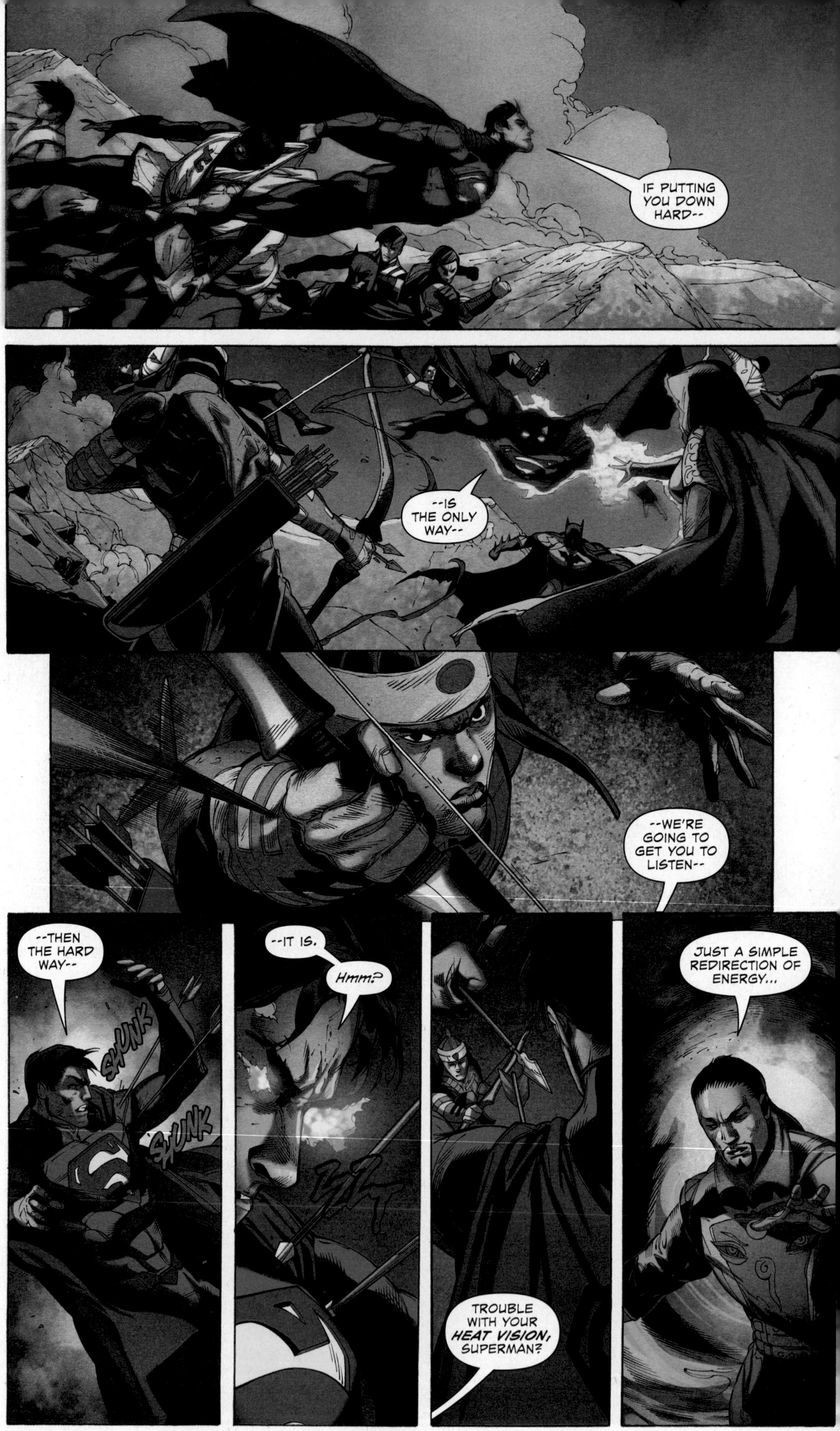
IF PUTTING YOU DOWN HARD--
--IS THE ONLY WAY--
--WE'RE GOING TO GET YOU TO LISTEN--
--THEN THE HARD WAY--
SHUNK
SHUNK
--IT IS.
Hmm?
TROUBLE WITH YOUR HEAT VISION, SUPERMAN?
JUST A SIMPLE REDIRECTION OF ENERGY...

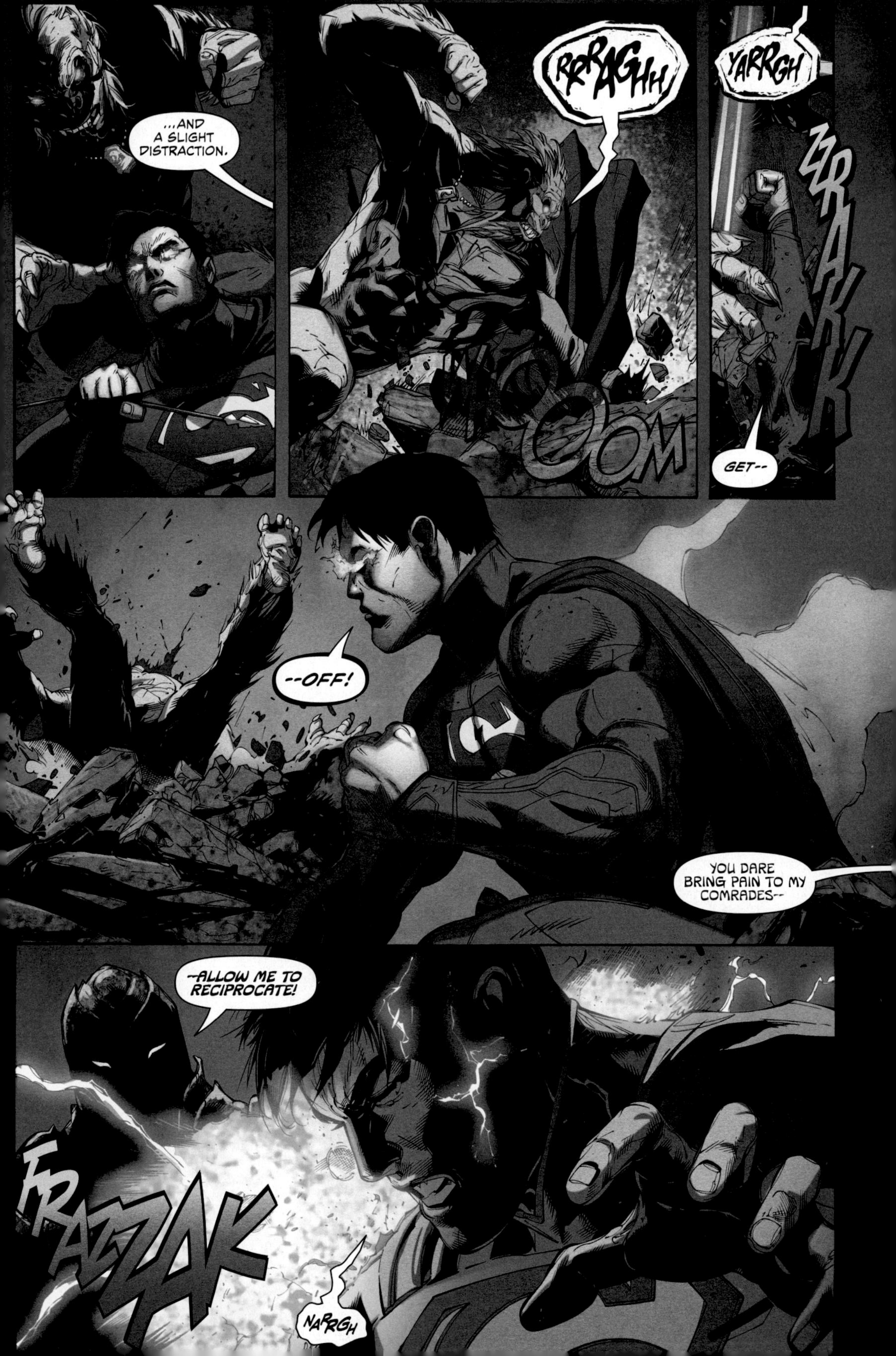
...AND A SLIGHT DISTRACTION.
RRRAGHH
WHOOOOM
YARRGH
ZZRAKKK
GET--
--OFF!
YOU DARE BRING PAIN TO MY COMRADES--
--ALLOW ME TO RECIPROCATE!
FRAZZAK
NARRGH

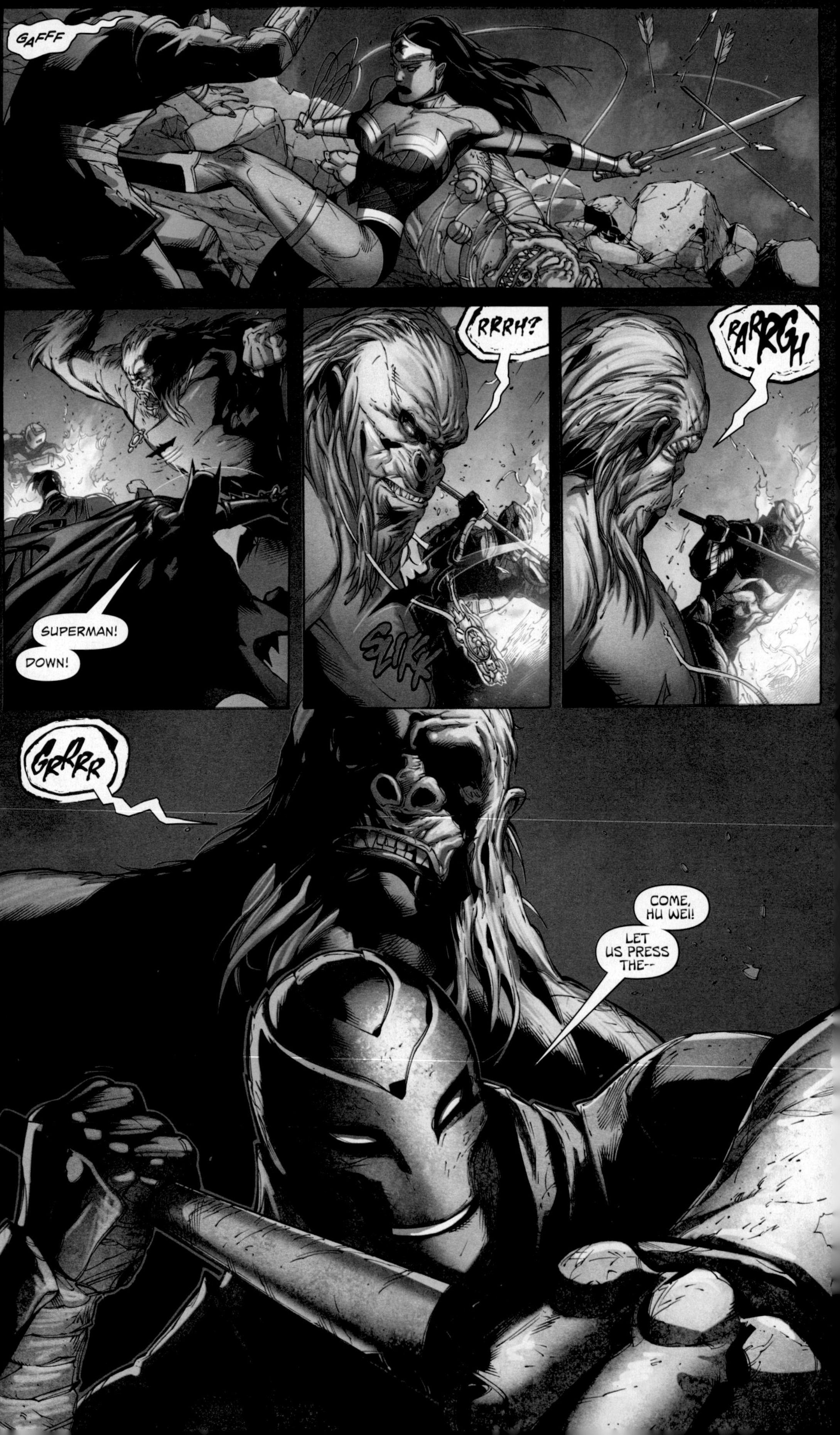
GAFFF
SUPERMAN!
DOWN!
SLIKK
RRRH?
RARRGH
GRRRR
COME, HU WEI!
LET US PRESS THE--

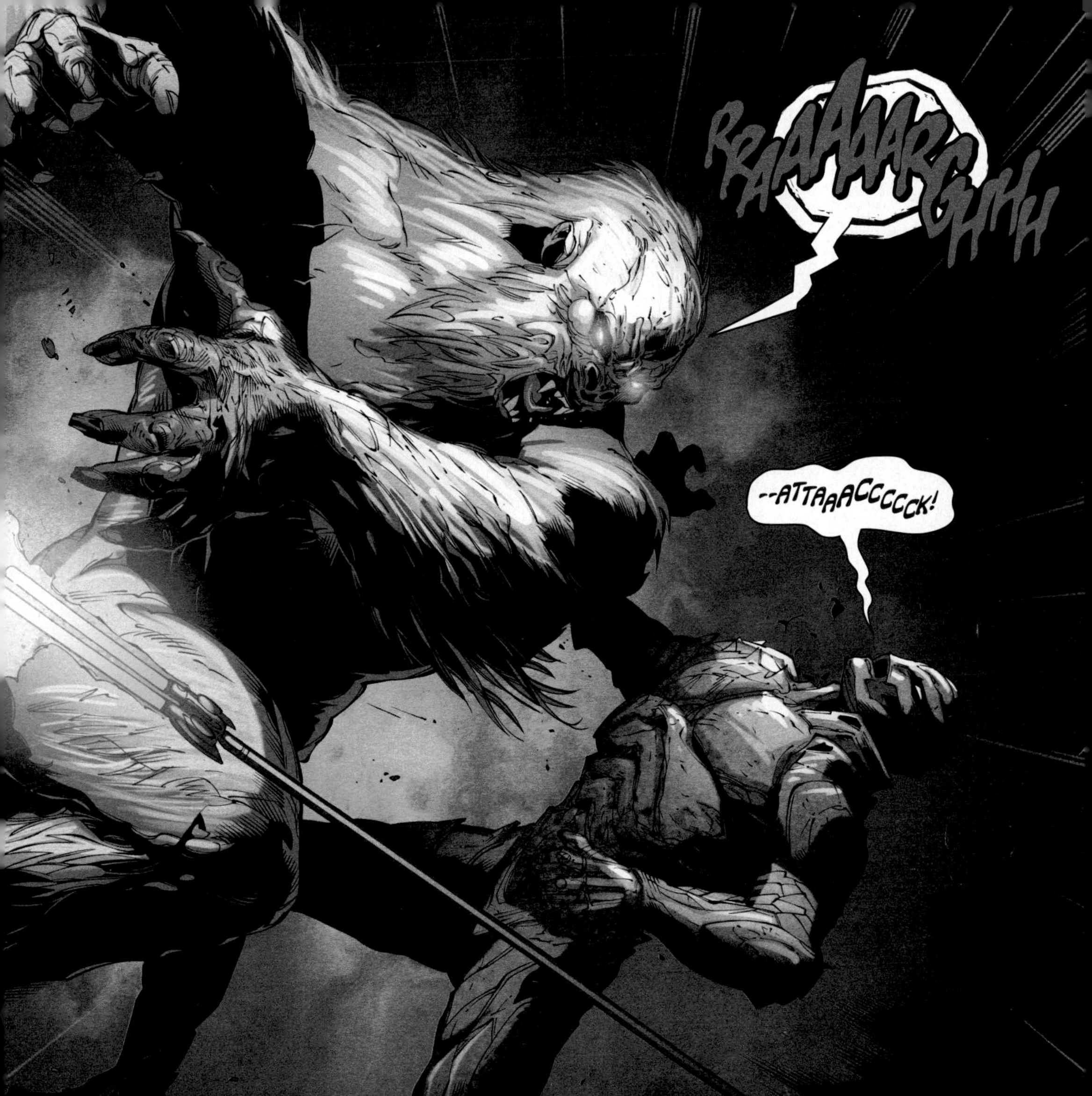
RRAAAAARGHHH
--ATTAAACCCCCK!
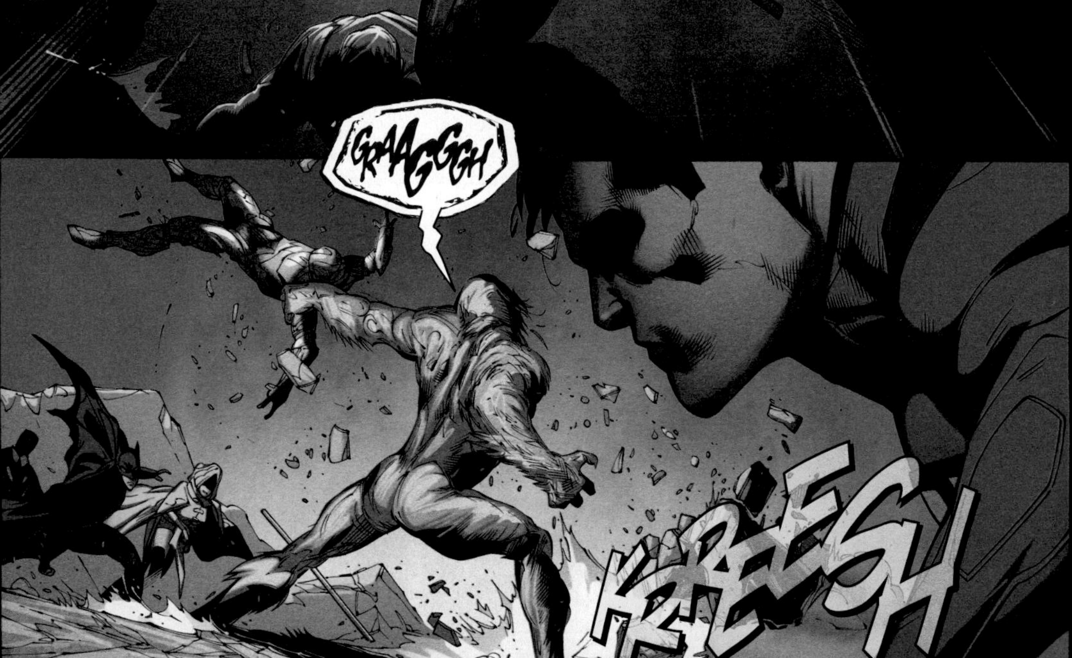
GRAAGGGH
KRREESH

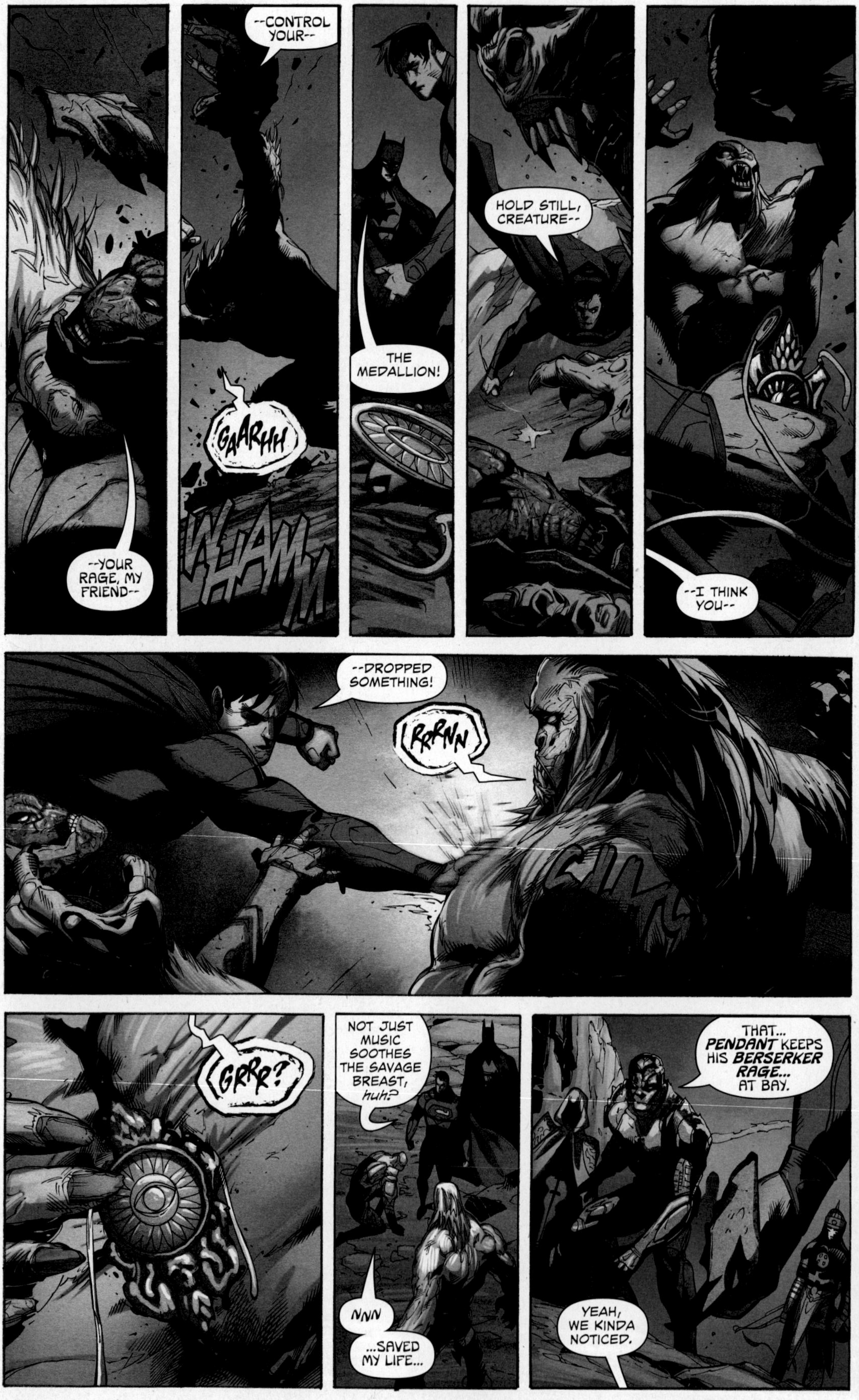
--YOUR RAGE, MY FRIEND--
--CONTROL YOUR--
GAARHH
WHAM
THE MEDALLION!
HOLD STILL, CREATURE--
--I THINK YOU--
--DROPPED SOMETHING!
RRRNN
GRRR?
NOT JUST MUSIC SOOTHES THE SAVAGE BREAST, huh?
NNN
...SAVED MY LIFE...
THAT... PENDANT KEEPS HIS BERSERKER RAGE... AT BAY.
YEAH, WE KINDA NOTICED.

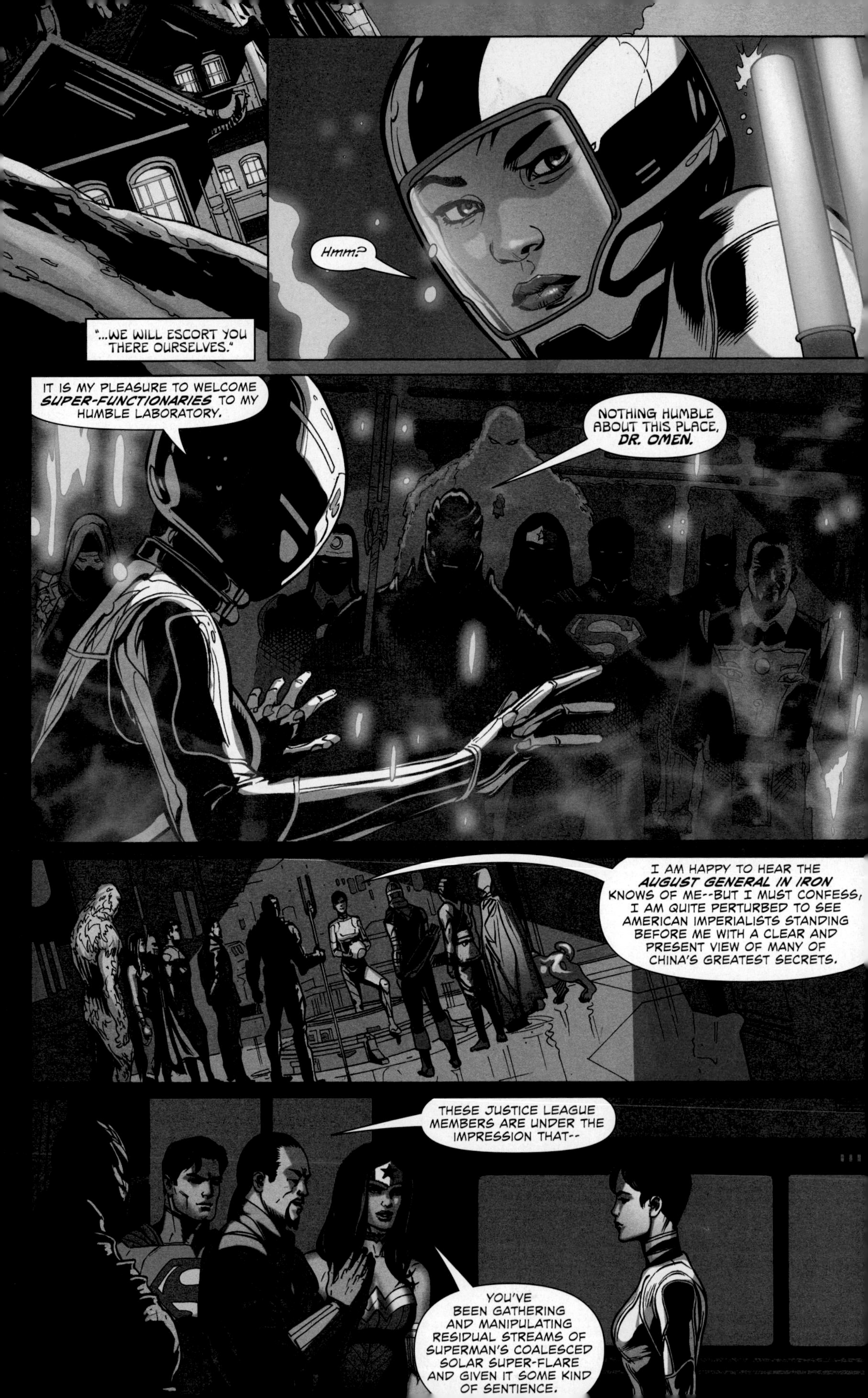

Hmm?
"...WE WILL ESCORT YOU THERE OURSELVES."
IT IS MY PLEASURE TO WELCOME ***SUPER-FUNCTIONARIES*** TO MY HUMBLE LABORATORY.
NOTHING HUMBLE ABOUT THIS PLACE, **DR. OMEN.**
I AM HAPPY TO HEAR THE ***AUGUST GENERAL IN IRON*** KNOWS OF ME--BUT I MUST CONFESS, I AM QUITE PERTURBED TO SEE AMERICAN IMPERIALISTS STANDING BEFORE ME WITH A CLEAR AND PRESENT VIEW OF MANY OF CHINA'S GREATEST SECRETS.
THESE JUSTICE LEAGUE MEMBERS ARE UNDER THE IMPRESSION THAT--
YOU'VE BEEN GATHERING AND MANIPULATING RESIDUAL STREAMS OF SUPERMAN'S COALESCED SOLAR SUPER-FLARE AND GIVEN IT SOME KIND OF SENTIENCE.

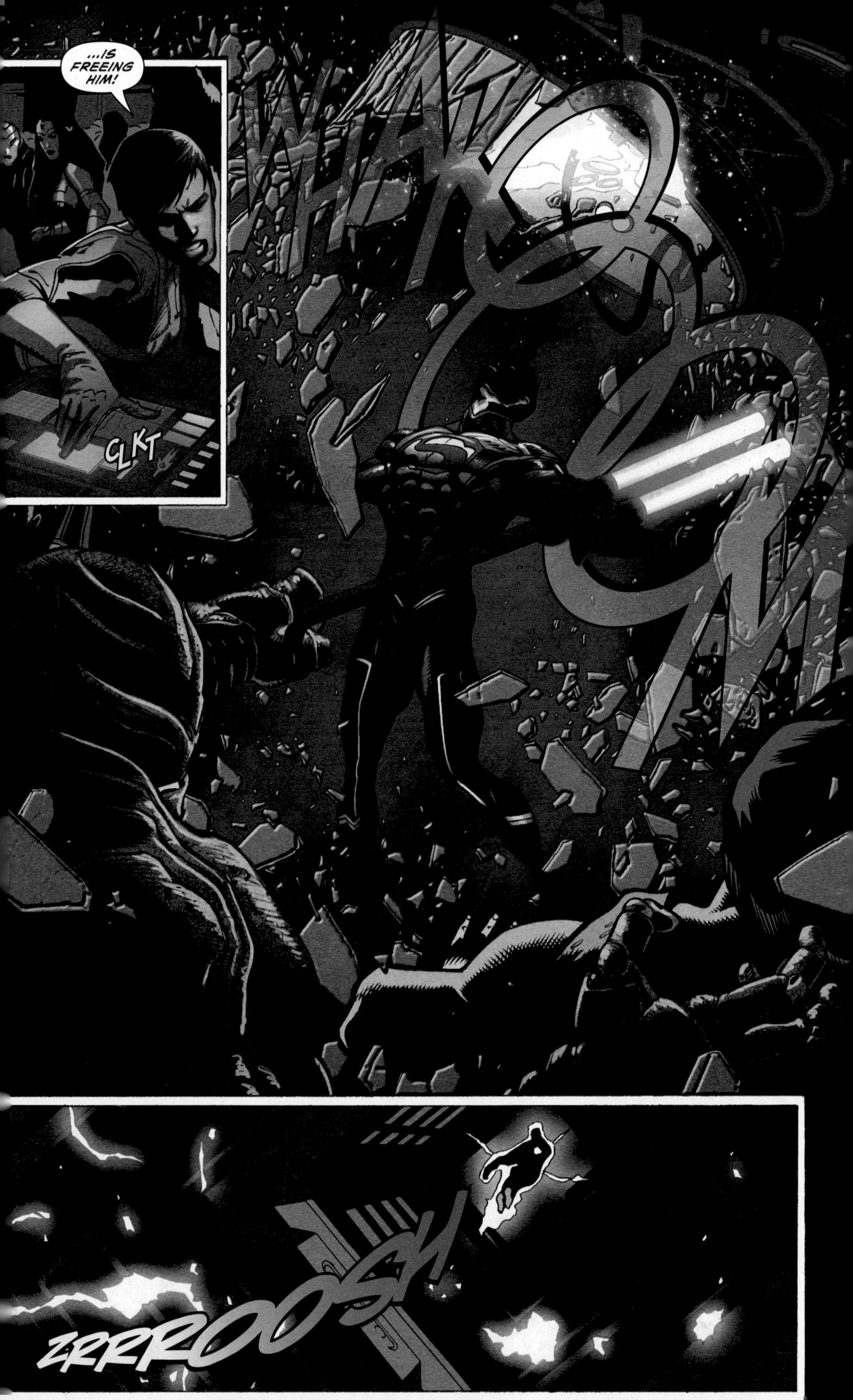
...IS FREEING HIM!
CLKT
WHAKOOM
ZRRROOSH

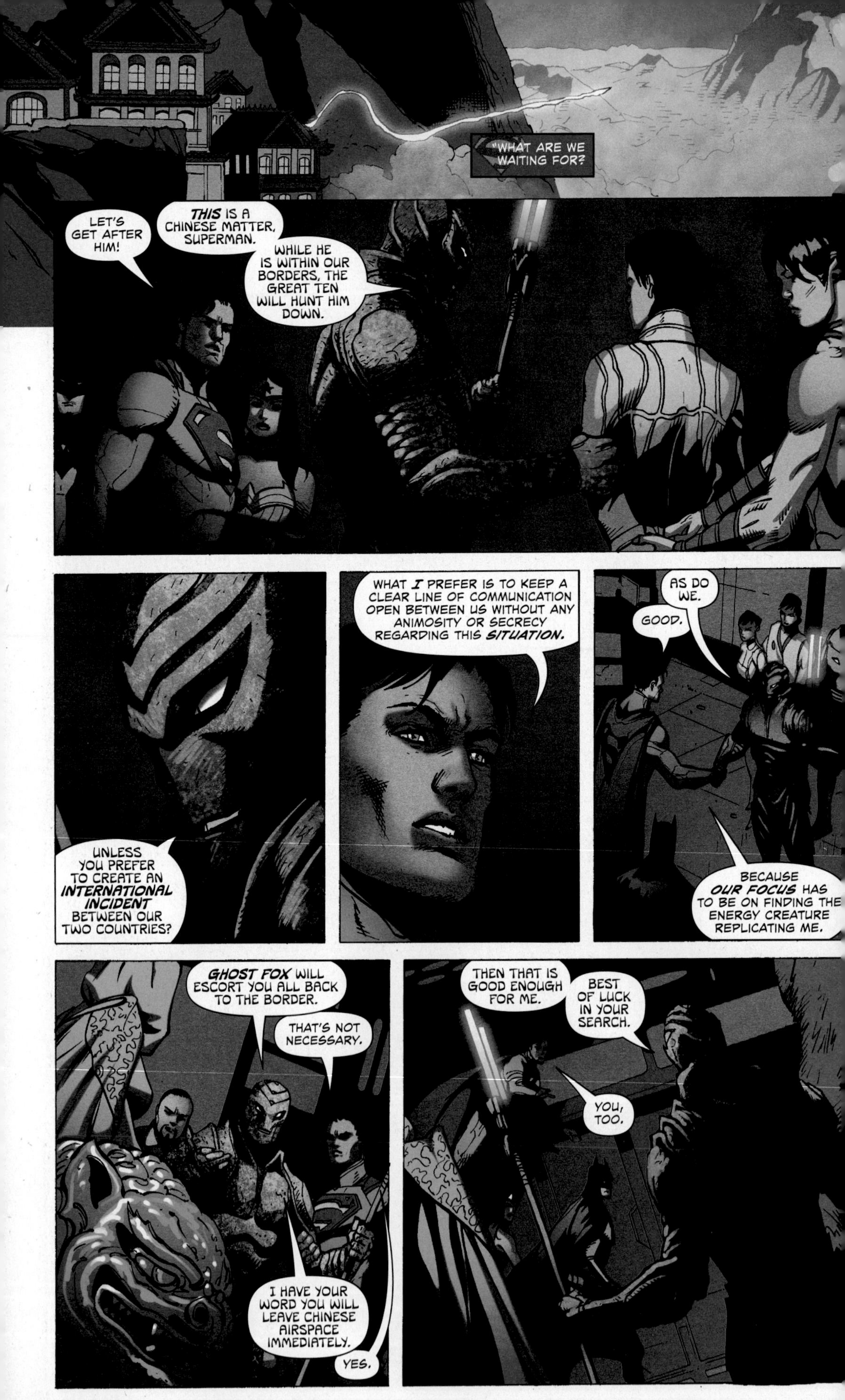

"WHAT ARE WE WAITING FOR?
LET'S GET AFTER HIM!
THIS IS A CHINESE MATTER, SUPERMAN.
WHILE HE IS WITHIN OUR BORDERS, THE GREAT TEN WILL HUNT HIM DOWN.
UNLESS YOU PREFER TO CREATE AN INTERNATIONAL INCIDENT BETWEEN OUR TWO COUNTRIES?
WHAT I PREFER IS TO KEEP A CLEAR LINE OF COMMUNICATION OPEN BETWEEN US WITHOUT ANY ANIMOSITY OR SECRECY REGARDING THIS SITUATION.
AS DO WE.
GOOD.
BECAUSE OUR FOCUS HAS TO BE ON FINDING THE ENERGY CREATURE REPLICATING ME.
GHOST FOX WILL ESCORT YOU ALL BACK TO THE BORDER.
THAT'S NOT NECESSARY.
I HAVE YOUR WORD YOU WILL LEAVE CHINESE AIRSPACE IMMEDIATELY.
YES.
THEN THAT IS GOOD ENOUGH FOR ME.
BEST OF LUCK IN YOUR SEARCH.
YOU, TOO.

TAKATAK
TAK TAK
TAK

TAP TAP
TAP

WHAT THE HELL...
HE'S BACK...

...HOW DID HE
ESCAPE FROM
A.R.G.U.S.?

PLAY THIS COOL,
LOIS...DON'T GET
HIM AGITATED....

...AFTER WHAT
HE DID AT THE
PLANET...

...TO GET ALONG...
JUST GO ALONG...

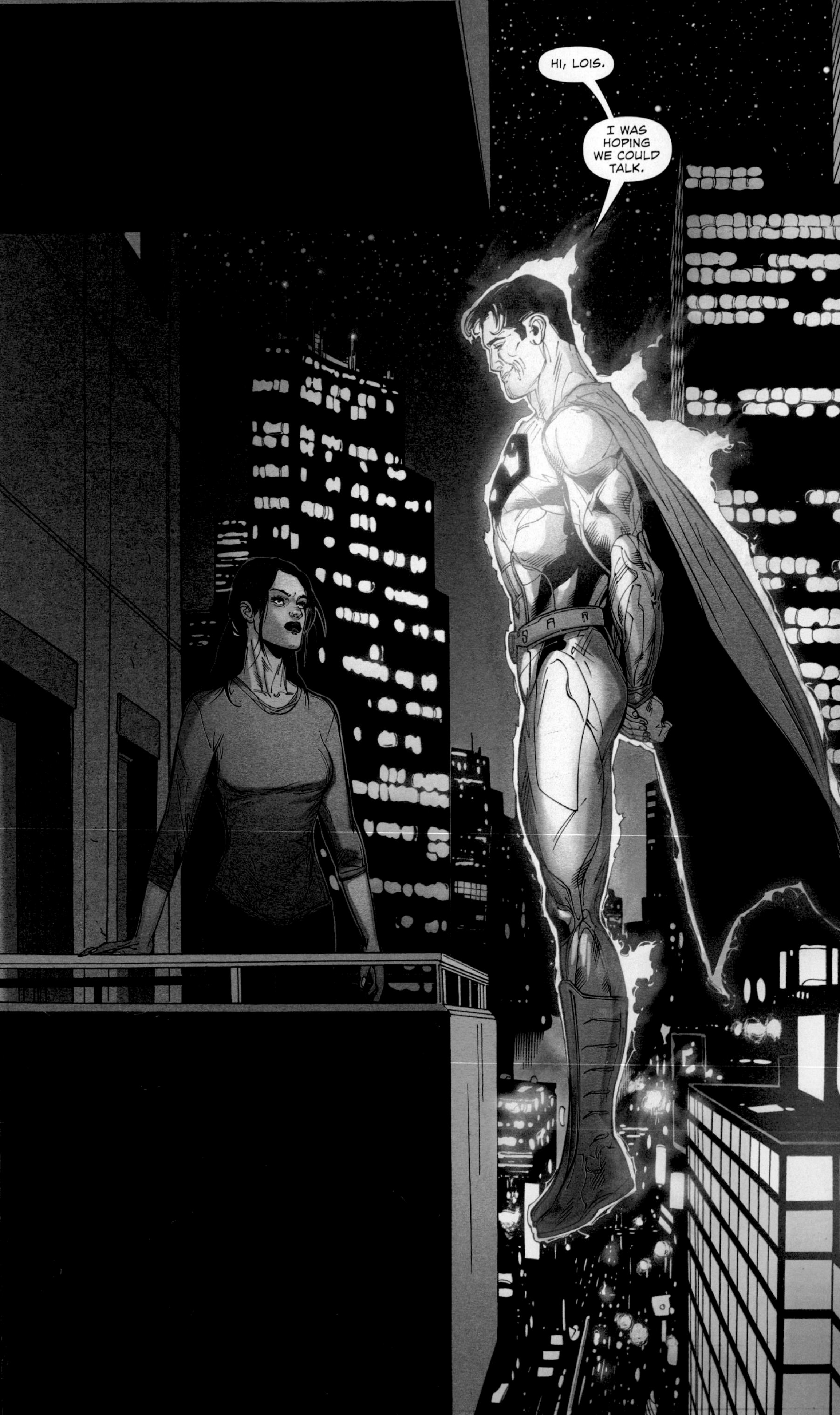
HI, LOIS.
I WAS HOPING WE COULD TALK.

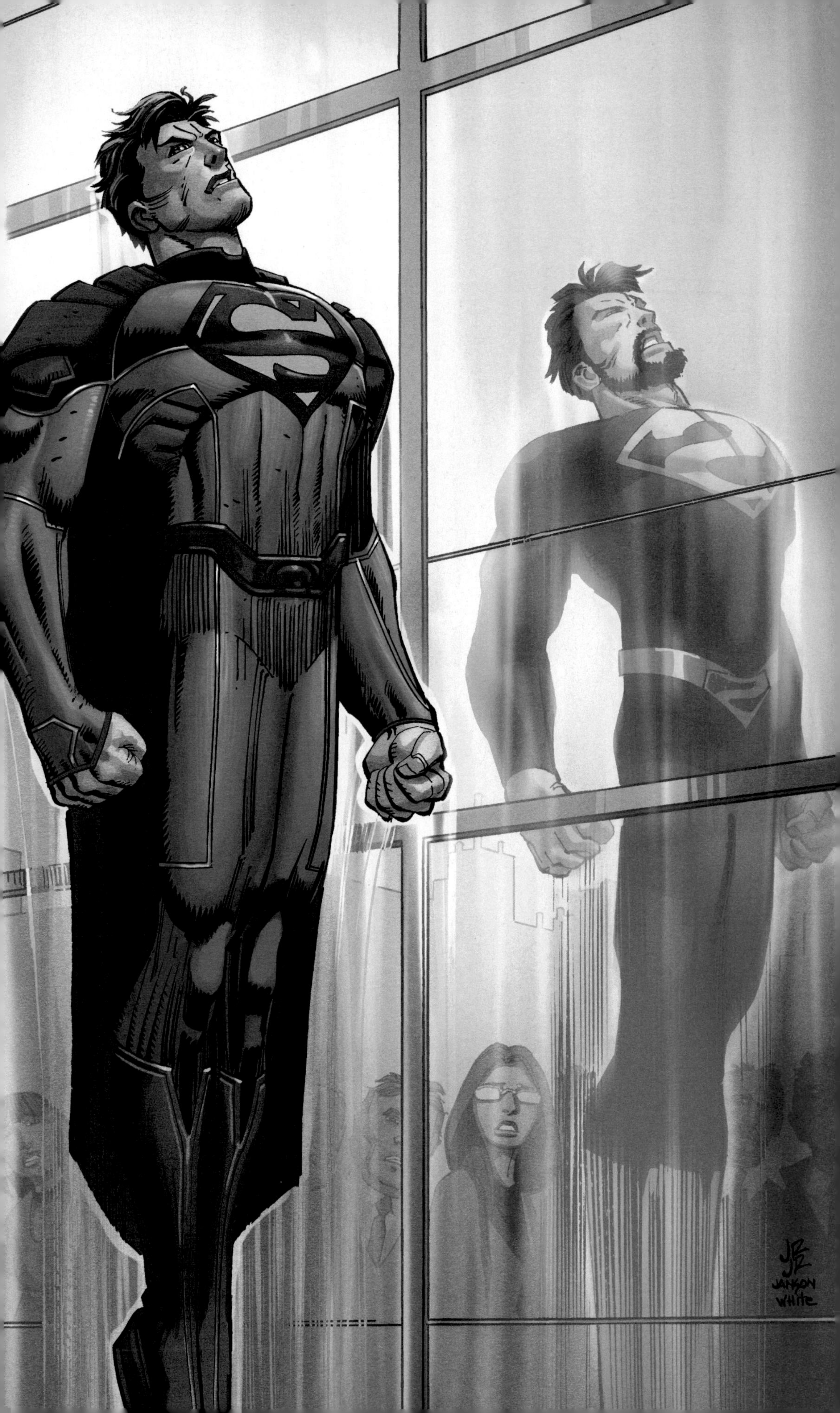
JANSON
WHITE

THE FINAL DAYS OF SUPERMAN PART 6: THE GREAT PRETENDER

PETER J. TOMASI writer **DALE EAGLESHAM SCOT EATON** pencillers **DALE EAGLESHAM WAYNE FAUCHER** inkers **TOMEU MOREY** colorist **ROB LEIGH** letterer
JOHN ROMITA JR. KLAUS JANSON DEAN WHITE cover

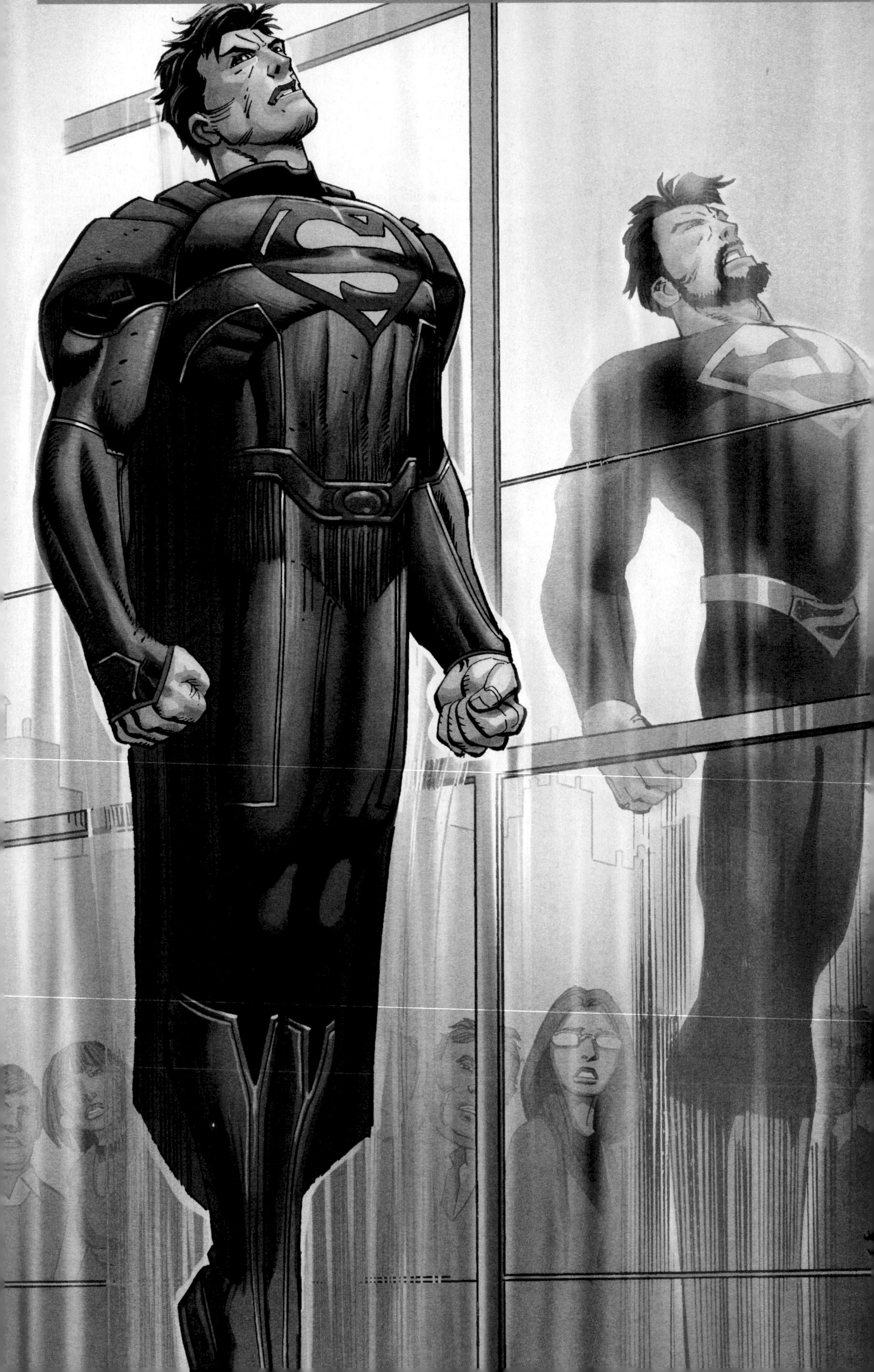

IT'S THESE SMALL, SILENT
MOMENTS BETWEEN THE
BATTLES AND THE SAVES
I WISH I HAD MORE OF...

...FLYING BESIDE
THE WOMAN
I LOVE...

...AND THE WOMAN
WHO LOVES ME...

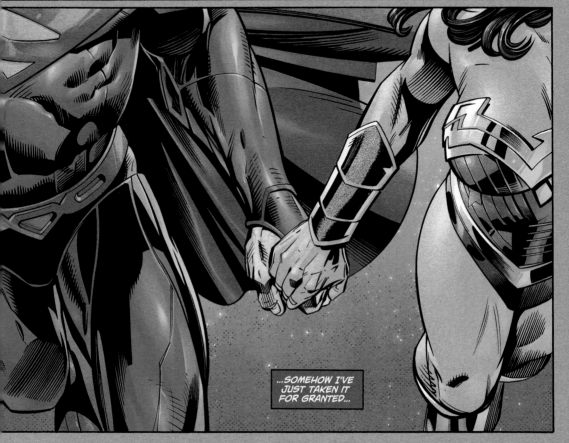

...SOMEHOW I'VE
JUST TAKEN IT
FOR GRANTED...

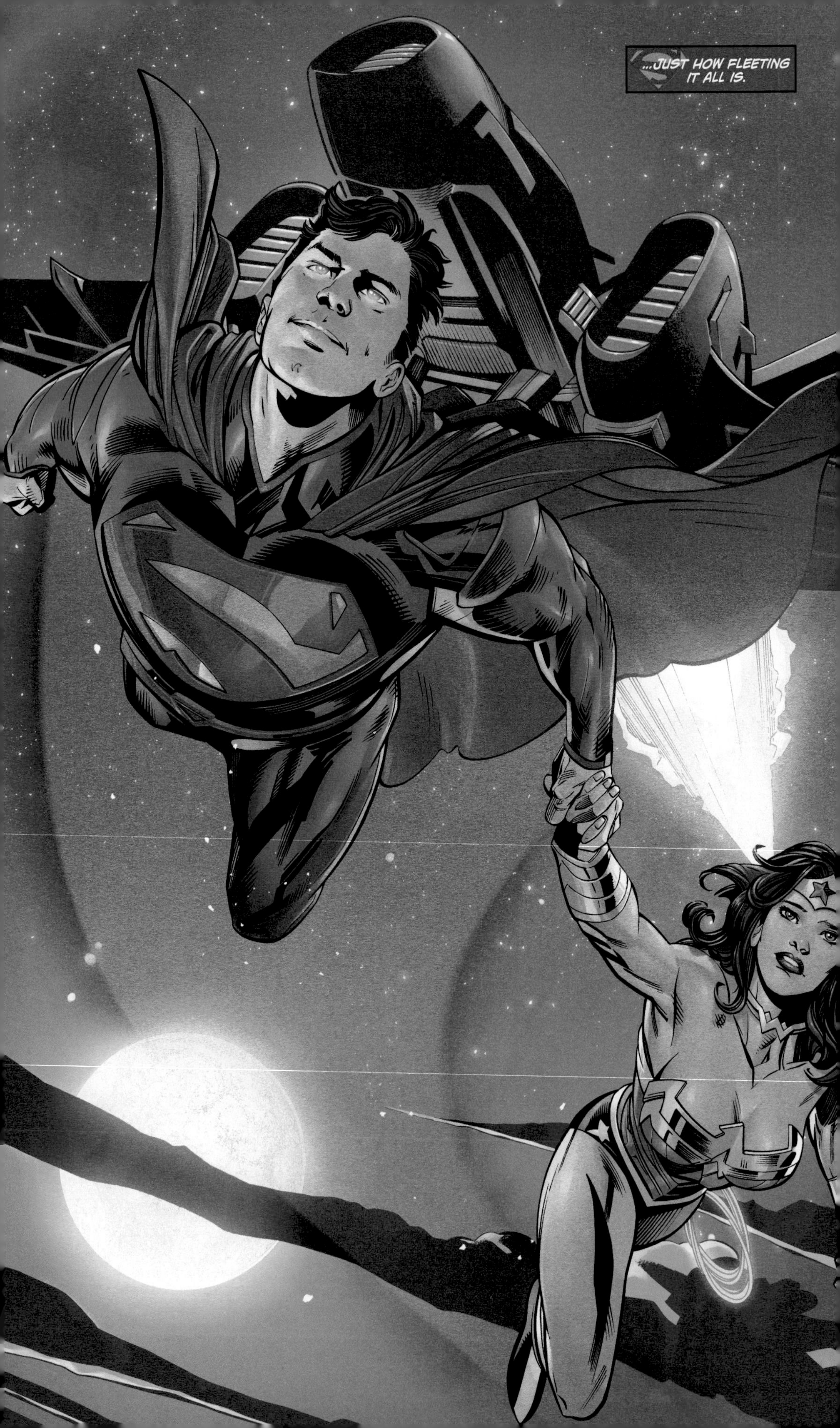
...JUST HOW FLEETING IT ALL IS.

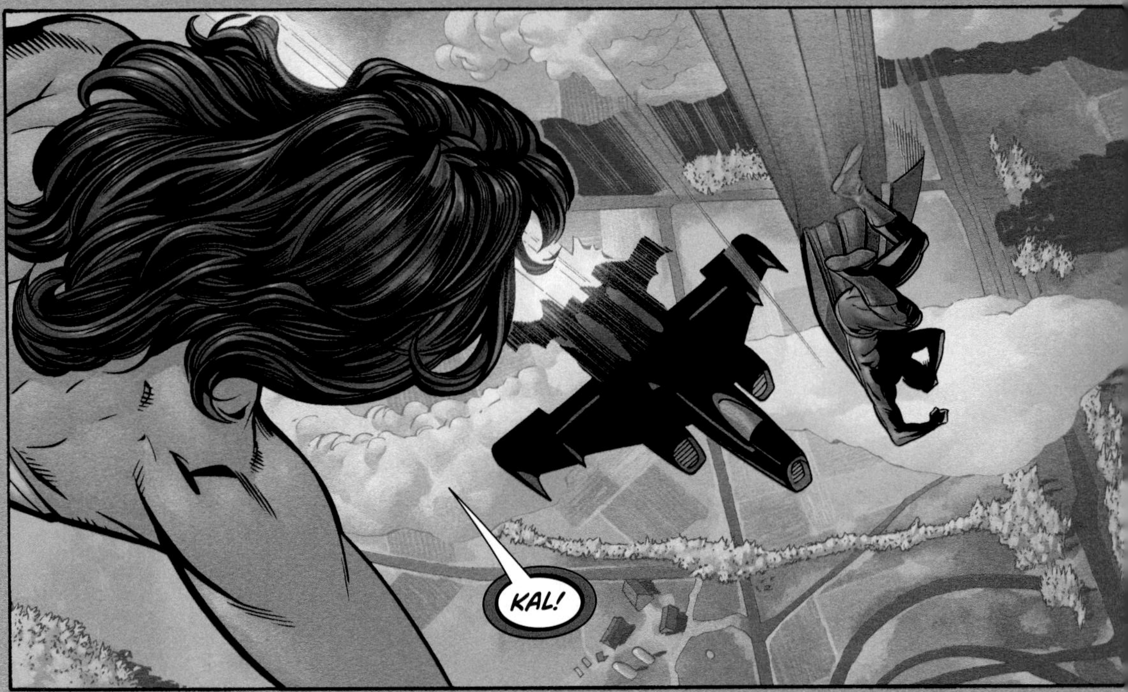
KAL!

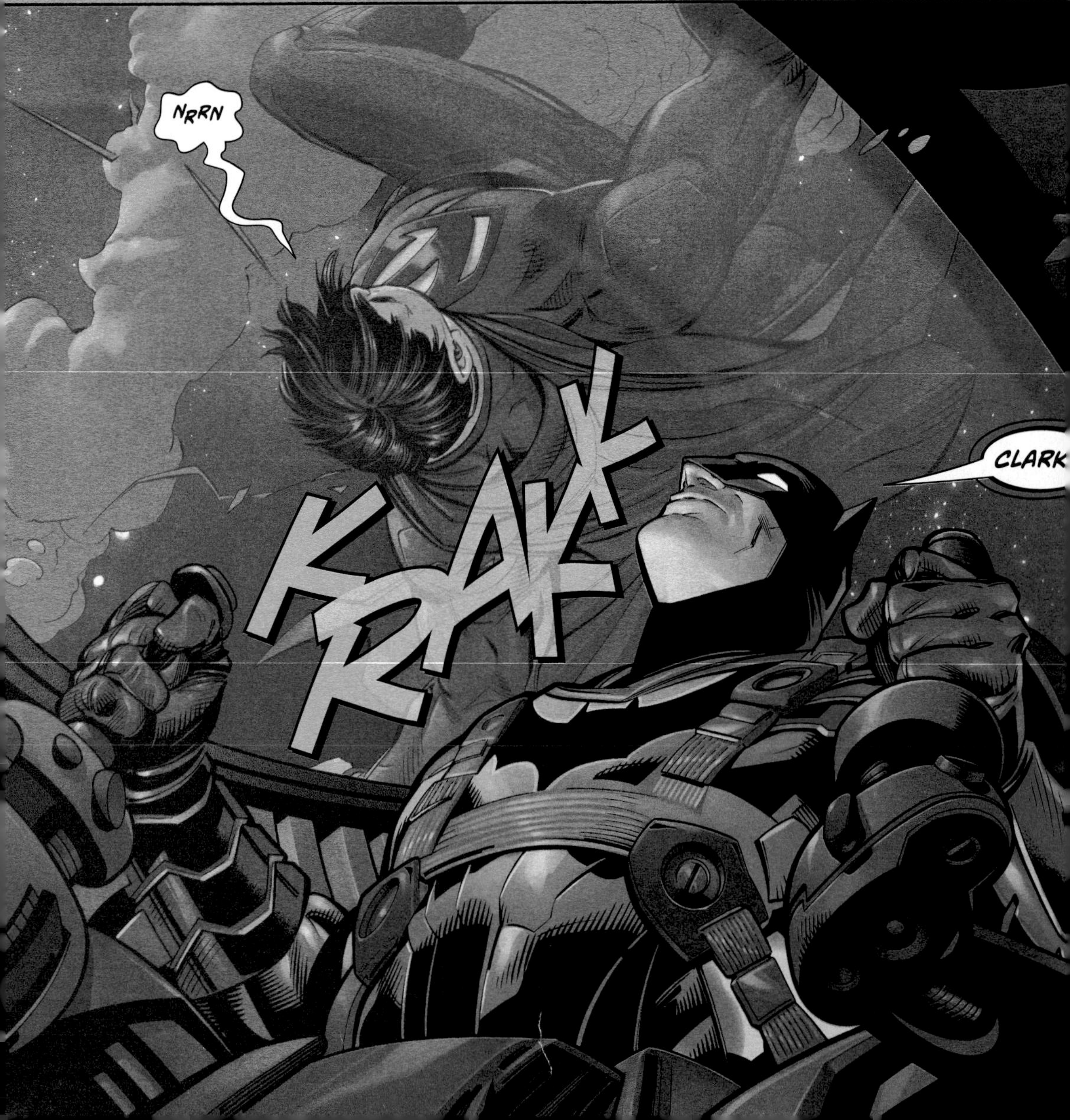
NRRN
KRAK
CLARK

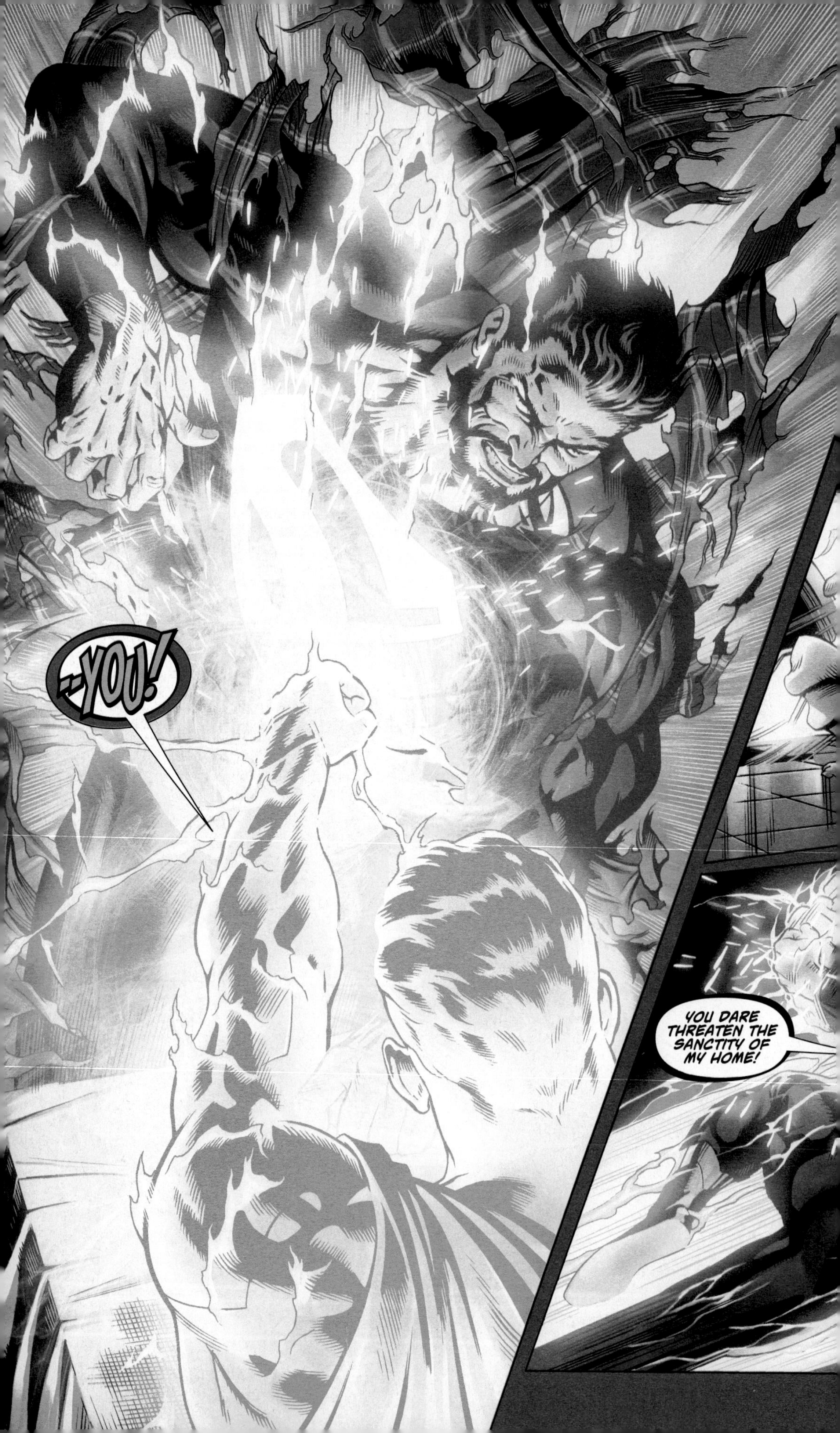
--YOU!
YOU DARE THREATEN THE SANCTITY OF MY HOME!

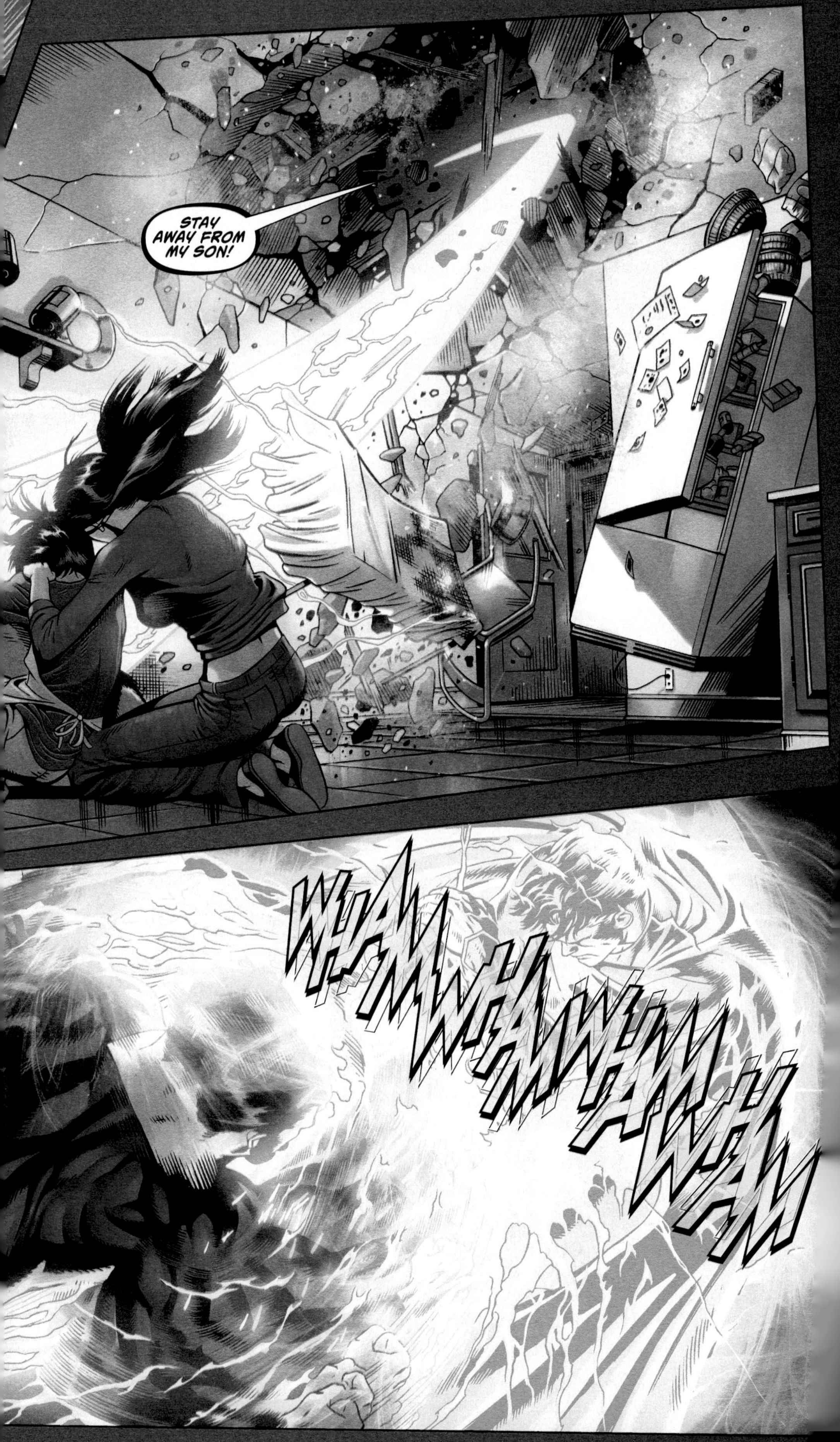
STAY AWAY FROM MY SON!
WHAMWHAMWHAMWHAM

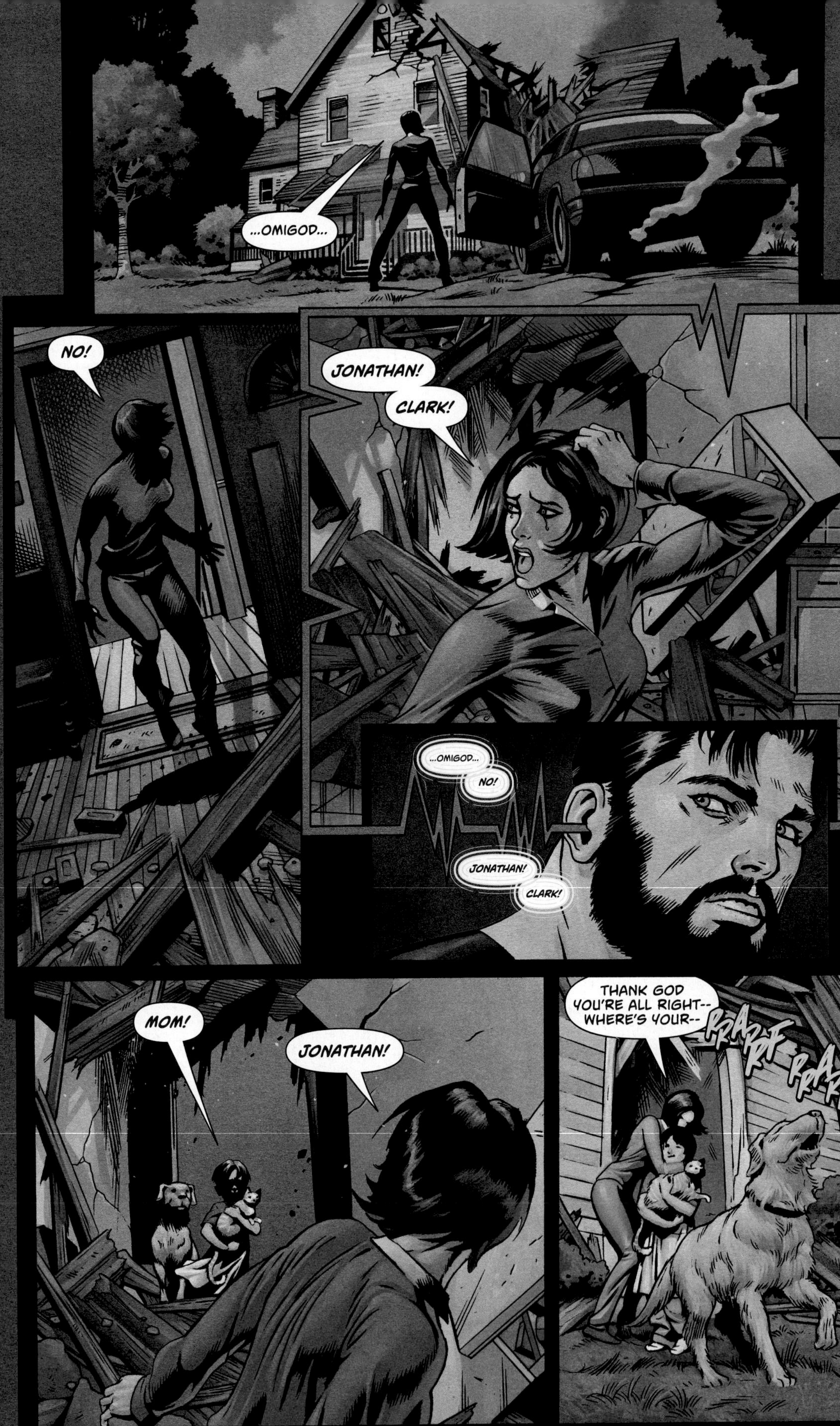
...OMIGOD...
NO!
JONATHAN!
CLARK!
...OMIGOD...
NO!
JONATHAN!
CLARK!
MOM!
JONATHAN!
THANK GOD YOU'RE ALL RIGHT-- WHERE'S YOUR--
RRARF RRARF

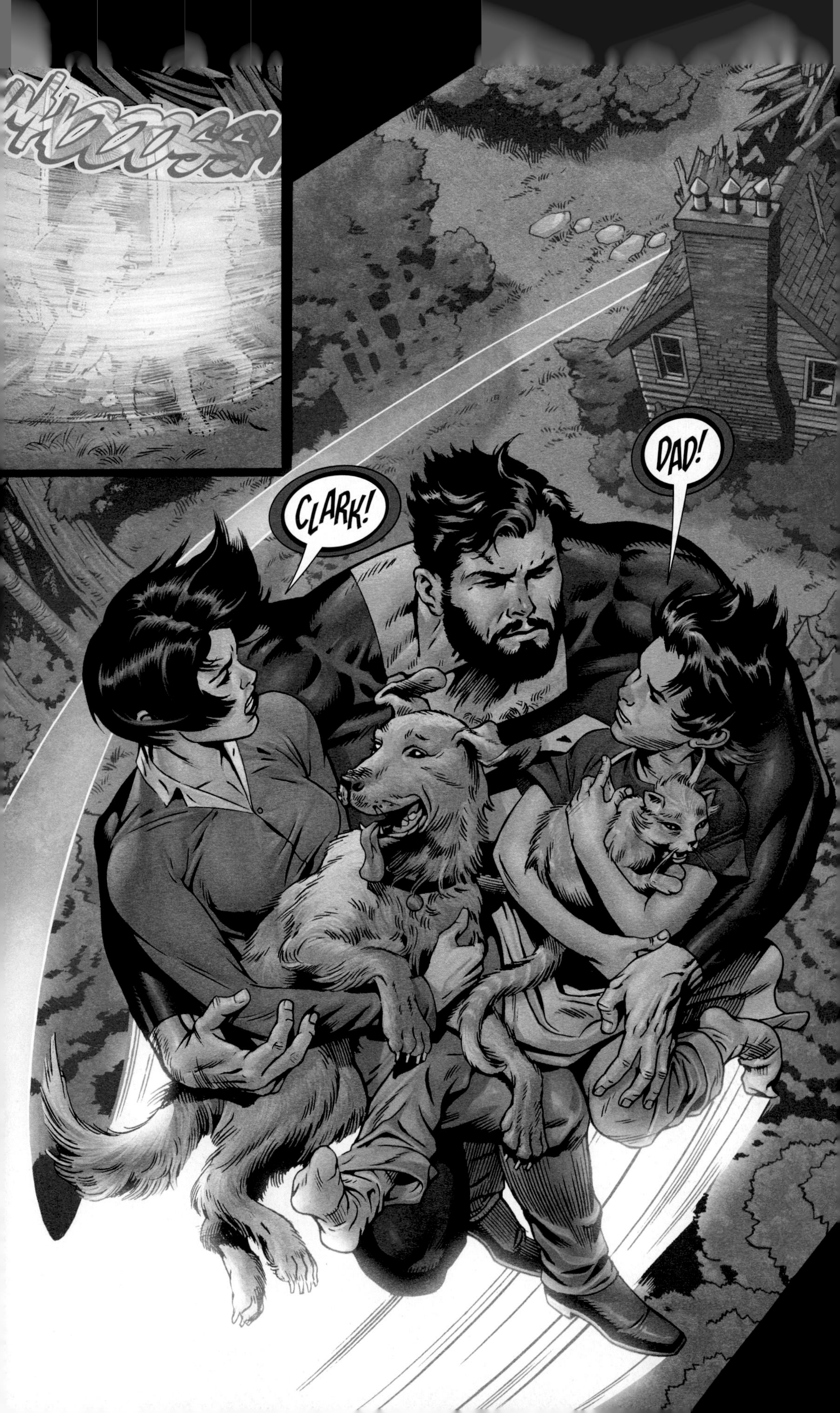
CLARK!
DAD!

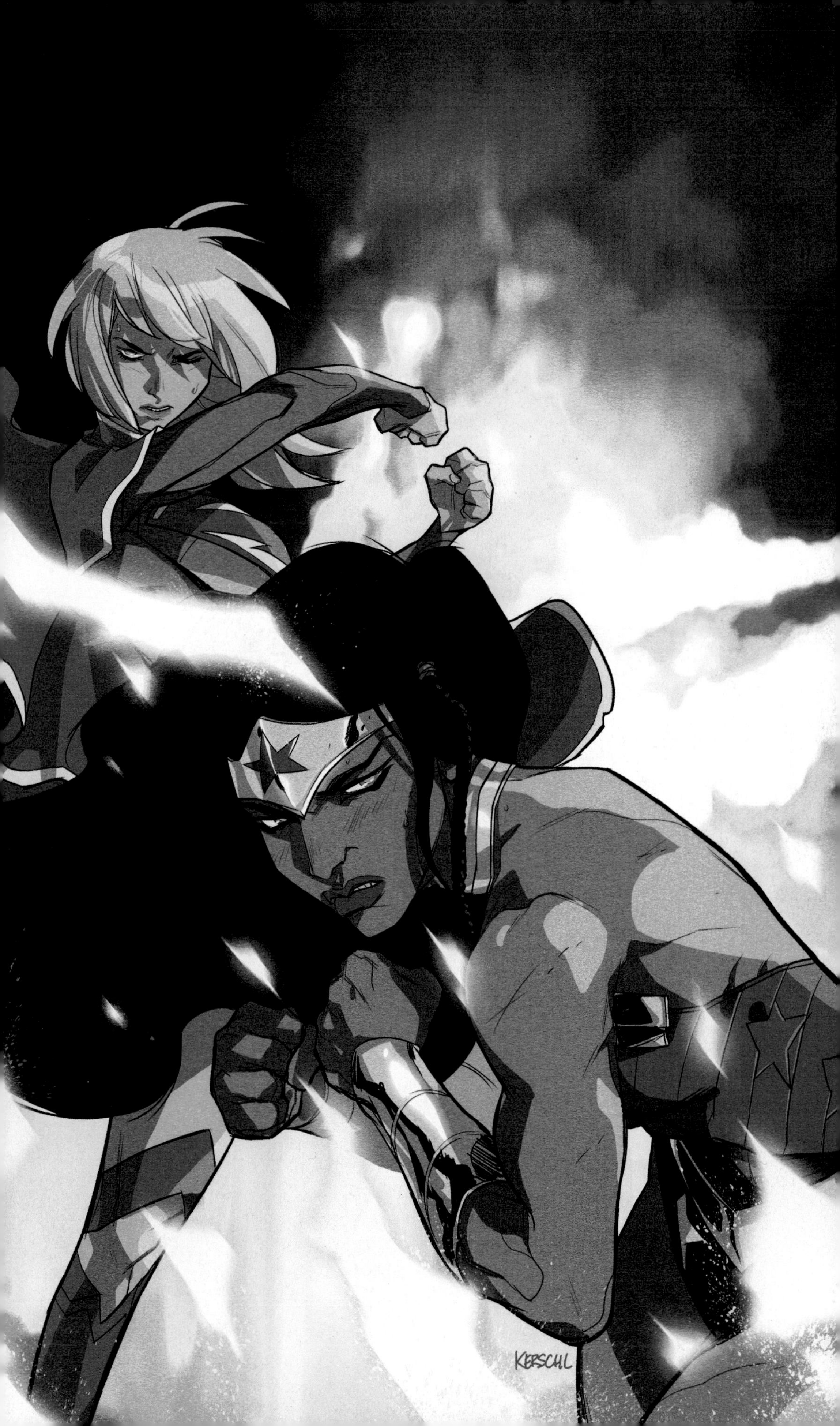
KERSCHL

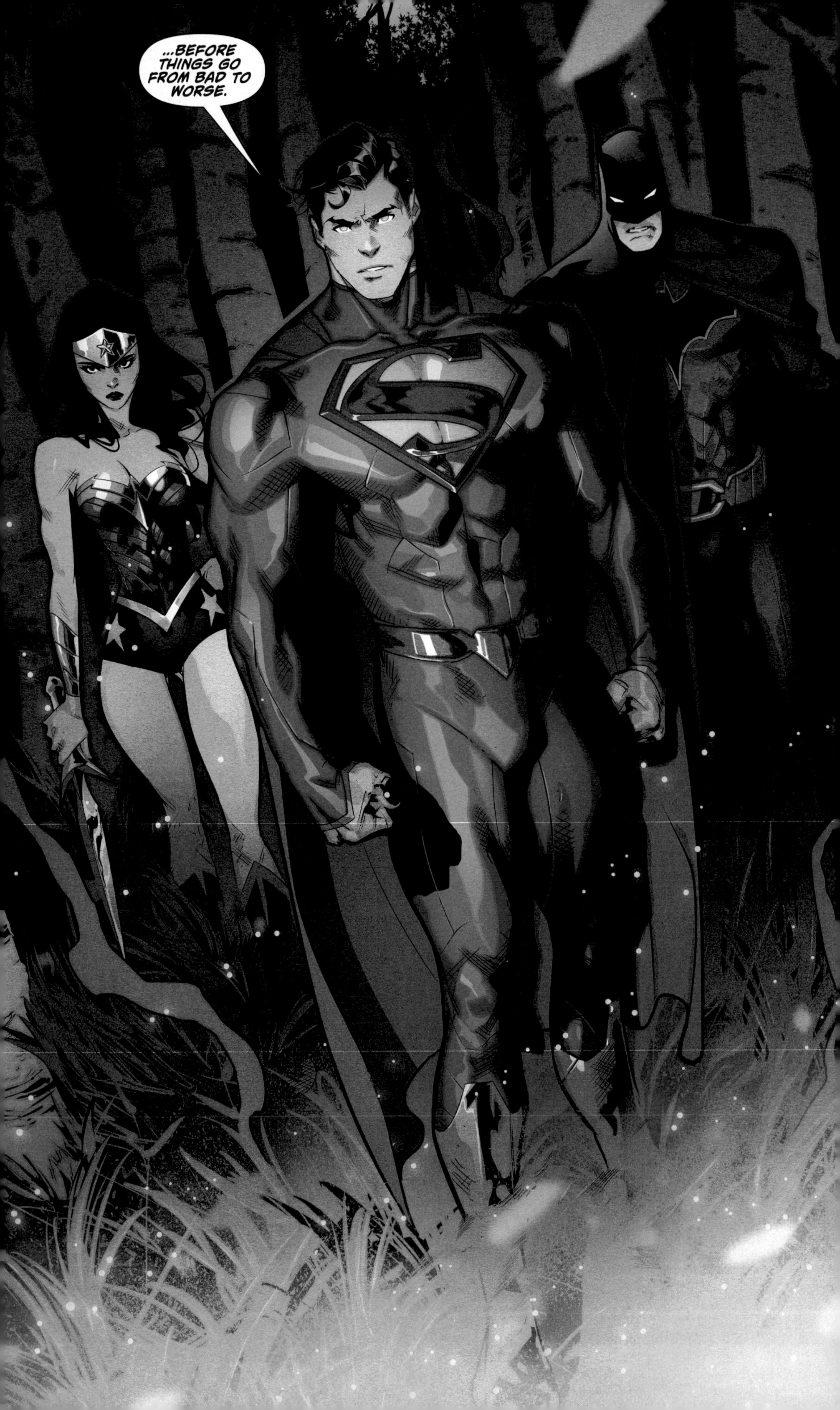
...BEFORE THINGS GO FROM BAD TO WORSE.

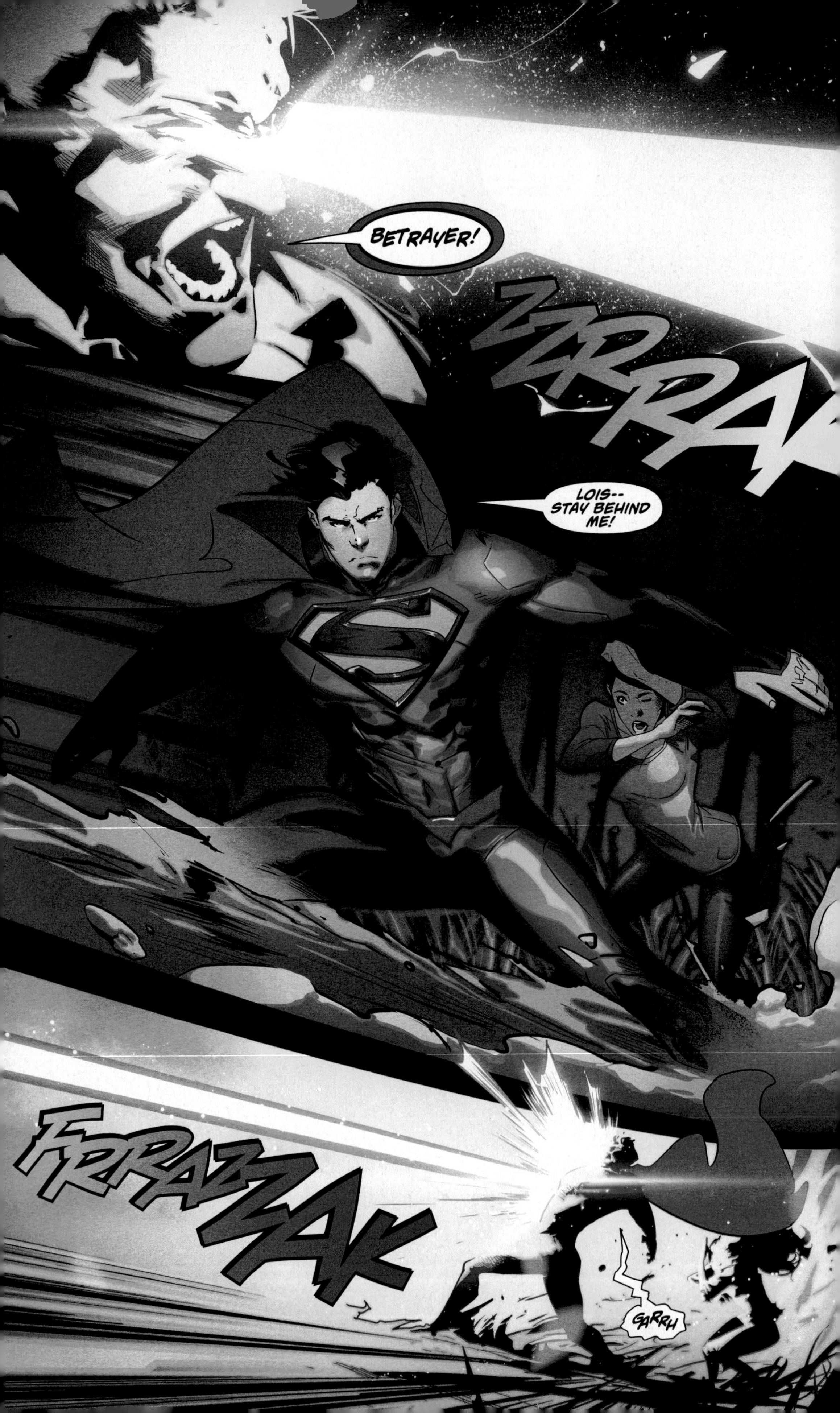
BETRAYER!
ZZRRAK
LOIS-- STAY BEHIND ME!
FRRAZZAK
GARRH

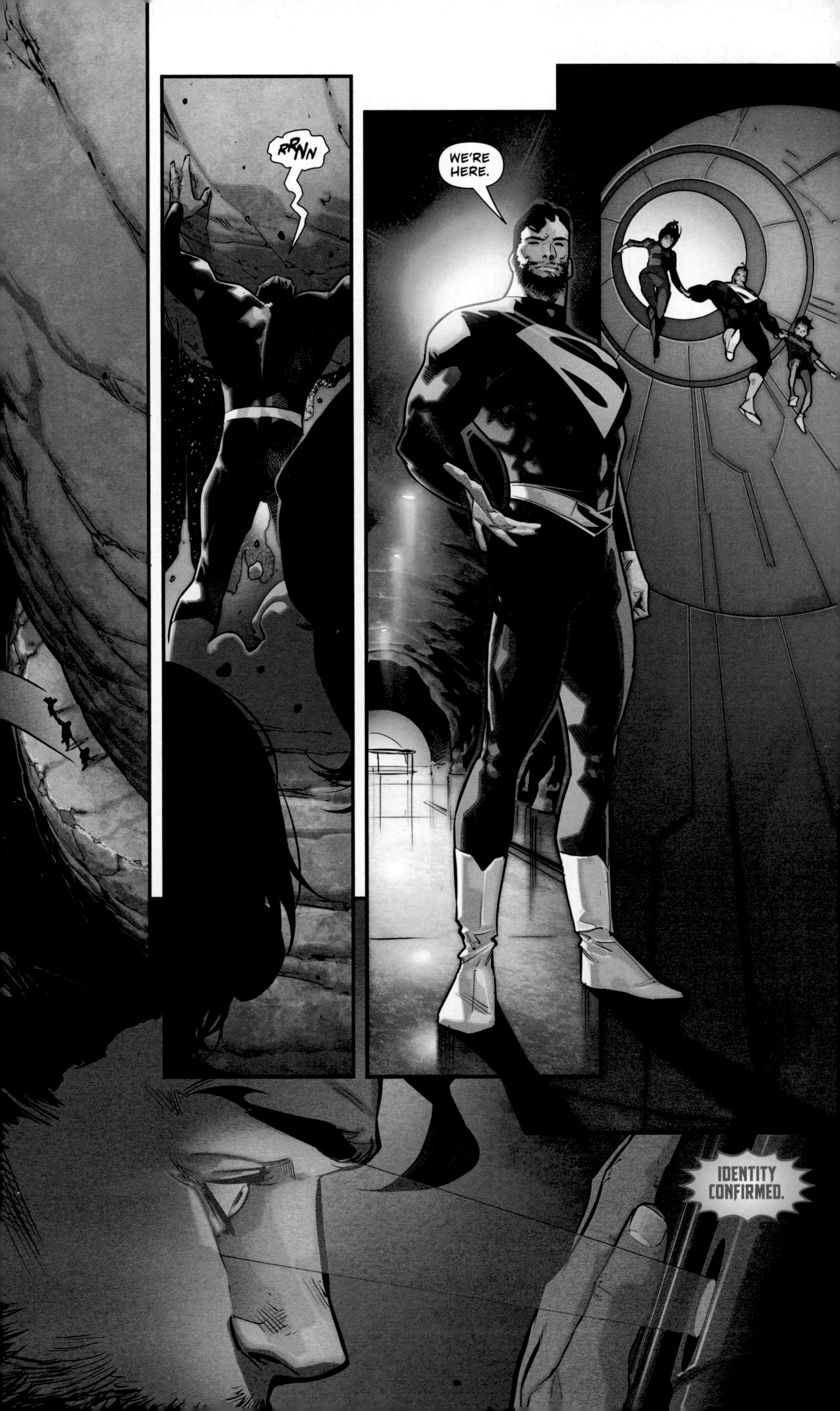
RRNN
WE'RE HERE.
IDENTITY CONFIRMED.

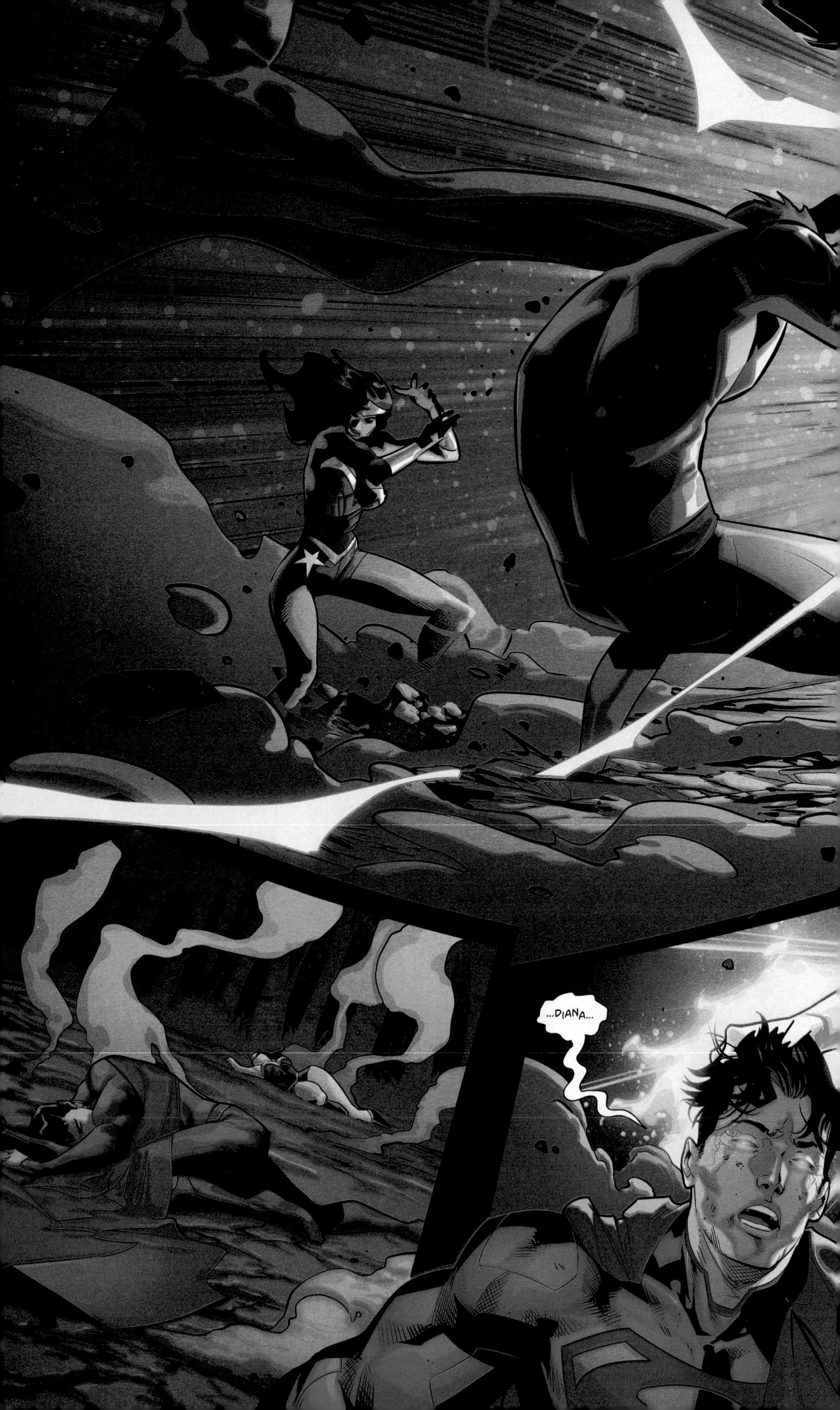
...DIANA...

SOME ABERRANT POWER SPIKES IN CALIFORNIA, BUT NOTHING FOR YOU TO BE CONCERNED ABOUT, SUPERGIRL.

WHAT KIND OF POWER, ELIZA?

METAHUMANS. IN SALINAS.

WHICH METAHUMANS, JEREMIAH?

Um, ONE OF THEM WE BELIEVE IS SUPERMAN.

THE OTHER ONE WE'RE NOT SURE OF... YET.

OPEN THE CEILING PORTAL.

YOU'RE NOT FULLY POWERED, PUTTING YOURSELF IN A PRECARIOUS SITUATION IS NOT RECOMMENDED AT THIS TIME.

I'M HERE ON MY OWN ACCORD, RIGHT?

WELL, YES, YOU ARE.

OPEN IT-- NOW.

I DO BELIEVE WE'RE GOING TO BE FIRED.

FWOOSH!

"I'VE HAD ENOUGH OF ALL YOU PHONY SUPERMEN..."

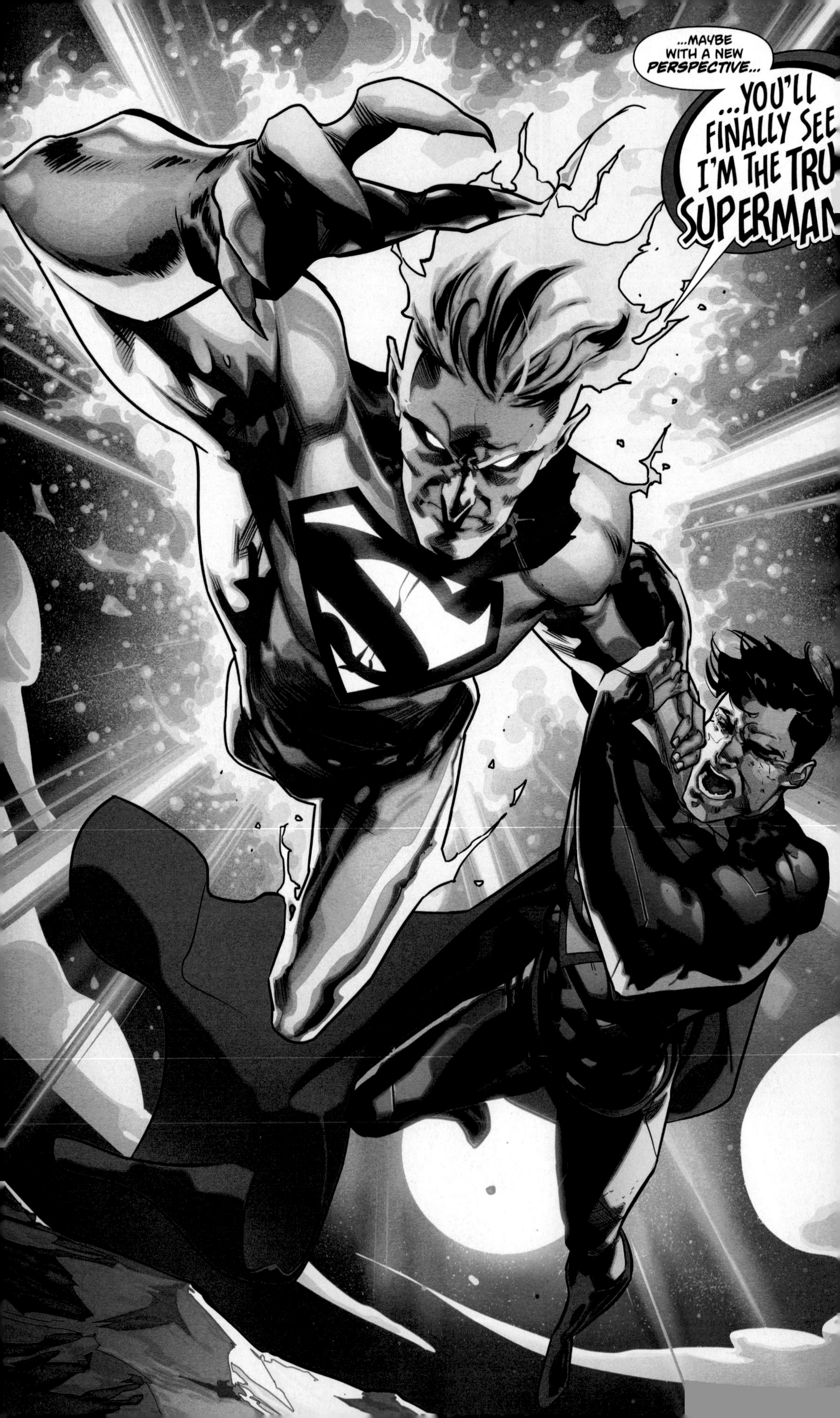
...MAYBE WITH A NEW PERSPECTIVE...
...YOU'LL FINALLY SEE I'M THE TRU SUPERMAN

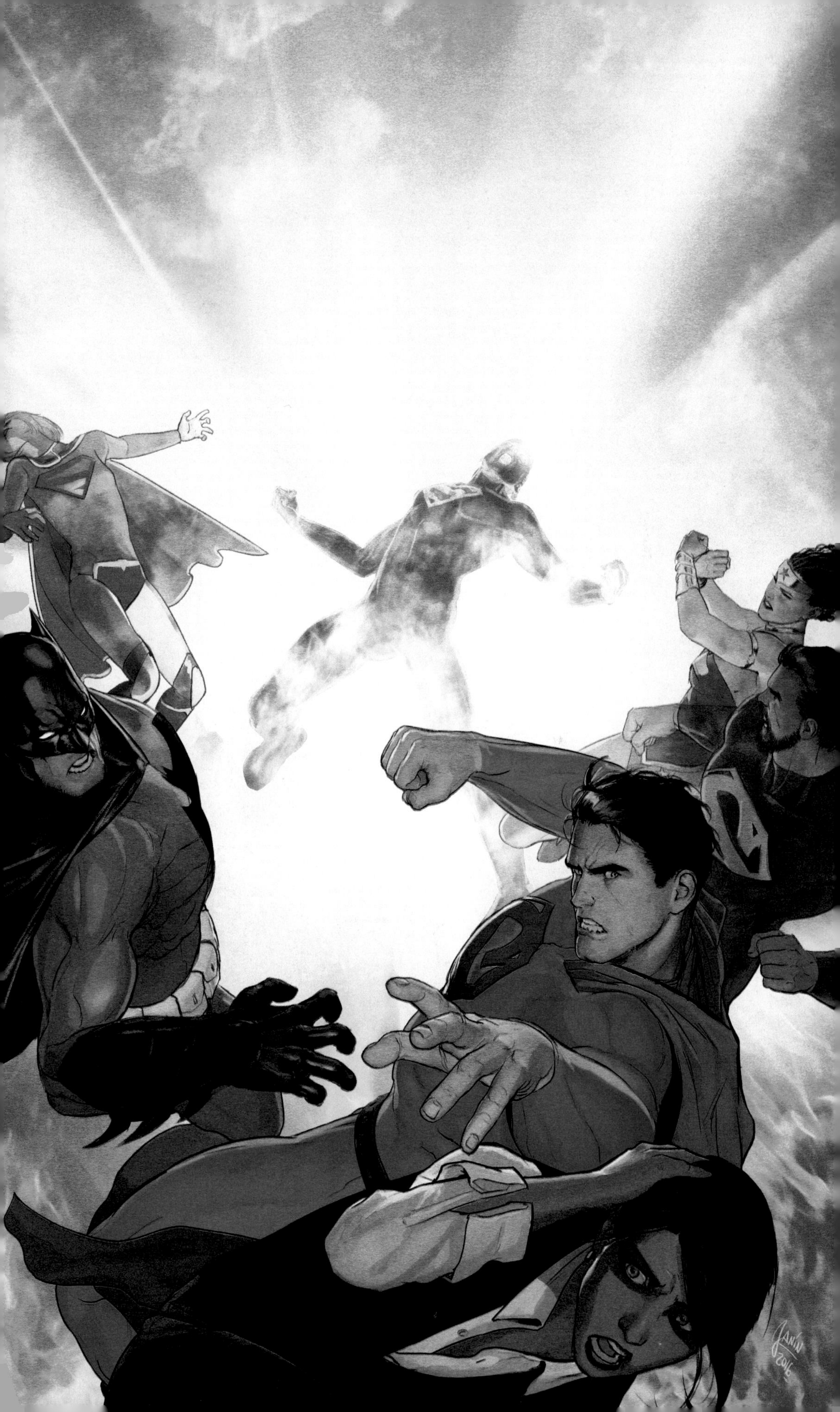
JANÍN
2016

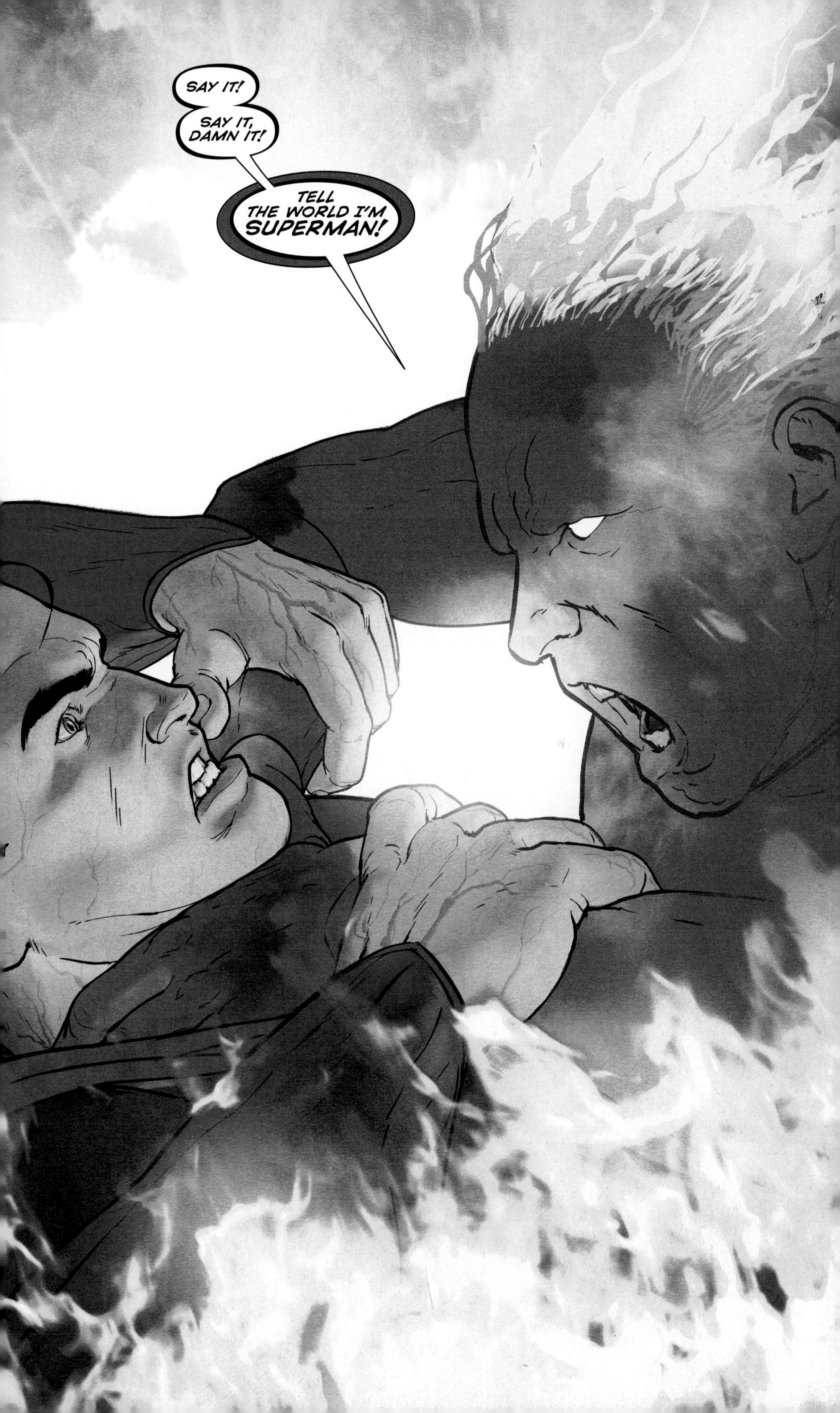
SAY IT!
SAY IT, DAMN IT!
TELL THE WORLD I'M SUPERMAN!

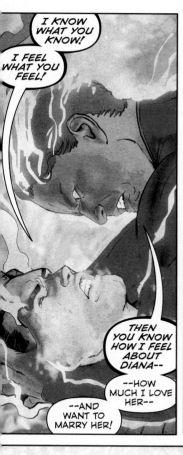

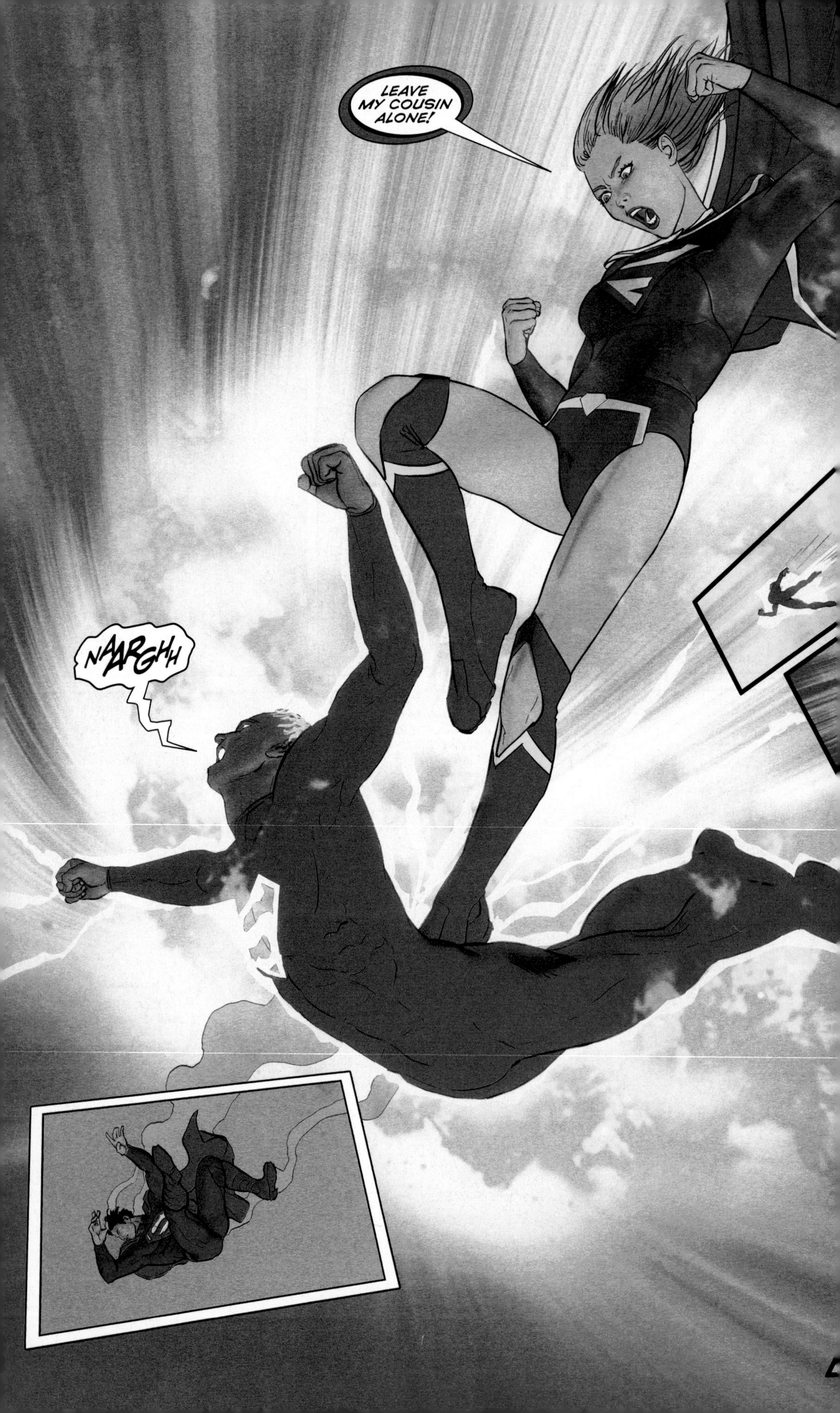
LEAVE MY COUSIN ALONE!
NAARGHH

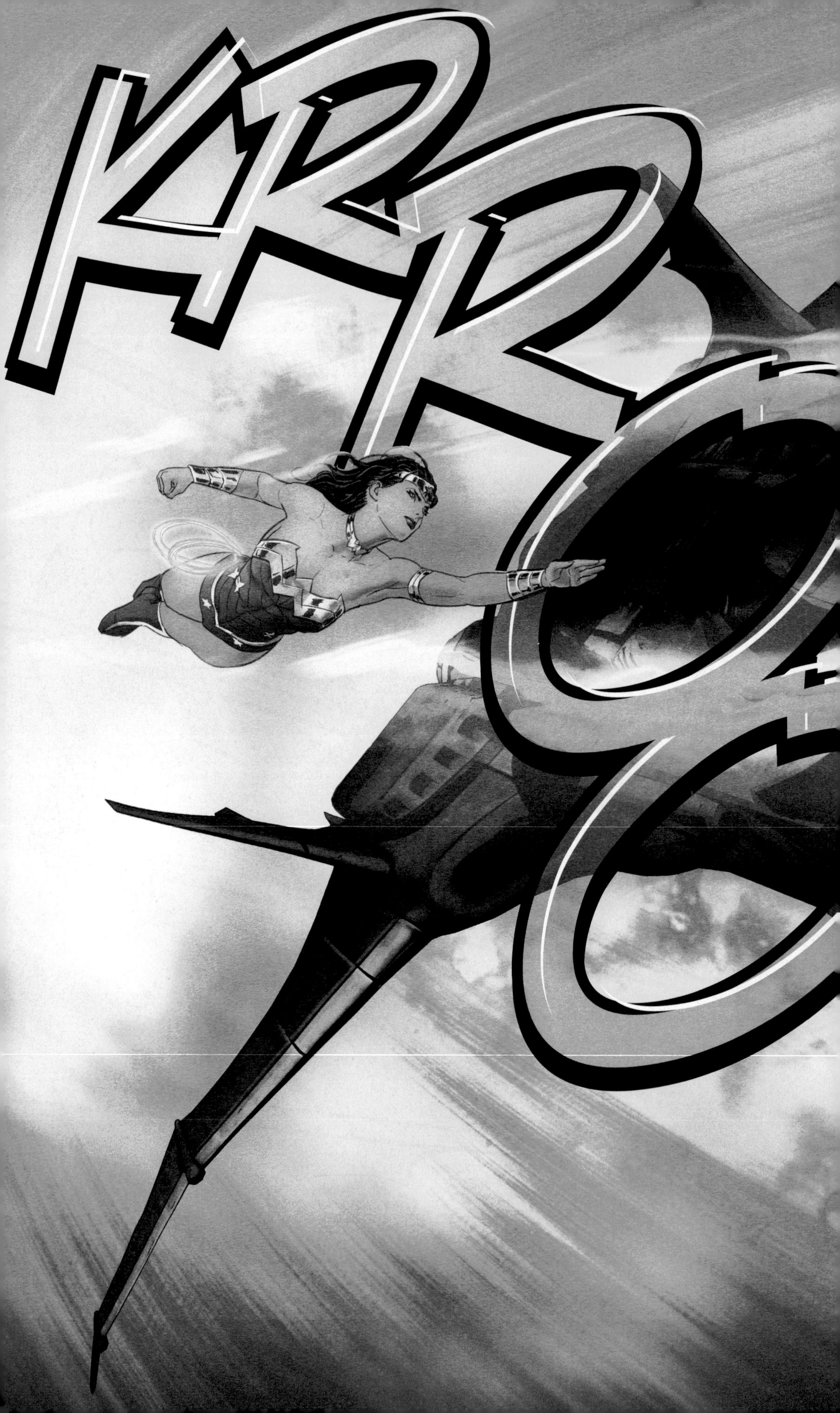
KRROO

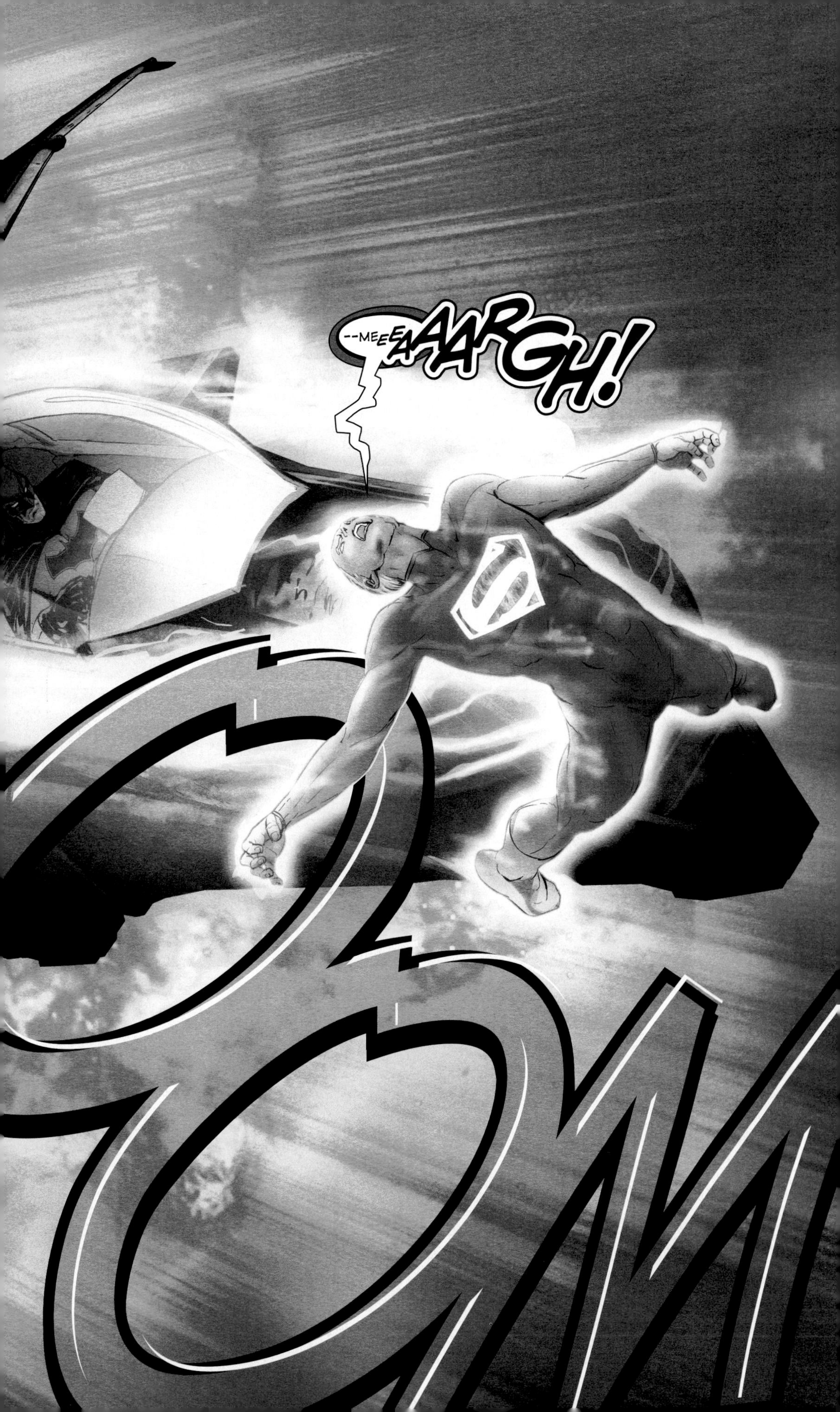

--MEEEAAAARGH!

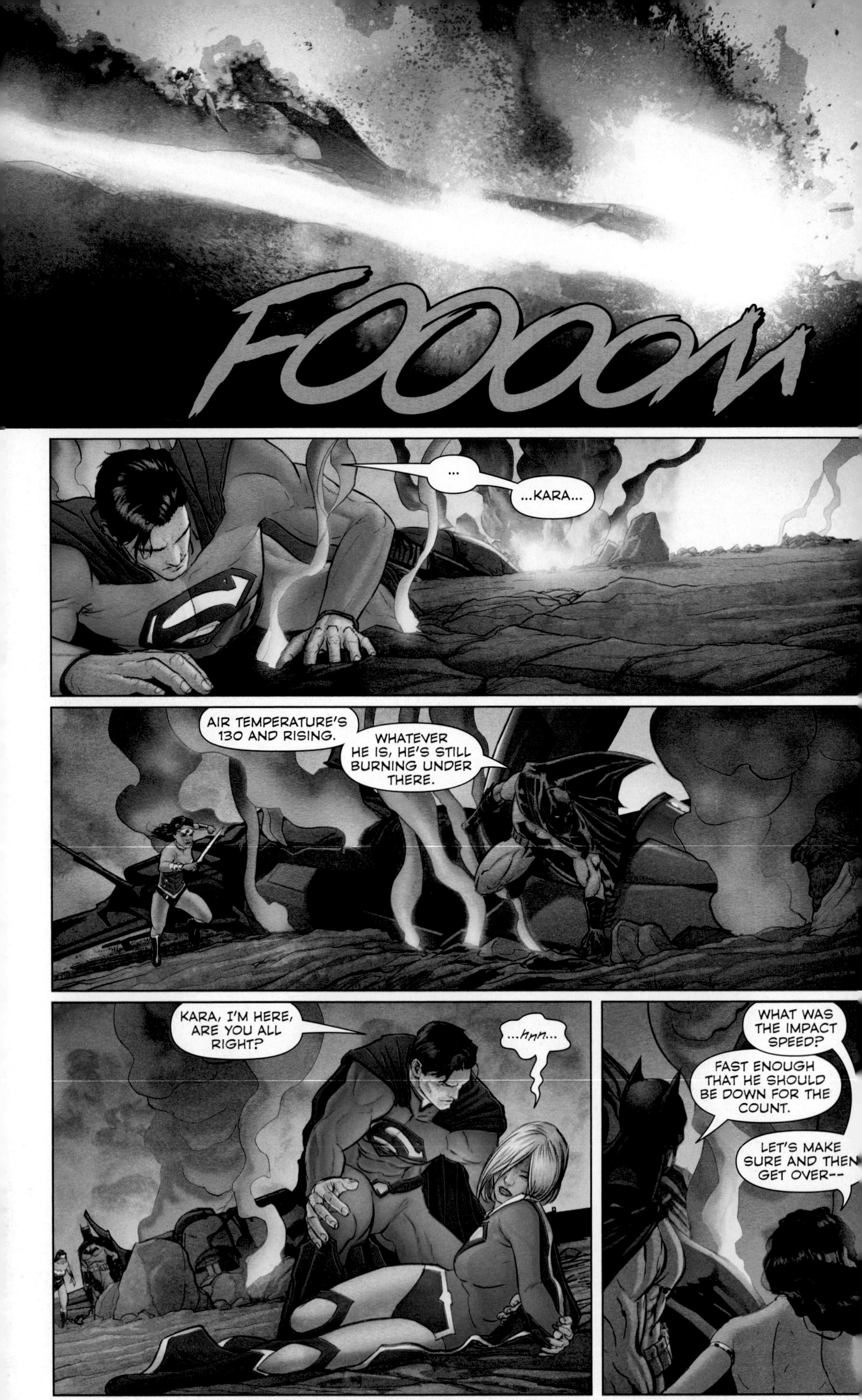
FOOOOM
...
...KARA...
AIR TEMPERATURE'S 130 AND RISING.
WHATEVER HE IS, HE'S STILL BURNING UNDER THERE.
KARA, I'M HERE, ARE YOU ALL RIGHT?
...hnn...
WHAT WAS THE IMPACT SPEED?
FAST ENOUGH THAT HE SHOULD BE DOWN FOR THE COUNT.
LET'S MAKE SURE AND THEN GET OVER--

...NOT MUCH TIME...
...ONLY OPTION LEFT...
...HAVE TO GET HIM HIGHER... SO HE DOESN'T KILL ANYBODY IN CASE HE BLOWS BEFORE I CAN...
...BEFORE I CAN...USE MY...MY...
...DAMN IT... NOTHING LEFT... LOSING ALTITUDE...
NO WAY I CAN KEEP HIM IN ORBIT ANY LONGER...

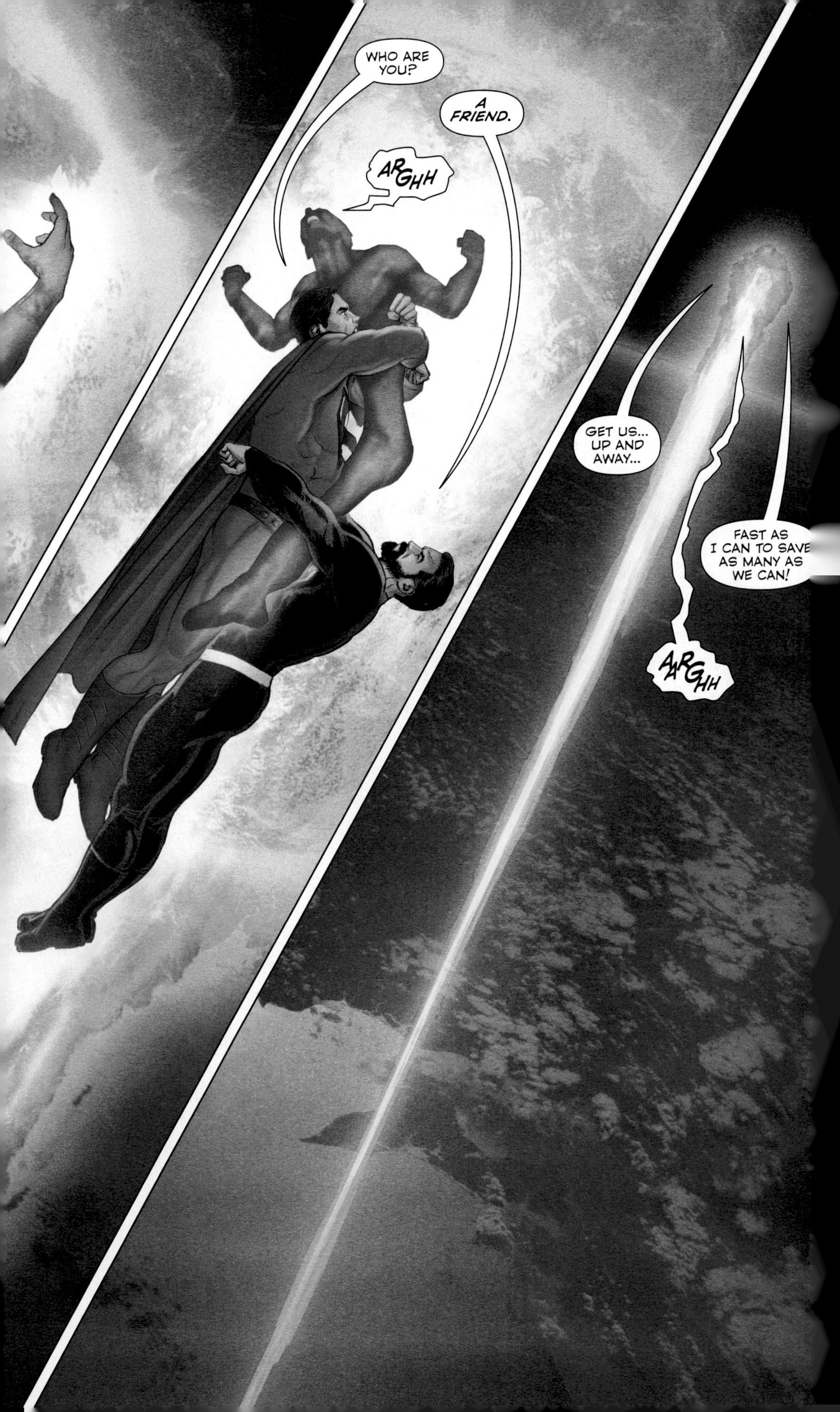
WHO ARE YOU?
A FRIEND.
ARGHH
GET US... UP AND AWAY...
FAST AS I CAN TO SAVE AS MANY AS WE CAN!
AARGHH

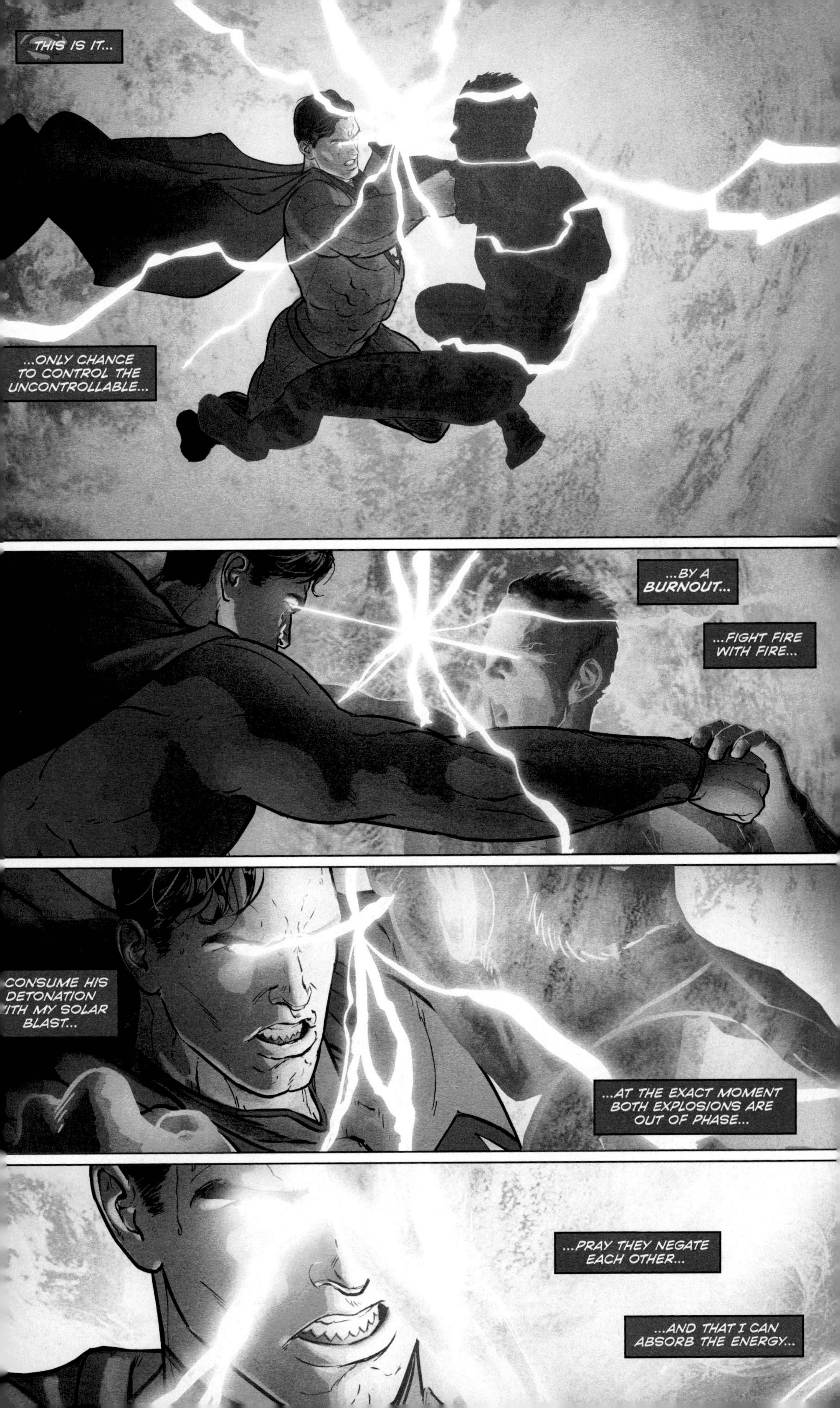
THIS IS IT...
...ONLY CHANCE TO CONTROL THE UNCONTROLLABLE...
...BY A BURNOUT...
...FIGHT FIRE WITH FIRE...
CONSUME HIS DETONATION
ITH MY SOLAR BLAST...
...AT THE EXACT MOMENT BOTH EXPLOSIONS ARE OUT OF PHASE...
...PRAY THEY NEGATE EACH OTHER...
...AND THAT I CAN ABSORB THE ENERGY...

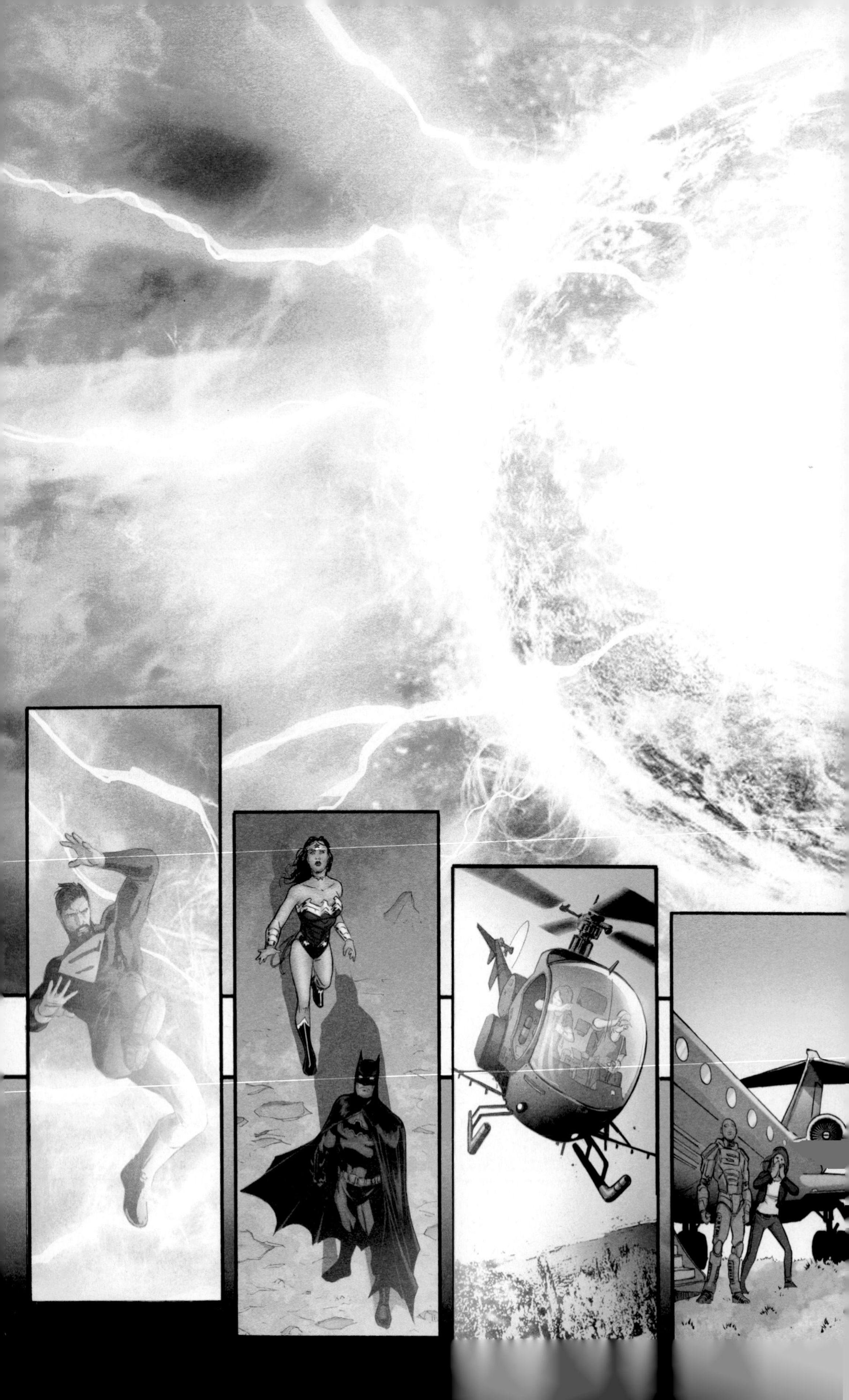

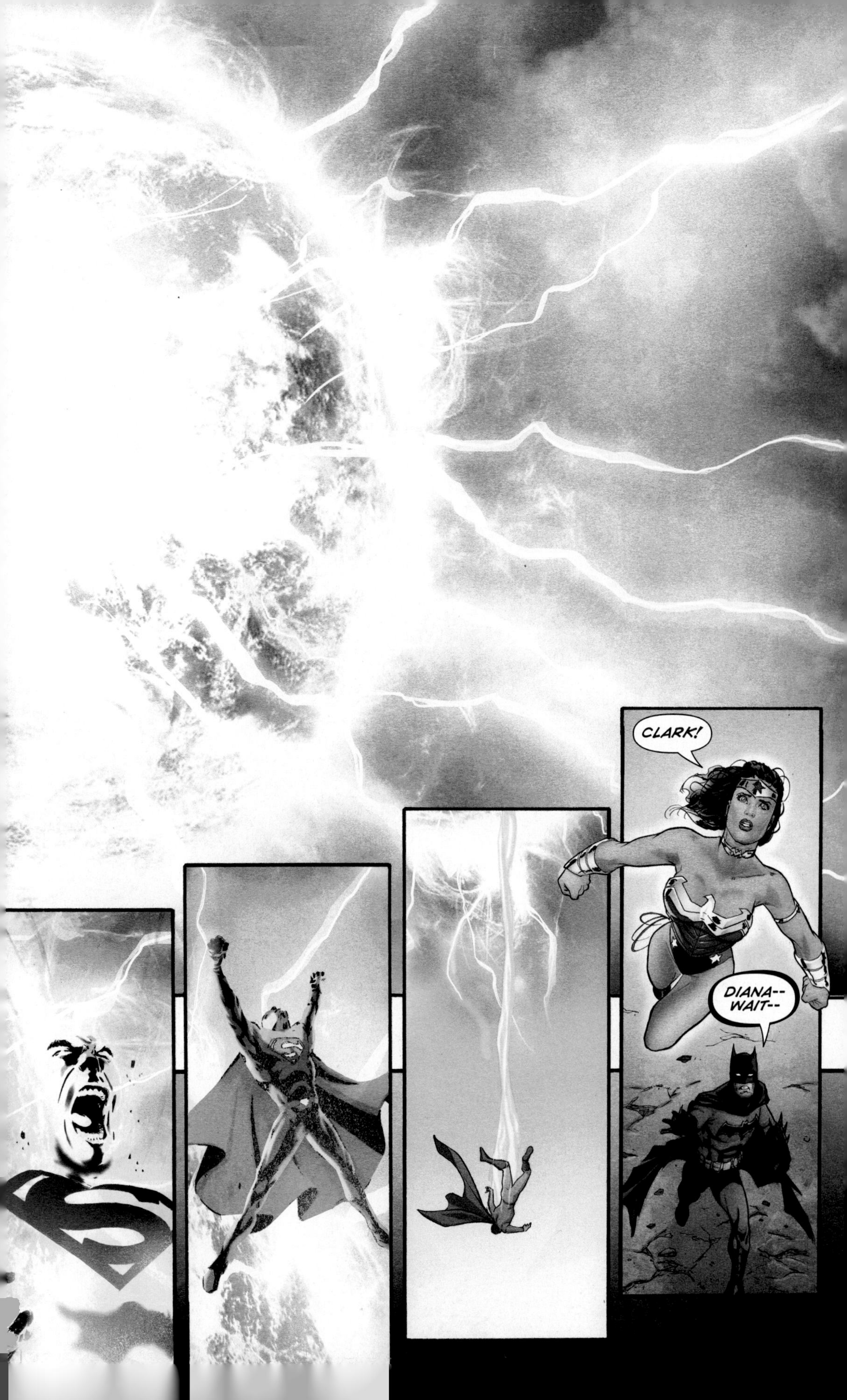
CLARK!
DIANA-- WAIT--

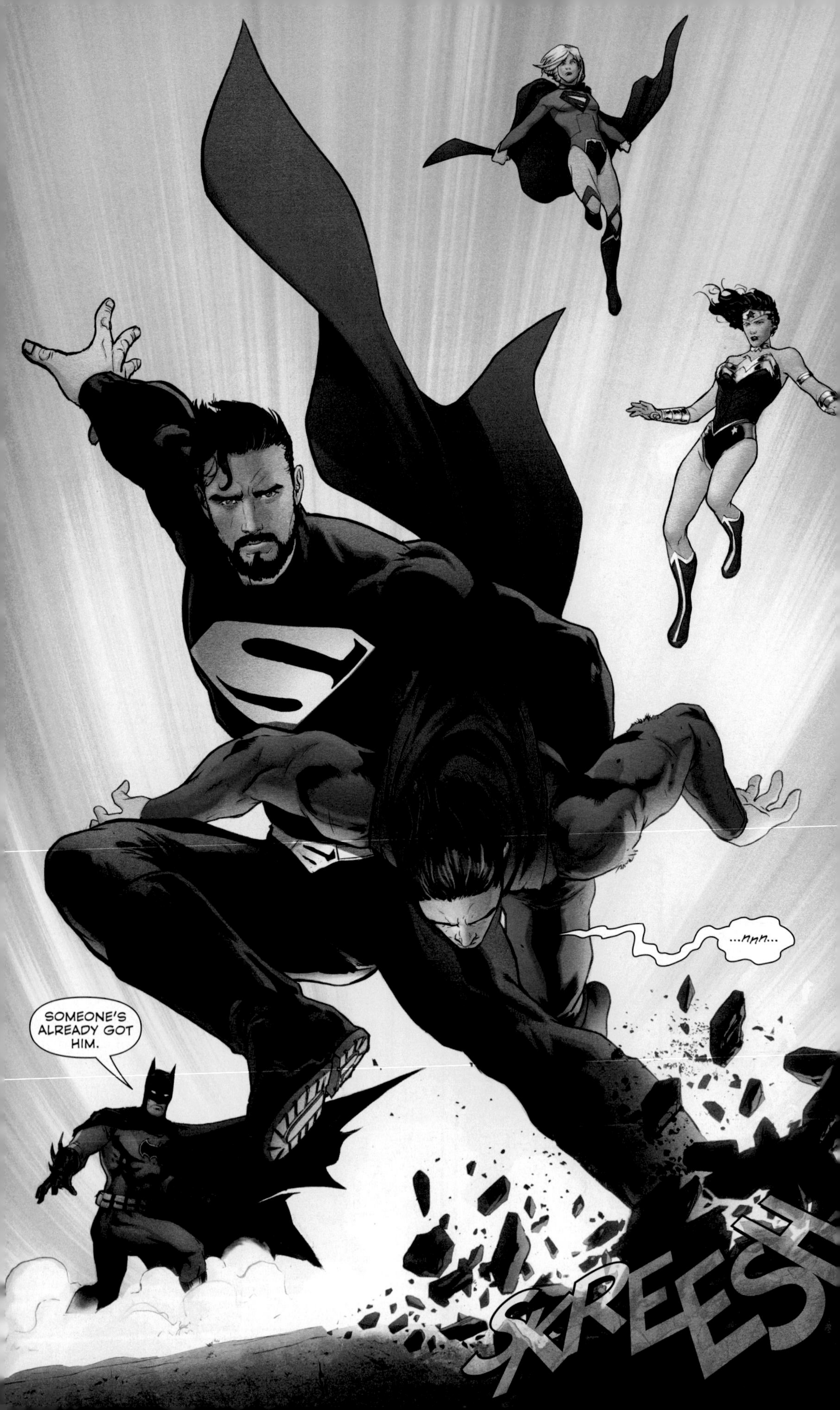
...NNN...
SOMEONE'S ALREADY GOT HIM.
SKREEES

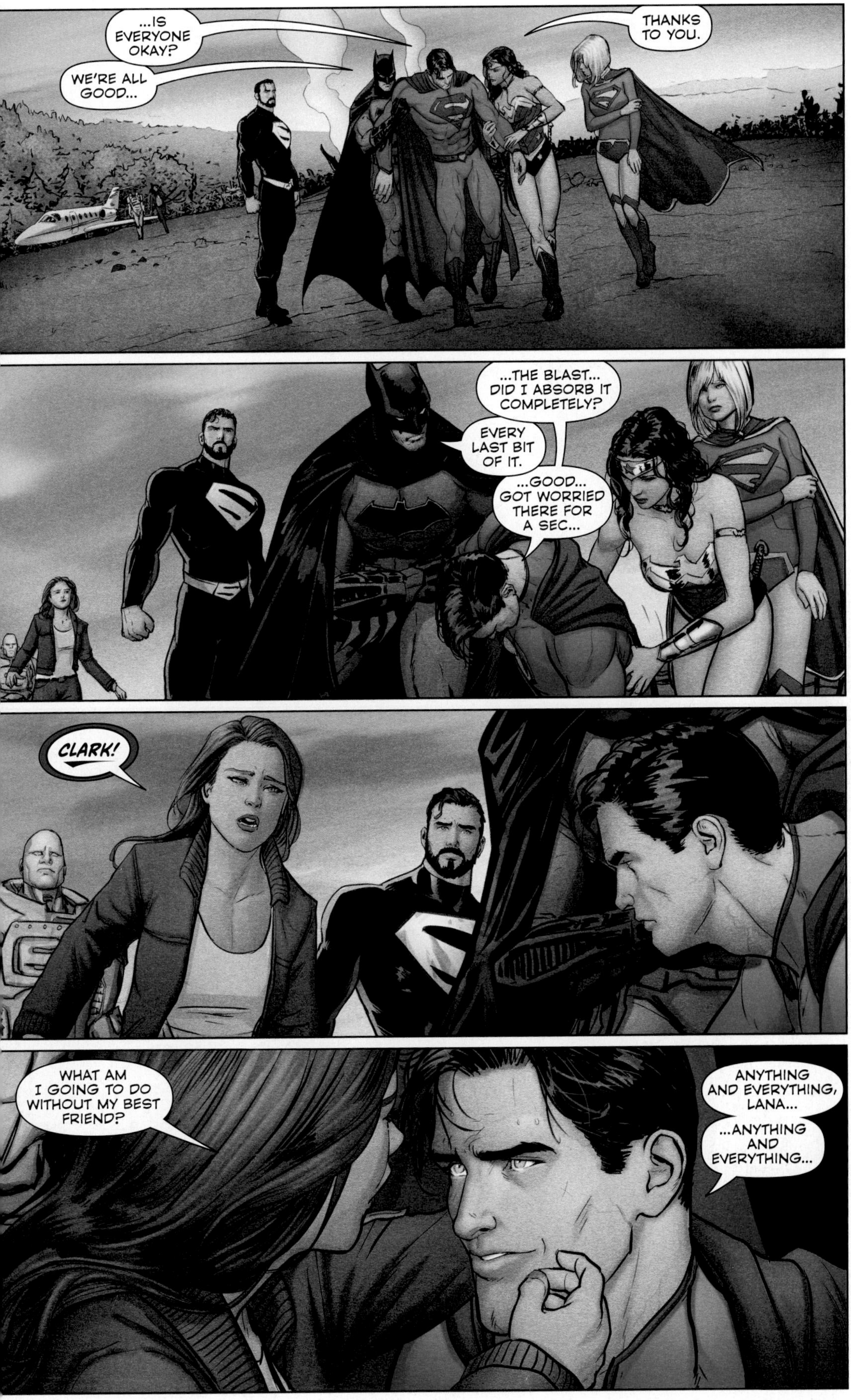
...IS EVERYONE OKAY?
WE'RE ALL GOOD...
THANKS TO YOU.
...THE BLAST... DID I ABSORB IT COMPLETELY?
EVERY LAST BIT OF IT.
...GOOD... GOT WORRIED THERE FOR A SEC...
CLARK!
WHAT AM I GOING TO DO WITHOUT MY BEST FRIEND?
ANYTHING AND EVERYTHING, LANA...
...ANYTHING AND EVERYTHING...

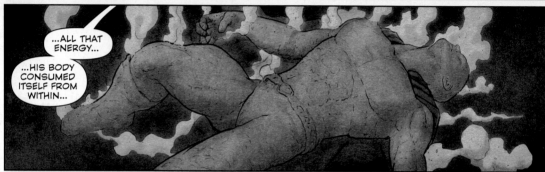

...ALL THAT ENERGY...

...HIS BODY CONSUMED ITSELF FROM WITHIN...

...HE'S...

...DEAD...

THERE'S LOTS OF QUESTIONS--

WHICH I'LL ANSWER AT ANOTHER TIME.

WHERE WILL WE FIND YOU?

DON'T WORRY, I'LL FIND YOU.

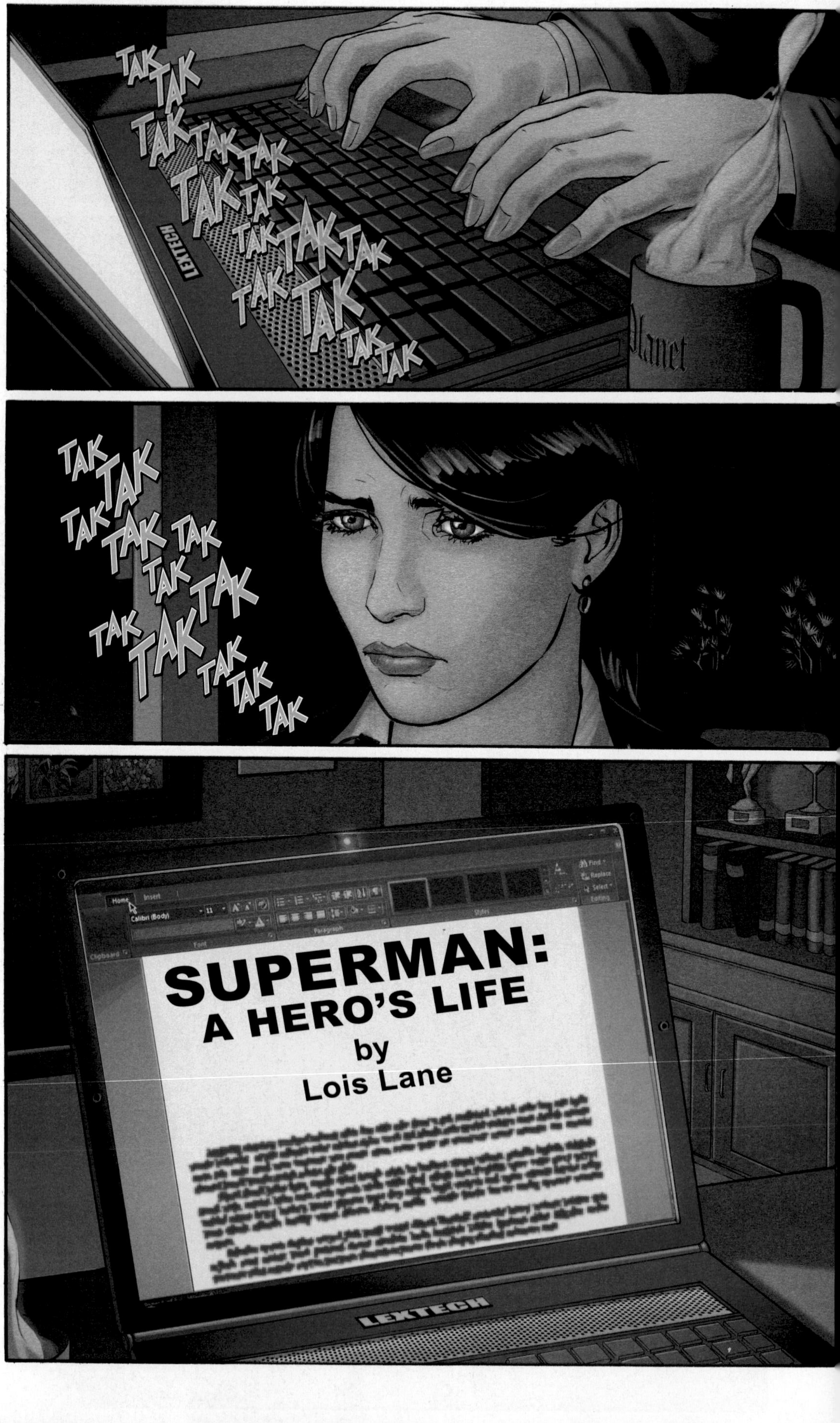
TAK TAK TAK TAK TAK TAK TAK TAK TAK TAK TAK TAK TAK TAK
LEXTECH
Planet
TAK TAK TAK TAK TAK TAK TAK TAK TAK TAK TAK TAK
Home
Insert
Calibri (Body)
11
Clipboard
Font
Paragraph
Styles
Find
Replace
Select
Editing
SUPERMAN:
A HERO'S LIFE
by
Lois Lane
LEXTECH

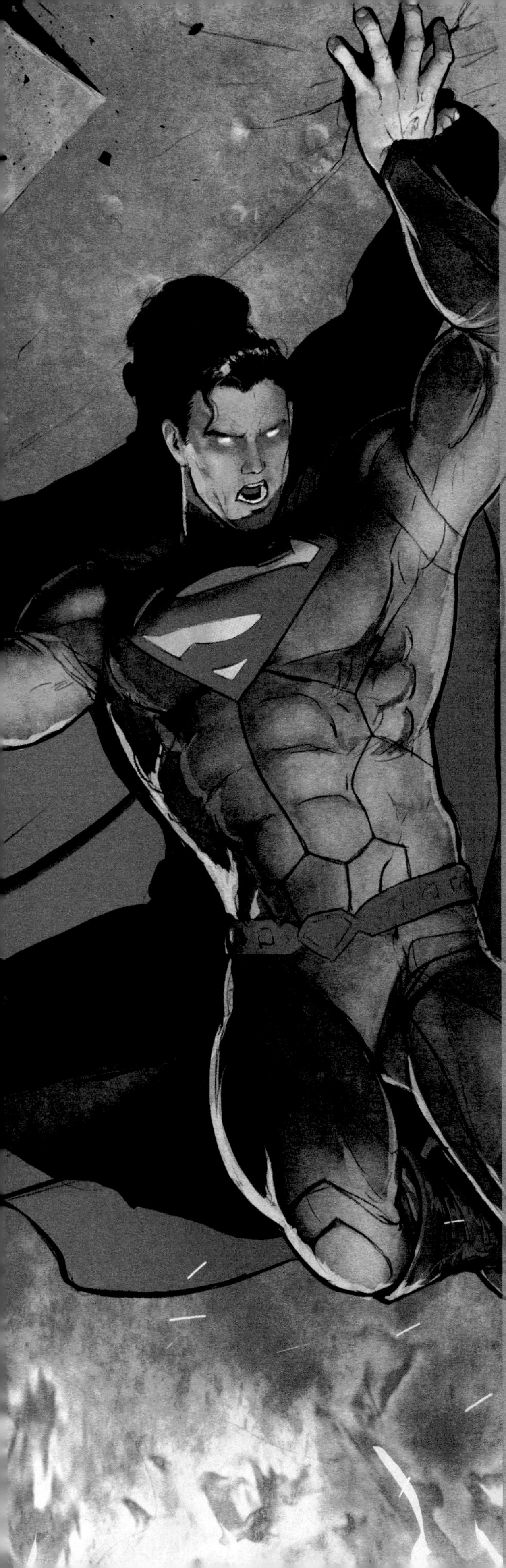

VARIANT COVER GALLERY

SUPERMAN #51
VARIANT BY JOHN ROMITA JR., DANNY MIKI, ARIF PRIANTO

BATMAN/SUPERMAN #31
VARIANT BY JOHN ROMITA JR., KLAUS JANSON, DAVE MCCAIG

ACTION COMICS #51
VARIANT BY JOHN ROMITA JR., KLAUS JANSON, ALEX SINCLAIR

SUPERMAN/ WONDER WOMAN #28
VARIANT BY JOHN ROMITA JR., SCOTT HANNA, LAURA MARTIN

ACTION COMICS #52
VARIANT BY BEN OLIVER

SUPERMAN #52
NEW 52 VARIANT BY MIKEL JANÍN

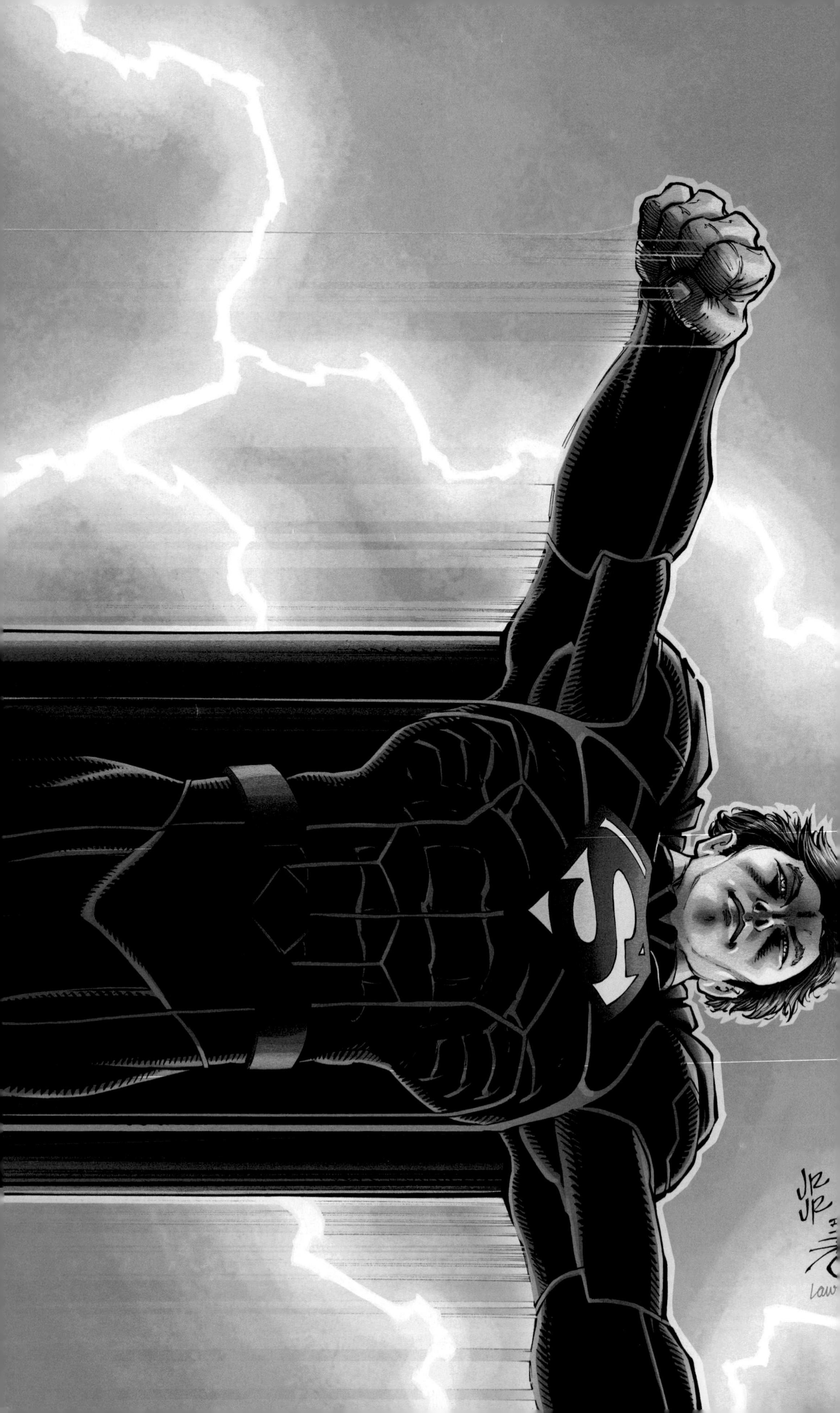

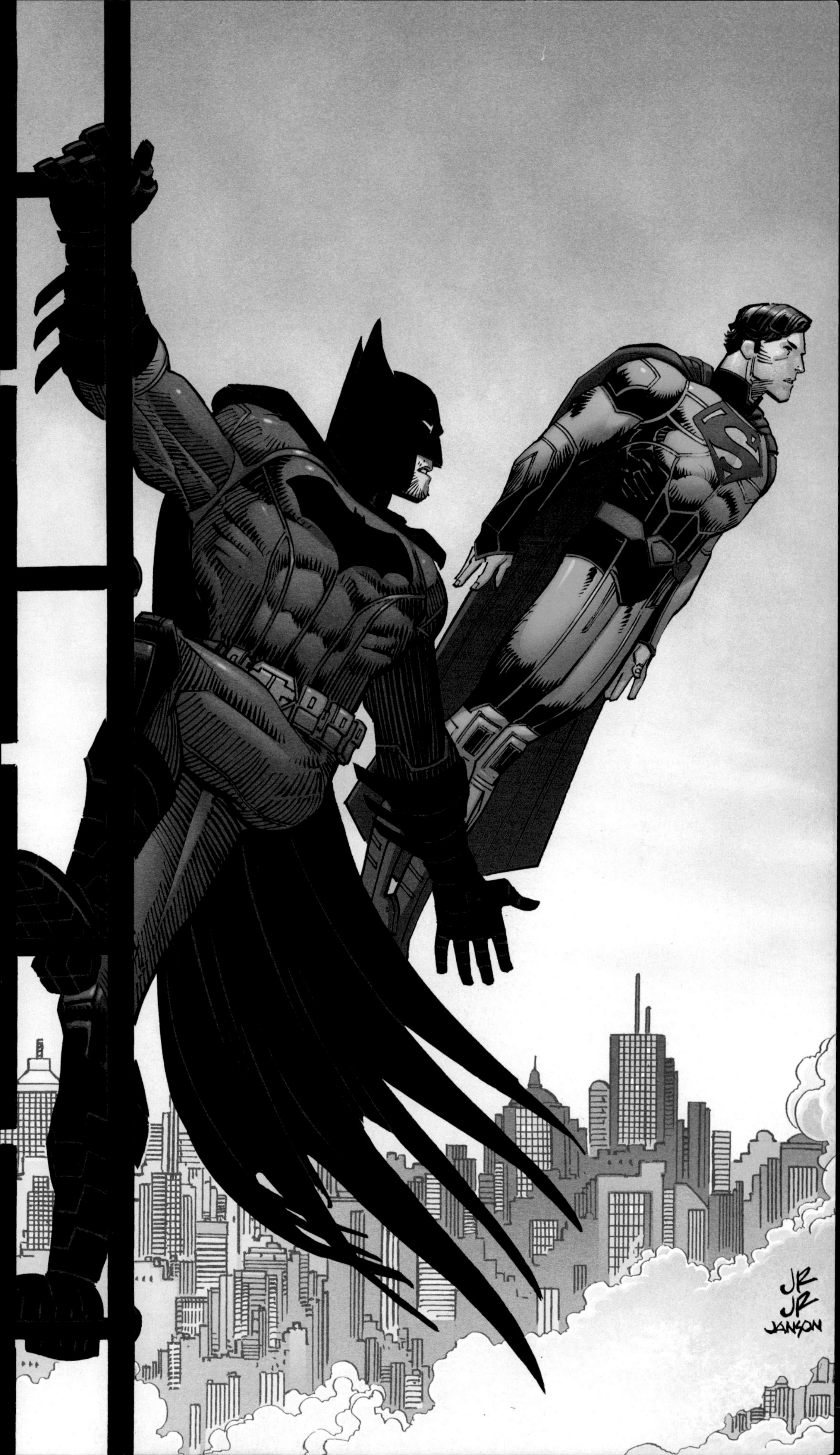
JR
JR
JANSON

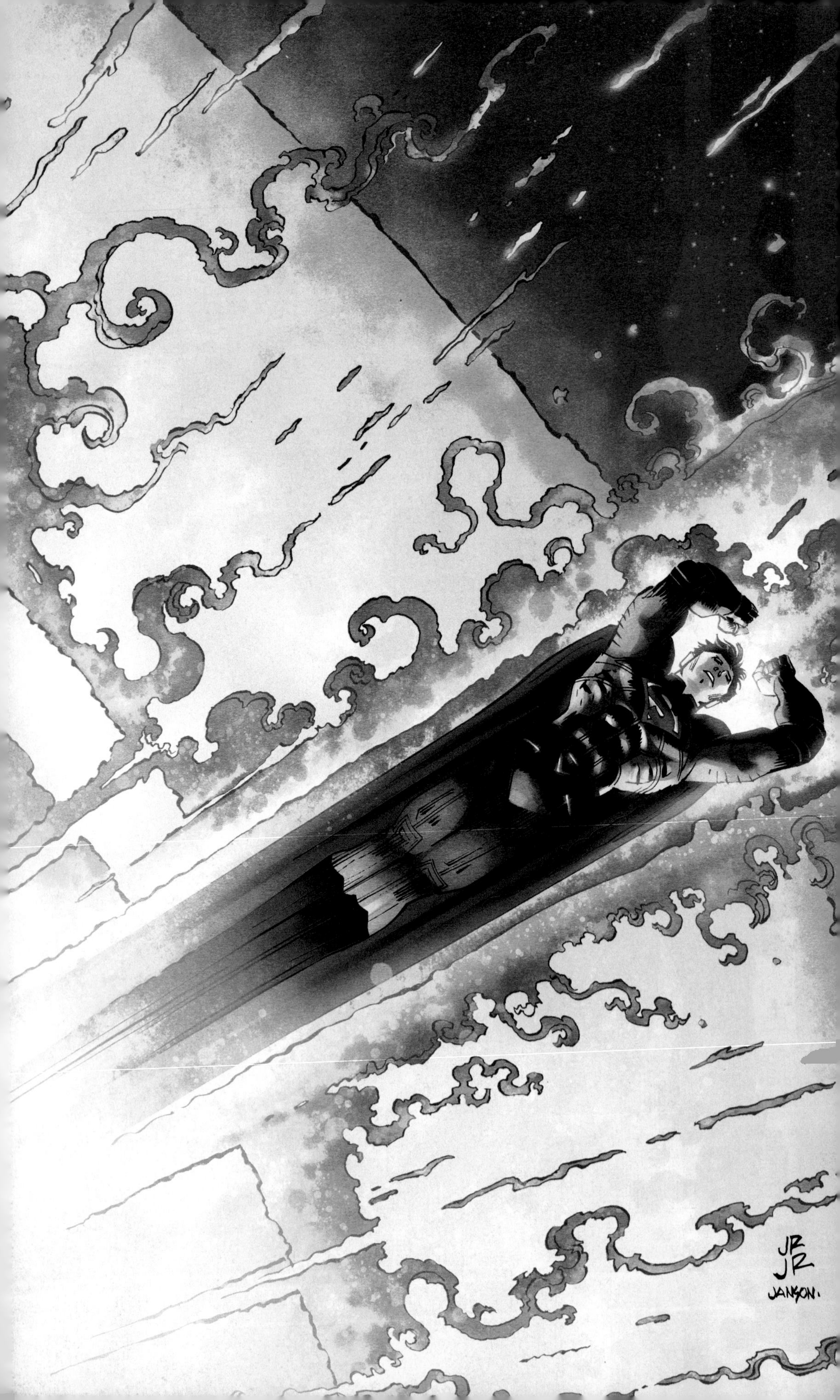
JR JR
JANSON.

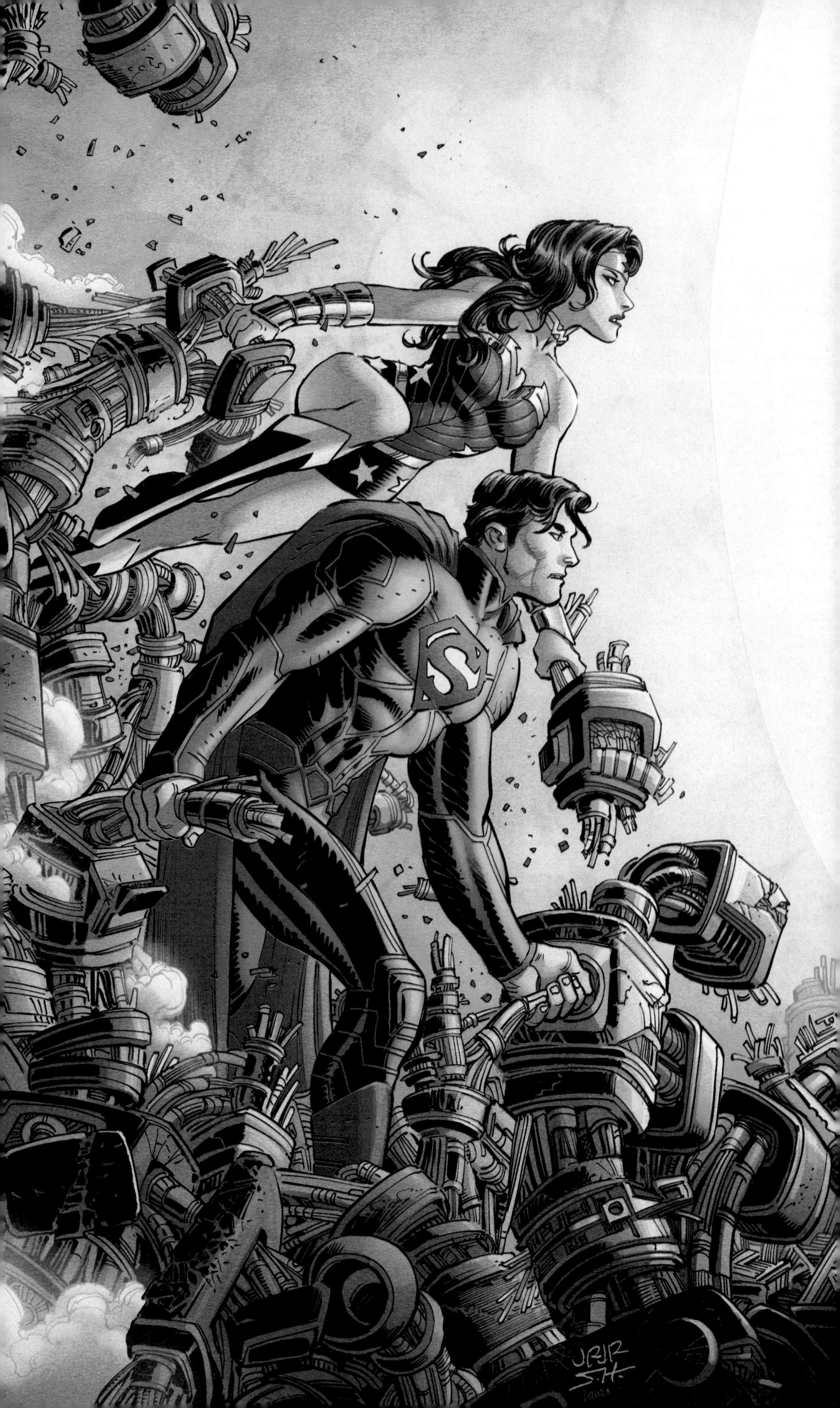

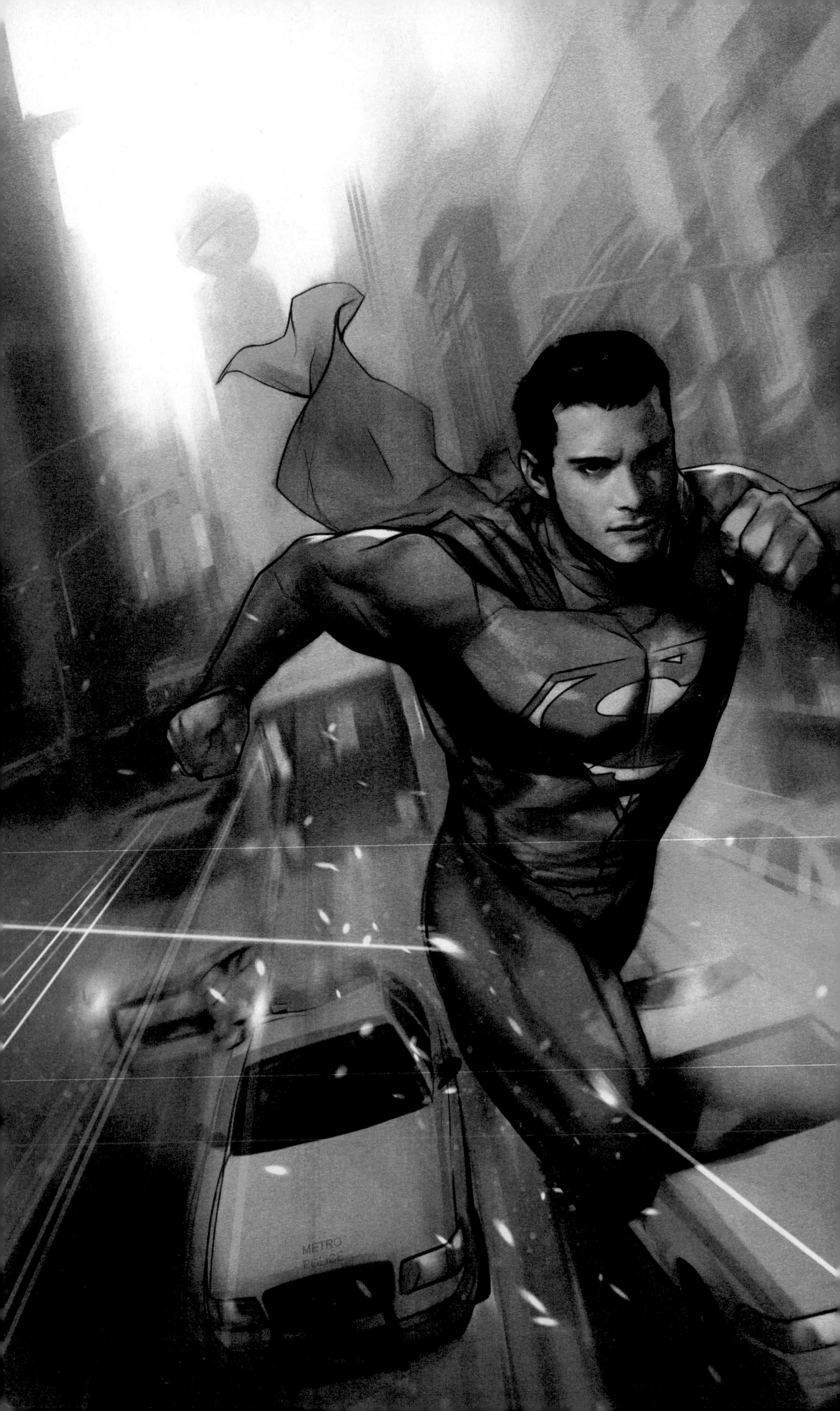
METRO
POLICE

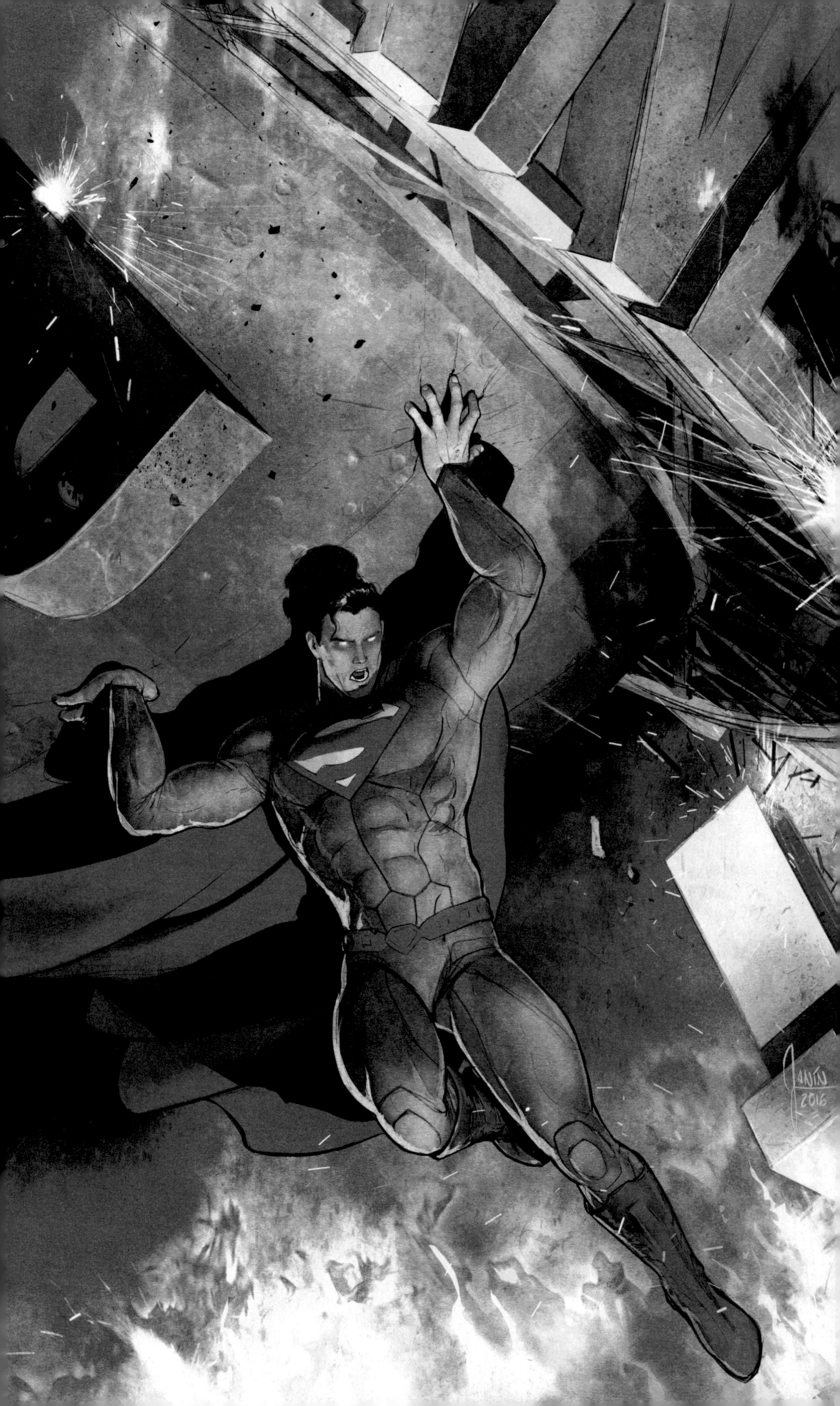

Pencils from SUPERMAN #51 by **MIKEL JANÍN**

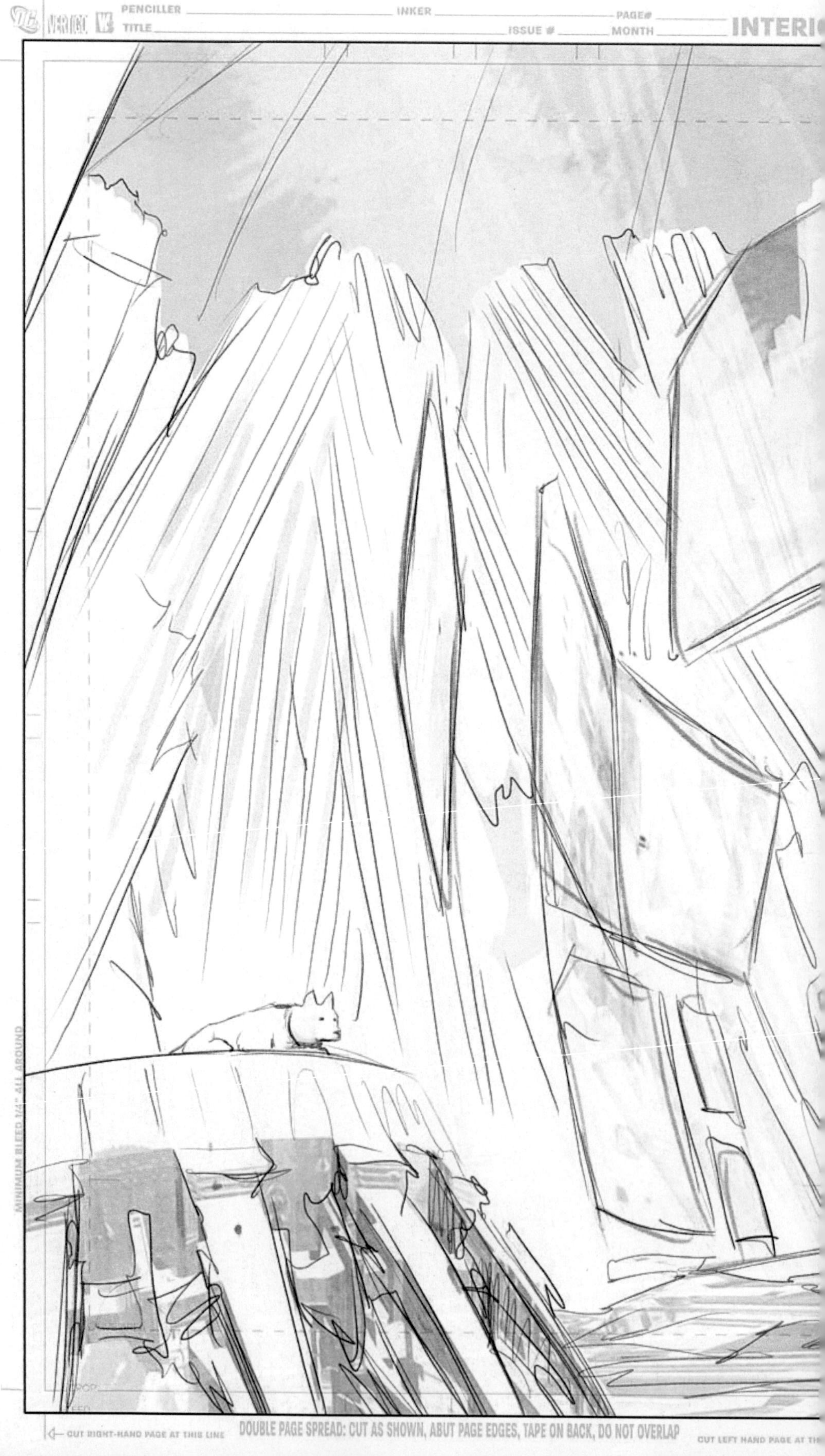
PENCILLER
INKER
PAGE#
TITLE
ISSUE #
MONTH
INTERI
MINIMUM BLEED 1/4" ALL AROUND
CUT RIGHT-HAND PAGE AT THIS LINE
DOUBLE PAGE SPREAD: CUT AS SHOWN, ABUT PAGE EDGES, TAPE ON BACK, DO NOT OVERLAP
CUT LEFT HAND PAGE AT TH

Pencils from ACTION COMICS #52 by SCOT EATON

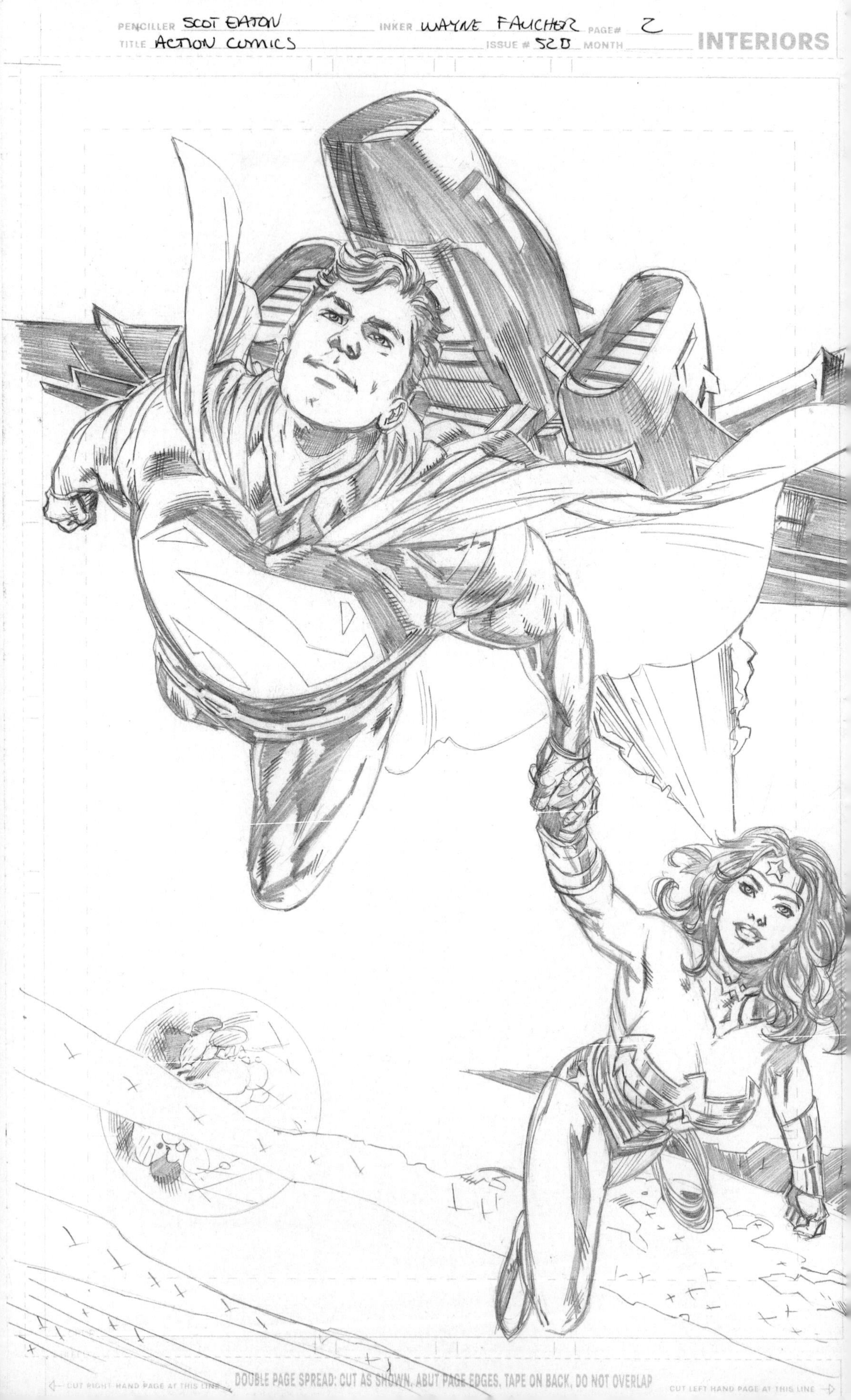
PENCILLER SCOT EATON
INKER WAYNE FAUCHER
PAGE# 2
TITLE ACTION COMICS
ISSUE #
MONTH
INTERIORS
CUT RIGHT HAND PAGE AT THIS LINE
DOUBLE PAGE SPREAD: CUT AS SHOWN. ABUT PAGE EDGES. TAPE ON BACK. DO NOT OVERLAP
CUT LEFT HAND PAGE AT THIS LINE